Matt Sorger will inspire you to harness life and experience the rewards of servi how living in the fruit of the Spirit will make you a conduit for the power of God at work all around us. This book is a must for anyone seeking to maximize their faith and the possibilities of their walk with Christ.

—PASTOR MATTHEW BARNETT
COFOUNDER OF THE DREAM CENTER IN LOS ANGELES

Every so often there is a book that comes along and "grabs you." *Power for Life* is one of those books! Matt Sorger is a dynamic, emerging hero in the kingdom of God. In this book he has captured many necessary keys to unlocking what you are called to do, called to be, and, most importantly, knowing how to embrace who you are! This is a book that will help you better understand the wounds and spiritual inheritance in your DNA. *Power for Life* will help you reconnect to your past so you can be connected to your future!

—CHUCK D. PIERCE
PRESIDENT, GLOBAL SPHERES, INC.
PRESIDENT, GLORY OF ZION
INTERNATIONAL MINISTRIES, INC.

Power for Life hits the mark for one of the most important and critical messages for this prophetic hour. There are few in Matt's generation who are able to articulate the depth of the marriage of intimacy, character, and power that he has been able to convey in his book. I am changed and renewed in my personal walk of faith through reading these pages. Every believer should read it and be transformed!

—CINDY JACOBS
GENERALS INTERNATIONAL

Matt Sorger's book *Power for Life* offers both spiritual and practical advice on living the way Jesus intended: in the fullness of His love and in the fullness of His power. Matt shows that the only way to abundant fruit and a power-filled life is through a lifestyle of intimacy and prayer. It is in this place that we discover our true identity as sons and daughters of God. Simply abiding in the Father's embrace will empower our lives beyond measure, because love never fails. To echo Matt's own words, it is the one thing that has a 100 percent success rate. The wonderful testimonies in this book will richly inspire your faith and leave you hungering for more of God's presence. I highly recommend Matt's book to all who are desperate to see the kingdom of God released in fullness, here on earth, as it is in heaven. Matt carries the presence and passion of God in a beautiful way, and this is clearly reflected in the pages of his book.

—HEIDI BAKER, PHD
FOUNDING DIRECTOR, IRIS MINISTRIES

Do you want to make an impact with your life for Jesus Christ? Do you need more of the power of God to accomplish your dreams? Then look no further. Matt Sorger is a modern-day revivalist crying in the wilderness that hope is on the way. Yes, you can leave an impact in your sphere of influence and accomplish your very dreams. Be equipped by scriptural truths combined with inspiring testimonies from my dear friend and partner advancing the kingdom of God. Receive power for your life!

—JAMES W. GOLL
ENCOUNTERS NETWORK, PRAYER STORM,
COMPASSION ACTS

Matt Sorger is one of the young promising evangelists for integrity and power. His book *Power for Life* reveals both of these emphases—integrity and power. The book is balanced. This is not charismania. I believe Matt teaches how to enter into the more. I am sure you will be blessed by reading and studying this book.

—RANDY CLARK
FOUNDER OF THE APOSTOLIC NETWORK OF
GLOBAL AWAKENING

The world is in desperate need of heroes. My dear friend Matt Sorger has provided you with a road map of the birth, growth, development, and release of the hero within you for the day in which you and I are living. His signposts are clear and scriptural, his intention is exceptional, his passion is admirable, and his promise to you is transferrable by the same Spirit that is working in him that has worked in all heroes of God in past generations. *Power for Life* will unleash God's greatness in you and through you and cause you to respond to a call that is issuing from His heart in this hour for those whose lives are clearly marked by God's presence! Thanks, Matt, for taking the time to pen these words; may they go deep into the hearts of the ageless generation that will be led by the Spirit to read them, apply them, and experience the fruit of them in this hour!

—Dr. Mark Chironna
The Master's Touch International Church
Mark Chironna Ministries

Matt Sorger is one of my favorite ministers! He is dedicated, passionate, and full of integrity. His book *Power for Life* is written from his own life experiences and study in the Word of God and is loaded with fresh revelation of the Word and practical wisdom to help you walk in the power of God. What Matt pens in this book is authentic and trustworthy—a great book for your library!

—Patricia King
Cofounder, XPmedia

In Matt's book *Power for Life*, you will learn how to connect to the power of God and direct it according to God's purposes so that you may be used as a conduit of God's glory. As you become a channel of God's presence, you will help bring the societal reformation we are believing for.

—Ché Ahn
Senior Pastor, HROCK Church
President, Harvest International Ministry

In his book *Power for Life*, Matt Sorger has presented how to harness and release the power of God in our lives. Its truth will set many free and help you fulfill your destiny. The kingdom of God will be advanced and the church more triumphant when the jewels in this book are applied. It will enhance your life as you discover the power and purpose God intends for you. Everyone needs to read this book and put in to practice its spiritual truths and practical principles. As a result, much more will be accomplished in your life and ministry.

—DR. BILL HAMON
BISHOP, CHRISTIAN INTERNATIONAL MINISTRIES
NETWORK (CIMN)

In his book *Power for Life*, Matt Sorger combines powerful biblical principles with artfully communicated life stories to present a handbook for believers to live lives of victory, vision, and purpose. You will be encouraged as Matt shares much of his own journey toward living the life of an overcomer. This book will inspire you to live stronger and reach higher than you ever have before.

—JANE HAMON
CHRISTIAN INTERNATIONAL MINISTRIES

Matt's book *Power for Life* has fresh insights into releasing the wonderful presence of the Holy Spirit in strategic areas of our lives. You have a resource here to not only propel you into God's supernatural but also to assist others in getting their breakthrough. I am grateful for tools like these that help us go from glory to glory.

—MAHESH CHAVDA
CHAVDA MINISTRIES INTERNATIONAL

Matt Sorger is a lover of God first, as well as a powerful dynamic minister that the Lord has raised up to demonstrate His glory to this generation. I was privileged to be part of his ordination to ministry and have been impressed at his humility and purity of heart. His new book, *Power for Life*, will release in you supernatural faith in Almighty God to do the impossible in your life. The dynamic ingredients for miraculous living are in this life-changing book. This is a must-read for the entire body of Christ. I highly recommend it!

—Bob Weiner
Weiner Ministries International

POWER
FOR
LIFE

POWER FOR LIFE

MATT SORGER

CHARISMA
HOUSE

Most CHARISMA HOUSE Book Group products are available at special quantity discounts for bulk purchase for sales promotions, premiums, fund-raising, and educational needs. For details, write Charisma House Book Group, 600 Rinehart Road, Lake Mary, Florida 32746, or telephone (407) 333-0600.

POWER FOR LIFE by Matt Sorger
Published by Charisma House
Charisma Media/Charisma House Book Group
600 Rinehart Road
Lake Mary, Florida 32746
www.charismahouse.com

Unless otherwise noted, all Scripture quotations are from the Amplified Bible. Old Testament copyright © 1965, 1987 by the Zondervan Corporation. The Amplified New Testament copyright © 1954, 1958, 1987 by the Lockman Foundation. Used by permission.

Scripture quotations marked KJV are from the King James Version of the Bible.

Scripture quotations marked NKJV are from the New King James Version of the Bible. Copyright © 1979, 1980, 1982 by Thomas Nelson, Inc., publishers. Used by permission.

Cover design by Justin Evans
Design Director: Bill Johnson

Visit the author's website at www.mattsorger.com.

Library of Congress Cataloging-in-Publication Data:
Sorger, Matt.
  Power for life / Matt Sorger.
    p. cm.
  Includes bibliographical references (p.   ).
  ISBN 978-1-61638-277-3 (trade paper) -- ISBN 978-1-61638-569-9
(e-book) 1. Christian life--Pentecostal authors. 2. Power (Christian theology) I. Title.
  BV4501.3.S659 2011
  248.4'8994--dc23
                                          2011020705

11 12 13 14 15 — 9 8 7 6 5 4 3 2 1
Printed in the United States of America

I dedicate this book to my family.

First to my parents, Richard and Veronica Sorger, for their selfless love and sacrifice and for being two of the most amazing people I know. You have taught me how to have faith, how to walk with God, and how to truly love others. Your example has been extraordinary, and I honor you as my parents and celebrate you as my friends.

Second, to my brother, Rick Sorger, for being my best friend and for cheering me on in my pursuit of God. Your encouragement and faith have inspired and empowered me to dream bigger and reach further.

And to my amazing sister-in-law and nephews, Sabrina, Ricky, and Eric. I love you!

ACKNOWLEDGMENTS

I WANT TO FIRST thank God for stepping into my life at the age of fourteen. You became my best friend as a teenager, and Your presence has been with me ever since. Thank You for showing me the truth, healing me on the inside, and making me the man of God You called me to be. As long as I have Your presence, I know everything will be OK. Thank You for loving me and empowering me to help others be all You have destined them to be.

Thanks and love to my family, staff, ministry team, partners, and intercessors. Without you I could never do what I do for God. You are loved, valued, and highly appreciated! Together we are seeing miracles happen.

Special thanks to every leader who has had an impact on my life. You know who you are. Thank you for believing in me and cheering me on. I honor you and thank God for your love and wisdom.

Contents

FOREWORD

I LOVE BOOKS THAT take me on a journey, especially when I know that the author has written from the wisdom and insights gained in his own experience. It's not that I mind "classroom theories." Theories have their place in creating avenues for future dreams and experiments. There just comes a time when I need to know the absolutes of this Christian walk that have been proven over time. *Power for Life* is a book of such absolutes, tested, proven, and recorded for our benefit. It is out of Matt Sorger's purity and teachable spirit that these pages were written. The keys and principles in it create a clear road map of how to value the presence of God and walk in a lifestyle of fullness of power and deep intimate relationship. Though it operates as a "how-to" manual, it also extends an invitation and stirs the heart's cry of the reader to cultivate greater intimacy with the Father. Matt's journey displays the fruit of discipline, the joy of sacrifice, and the fullness of the Holy Spirit resting and operating through a surrendered life.

This journey is all that one could hope for. It is the reason we are alive. But like the greatest adventures in life, it is dangerous. It's dangerous to old mind-sets, dangerous to mediocrity and complacency, and dangerous to religious boredom. Matt connects us to the power of God for a life of *victory and overcoming*. We were born for this! He also introduces us to the *sustaining nature of God's power.* Longevity is key in this Christian life. God looks to be able to trust

us with an increased measure of Himself. And finally, we are introduced to the process of *staying fresh*. Oh, how we need this right
now. So many have tasted of God's great work but have become
stale and dry, which is one of the most contradictory experiences in
our walk with Jesus.

It has been said that the one who gives the most hope will always
have the most influence. If that is true, and I believe it is, then
Matt Sorger and his book *Power for Life* are about to take center
stage. This wonderful book brings hope by unveiling the road map
to supernatural purpose in a way that is neither cheap and easy nor
impossible to obtain. The truths on these pages were acquired in
raw, life experiences. And it is our privilege to glean what Matt has
learned to steward so well.

King David knew something of this journey unto supernatural
purpose. He fulfilled his destiny in ways that few have before or
since. Inspired by the brilliance of God's desire for humanity, he
wrote, "May He grant you according to your heart's *desire*, and
fulfill all your purpose" (Ps. 20:4, NKJV). When God fulfills our
heart's desire, we are much more likely to fulfill His purpose for
our lives. Yet anyone who thinks that God loves to be directed
by the desires of a selfish people couldn't be more wrong. Therein
is the process revealed: God disciplines us in such a way that we
can bear up under His blessing. God desires to have a people who
won't be destroyed by His response to our desires. This, in part, is
where we fulfill our purpose. But when we strive for significance,
we undermine our significance.

Thankfully, Matt provides no shortcuts to Christian success.
Instead he reveals the divine process he has yielded to that has
brought him to a place of abundant fruitfulness for the King. This
is the privilege and pleasure of every believer—living for the glory
of another, Jesus Christ. An interesting picture is given in Scripture
of this process: a woman poured costly perfume over Jesus and
wiped it with her hair. While she did it for His sake, she walked
out smelling the same way Jesus did. It's the same for us: we live

to bring glory to the King. But we live in the same glory, smelling like Him.

We live in a time of great transition. What can be shaken is being shaken, and people are looking for solid ground to stand on. In our ministry we see highly trained professionals leaving their post in order to come and be trained in the ministry of saving the lost, healing the sick, and delivering the tormented. Their income and their station in life matter little any more. While many go back to their professions, it's not the position they seek. It's the hand of God upon their lives that becomes the great prize. These kinds of shifts are seen all through society as people are searching for their purpose. Even the world's wealthiest are giving away billions of dollars to try to fix what is wrong. And whether it's for saving the planet or destroying poverty, there is a cry in their hearts for significance. This is a God moment. A stable people can bring stability to a shaking world. This has become our moment.

Matt's life message demonstrates how to become trusted with heaven on earth. Our connection to the purposes of God—the sustaining presence of God's power working in our lives—puts everything in place, satisfying our desire to bring Him glory while allowing us to step fully into a position of eternal significance. Enjoy this great adventure!

—BILL JOHNSON
SENIOR LEADER OF BETHEL CHURCH, REDDING, CA
AUTHOR OF *WHEN HEAVEN INVADES EARTH* AND
FACE TO FACE WITH GOD

Fruit Produces Power

WHEN I WAS in my freshman year of college, the Lord spoke something very deep to my heart. He told me that the top of my list was the bottom of His, and the bottom of His list was the top of mine. At the top of His list was the refinement of my character, not the fulfillment of my ministry. He told me that He was going to cause my roots to go down so deep in Him that when success came to my life, I would not be moved. For years after receiving that word, I walked through some very deep refining fires in my life. God dealt with character issues in me that would become the foundation upon which He would release His power in me and through me. God first gave me the power to live holy and consecrated, and then He released His power through me to see others deeply touched by His presence. Even to this day character development is a daily process.

Power is defined in Webster's dictionary as "supplying a force to operate; to drive or push; to inspire, sustain; to conduct electricity; and the ability to do or act."

Power for life is about having the internal force and ability to live life to it's maximum potential. The power of God will be conducted in and through our lives as the fruit of the Spirit are cultivated and grown within us.

When I was a young person in school, I can remember another student using fruit to conduct electricity for a science project. I found it fascinating how a lemon could be used to light a light bulb. Fruit is a great conductor of electricity or power, and spiritual fruit will be a conductor of God's power in your life.

Let's Get Back to the Basics

Spiritual fruit are the qualities of God's nature you possess in your life. Galatians 5:22–23 states, "But the fruit of the [Holy] Spirit [the work which His presence within accomplishes] is love, joy (gladness), peace, patience (an even temper, forbearance), kindness, goodness (benevolence), faithfulness, gentleness (meekness, humility), self-control (self-restraint, continence)."

Many relegate the fruit of the Spirit to a Sunday school lesson, but it is much more than that. It's the very essence of God's power in us. While it is foundational, it is not trivial. It's a deception to think fruit is for the immature. The very proof of our maturity is our ability to walk in each of these qualities. It's one thing to know them, but it's another thing to live them. We learn about fruit as kids, but as we grow up, many times they're left unattended. Unattended fruit becomes rotten.

I was traveling on the road in ministry and was given a basket of fruit in my hotel room, but the fruit was rotten. As a result the fruit was swarming with fruit flies that eventually filled my entire hotel room. I had to throw the fruit out and clean my room. Rotten fruit attracts flies. The same thing happens in our lives when we neglect the basic yet profound principles of God's way to live. Our lives become rotten and attract darkness.

Many times people separate fruit from power. They think they are unrelated. They fail to realize that a lifestyle of fruit actually releases God's power in extraordinary ways.

Unleashing the Power Within You

Remember Winston Churchill, Abraham Lincoln, Mother Teresa, Martin Luther, Kathryn Kuhlman, Oral Roberts, and Billy Graham? They lived lifestyles that demonstrated the fruit of the Spirit. They were conductors of the power of God. Where are the heroes like that?

As we stand on the brink of social reformation and societal transformation, in a world where darkness clashes with light, people are in desperate need of something and someone to believe in—leaders, friends, and pastors with integrity and truth.

They want to know, who is standing for the lost, hurting, wounded, poor, and needy? Who is standing in truth and love? Is it you?

I was a very imaginative child growing up. I loved the thought of flying through the air and leaping over tall buildings in a single bound. In the classic story of Superman, Clark Kent was an unassuming reporter by day but had superhuman strength and ability hidden beneath the surface of his calm demeanor. In a moment, a transformation would take place, enabling Clark Kent to become Superman. He had the ability to overcome the greatest obstacles with superhuman strength, but many couldn't see it on the surface.

The same is true for you. You may not be able to literally leap over a tall building, but your power far exceeds that of Superman. For you have the Greater One living on the inside of you, enabling you to do the unimaginable. But you must first see and know the hero God has created you to be, and that starts by knowing the Hero who already lives in you.

The Power of Three

I have divided this book into three power-filled sections to help you get in position to live a life that is marked with the supernatural presence of God.

In the first section, "Plugging Into the Power Source," you will learn how to plug into God's power. God's power is granted to us so we can live true, authentic, overcoming lives filled with victory and freedom every day! This power is not just for a momentary experience. It's for life! His power is there for you on Monday morning when you have to get up and go to that job you dislike. His power is there for you when you are facing a difficult trial and circumstance. His power is there for you when you wake up in a bad mood and feel discouraged and defeated. His power is there for you when you face that same struggle and temptation you have fought before. His power is there for you when an unexpected crisis hits your life. His real, authentic, supernatural power is there to help you live your life every day in His fullness and abundance.

Once you plug into God's power, you will then move on to section two, "Harnessing the Power," where you will learn how to see God's power harnessed and sustained in your life for the long haul. Harnessing enables us to sustain, protect, nurture, and mature God's power in our lives.

You will be challenged to ask yourself the question, "Can God trust me?" This is why the harnessing process to develop strong, godly character is so important. The more He can trust us, the more He will give us because He knows we will be able to carry, sustain, and then release His power through our daily lives without endangering ourselves or those around us.

In the third section, "Releasing the Power," not only will you learn how to plug into and sustain God's power, but you will also be equipped to see that power supernaturally released through your life. The power of God is not just for you; it is for everyone you will come in contact with. God infuses you with His power so you can live a triumphant life and then pass that victory onto others. You must release His power in order for it to stay fresh and alive within you.

Biblically, there is a law of release. When you endure life's processing and challenges, release is imminent. Job was released into a double portion. Joseph was released into the palace. Israel was released into the Promised Land. David was released into kingship.

Jesus was released into divine power and ministry. The disciples were released into apostleship. The one hundred twenty in the Upper Room were released into power. Paul was released to the Gentiles. And each one of you reading this book right now has promises and a destiny over your life God is waiting to release you into.

The Choice Is Yours

One thing you need to know is that power for life is a choice! God has created us all with free will—your ability to make choices. Choices are containers for power. Make the right choices, and your life will be transformed! True power comes from the life you live. Your hidden lifestyle will either release God's abundant blessings or bring you into low-level living. The choice is yours.

> No trumpets sound when the important decisions of your life are made. Destiny is made known silently.[1]
>
> —Agnes DeMille

Make the decision to not live one more second beneath the fullness of everything God has for you. No more defeat. No more depression. No more negativity. No more fear. No more complacency, apathy, or lethargy. This is your life, and you only have one, so live it to the full.

CHAPTER 1

Don't Squeeze My Fruit

A PASTOR WALKED INTO his church on a Sunday morning and shared with his staff before the service started how he wanted to quit the ministry and was going to tell the people that day. Rather than sitting on the platform as he normally did, he chose to sit on the front row. During worship he sat there with his arms folded with a blank look on his face. He made no attempt to worship God. He was stone cold in his spirit. Right before he got up to preach, he whispered to his assistant, "Watch me preach. The people won't know the difference."

As he stood at the pulpit to preach, he opened up his mouth and spoke with the same eloquence he spoke with every Sunday. The words sounded great. In fact, they were impressive. When he finished preaching, he closed his Bible, walked off the platform, and disappeared into a back room. No one was the wiser. They clapped and applauded as usual. They left the service that day hearing a great message, but they were untouched and unchanged by the Spirit of God. They had fallen for charismatic hype. Things looked great on the outside, but there was no fruit on the inside. There was no power. No lives changed. Just empty ritual.

One day Jesus was walking down the road, and He spotted a

fig tree up on the embankment. Jesus got excited because He was hungry and saw that the fig tree was full of lush, green leaves. I imagine He hoped to find it full of ripe figs. But He got a little closer and saw that there was not one fig on the whole tree! There were all those leaves and no figs. With a single word He cursed the fig tree, and it instantly withered up and died. The disciples marveled at Jesus's power and authority, that even fig trees obeyed His command (Mark 11:12–14).

Jesus used the experience to teach them a lesson on faith that if they would just believe, they too could speak to even a mountain and it would have to move out of their way. But I believe this passage was designed for us to learn a few other things.

The first lesson has to do with us. Just as the fig tree looked lush and fruitful from a distance, there are many of us who look good from a distance. We smell good, sound good, and speak well. Surely there is spiritual fruit hidden in between all those leaves of gifts and talents.

Even some preachers, who can whip a crowd into a frenzy knowing just the right words to say to get a reaction from the people, can fool us into thinking there is fruit there. But I have come to learn that eloquent speech cannot always be equated with the true power of God. In fact, if you look a little closer, what you often find is form of godliness that lacks the true power of God to transform people's lives. Whooping and hollering are not the power of God. Shouting and dancing are not always the power of God.

We must long to have more than an exterior that looks good from a distance. We can polish ourselves up with fancy suits and ties, and hats and dresses. We can say all the right words and be stellar actors or actresses. But when Jesus comes closer, He doesn't want to see just leaves. He wants the fruit. He wants something deeper. He wants His hunger to be satisfied. God longs for people who won't just look good on the outside but will be true and genuine deep down in the fiber of their being, people who are truly living what they are portraying and who live in the pure authentic power of the living God. It's not enough to look good from a distance. Jesus is looking for fruit in the lives of His people.

The other lesson taught from the story of the fig tree has to do with our natural talents and spiritual gifts. Natural talents are abilities and strengths you are born with. For example, some are naturally gifted public speakers. Others have amazing musical abilities and can sing people to goose bumps and tears. Some are born with outstanding athletic inclinations, while others have a genius IQ. These are natural God-given talents and look great from a distance.

Then there are the supernatural gifts of the Spirit found in 1 Corinthians 12:8–10. These include "[the power to speak] a message of wisdom, and to another [the power to express] a word of knowledge and understanding according to the same [Holy] Spirit; to another [wonder-working] faith by the same [Holy] Spirit, to another the extraordinary powers of healing by the one Spirit; to another the working of miracles, to another prophetic insight (the gift of interpreting the divine will and purpose); to another the ability to discern and distinguish between [the utterances of true] spirits [and false ones], to another various kinds of [unknown] tongues, to another the ability to interpret [such] tongues."

From a distance the operation of the gifts of the Spirit in our lives can also look great. The gifts are given to imperfect vessels by God's grace and are without repentance (Rom. 11:29). As a person is seeking relationship with God, he or she can start off right and begin operating in gifts of the Spirit. But it's not enough just to start right; we also have to finish right. It's possible to begin strong but then ride on the gifts and abilities God has given and stray from Him in your heart. This is the danger of seeking talents and gifts apart from fruit.

Jesus made it very clear: "Therefore, you will fully know them by their fruits" (Matt. 7:20). What truly marks us as people who live a Spirit-empowered life is the fruit we produce.

Pruned if You Do and Pruned if You Don't

If you are a gardener or have a green thumb and grow plants in your home, you know that one of the best ways to get good fruit or full blossoms from your favorite bush is to prune or even cut it back completely during the right season. In John 15:2 Jesus compares us to branches. He says that if a branch does not produce fruit at all, it is to be cut off. And the branches that do produce fruit, He prunes and cuts back. You don't have to be doing something wrong to be pruned. It's actually when you are doing things right that pruning takes place. So look, you are pruned if you do and pruned if you don't. You might as well deal with it and let God produce His fruit in you. But there is one sure thing: it's better to be cut back than to be cut off.

So how does God prune us? Well, He does it in two major ways. First we know that His Word prunes us.

> You are cleansed and pruned already, because of the word which I have given you [the teachings I have discussed with you].
>
> —John 15:3

As we read His Word, our true condition is revealed and our hearts are exposed. Hebrews 4:12 says that the Word of God is "active and full of power...penetrating to the dividing line of the breath of life (soul) and [the immortal] spirit, and of joints and marrow [of the deepest parts of our nature], exposing and sifting and analyzing and judging the very thoughts and purposes of the heart." Through His Word, God shows us where we have missed it so that we can begin to live in a way that truly pleases Him. Also as we read and think on His Word, His Word contains a cleansing power that works in us, causing us to be the person He has destined us to be. His Word lights our paths and gives us the right direction for all aspects of our lives. His Word gives us the power to live a life that produces fruit.

> Every Scripture is God-breathed (given by His inspiration) and profitable for instruction, for reproof and conviction of sin, for correction of error and discipline in obedience, [and] for training in righteousness (in holy living, in conformity to God's will in thought, purpose, and action).
> —2 Timothy 3:16

God's Word puts before us the image of Christ, who perfectly lived out the fruit of the Spirit and walked in the power of God. By beholding His Word, we are pruned, groomed, corrected, and encouraged to be like Him.

Our relationships with others are also used to prune us. That's right. God puts all those "fruit testers" around us to make sure we are producing the right fruit. He creates all these people, each with different personalities. Some He creates strong-willed. Others He creates meek and mild. God creates all these different types of people and throws them all together. It's one big fruit salad! But it's really as these people interact with each other that true fruit is produced or the lack of it is exposed.

You know, there are two spiritual beings trying to kill you. "What?" you may ask. "Kill me?" Yes, kill you. God and Satan. Satan comes as a thief to steal, kill, and destroy for your harm. Satan comes to try to destroy God's plan and purpose for your life. God comes to kill our carnal and fleshly ways so we can experience His resurrection power! That kind of death is for our good. He allows every area of our life to become crucified with Christ so we can experience His power in those areas. Paul said, "I have been crucified with Christ; it is no longer I who live, but Christ lives in me; and the life which I now live in the flesh I live by faith in the Son of God, who loved me and gave Himself for me" (Gal. 2:20, NKJV).

Before we can receive resurrection power, we have to first experience His death. As we die to self, His power is released in us, enabling us to be who He has called us to be. And what better way to die than by all the interactions we have with people around us on a daily basis? Every time one of our buttons gets pushed and we choose to respond with love and grace, we die. When we are by ourselves, we are all little angels. There we are in prayer enjoying the presence of God. We are floating on a cloud. Everything is peaceful and perfect! Then the wife, the husband, or the kids come home. Shoes are left everywhere, clothes are thrown on the floor, or dishes are left in the sink. Suddenly the halo disappears, and the horns come out. Where did the little angel go? Buttons of the flesh start to get pushed, and the internal fruit start to be seen on the outside. This kind of reveal can only happen through our interactions with people. It's those closest to us who will really see what kind of fruit we have.

Picture this scenario with me. There you are at home having a "discussion" with your husband or wife or kids. It's a bit heated. Voices are raised; emotions are flared. Then the phone rings. "Hello," you say with a perfectly calm, relaxed voice. It's the pastor. "Well, hello, Pastor, so good to hear from you. Oh, yes, I am so excited about the bake sale on Saturday. For sure, I will be there with my cookies. Amen. God bless. Praise the Lord. I'm saved, sanctified, and filled with the Holy Ghost! Talk to you later, Pastor." Once the phone hangs up, the yelling picks up right where it left off.

It seems that we can have full control over what fruit we display and produce depending on who is around. Our family tends to see the worst in us. Why? We feel the most comfortable, and also because family is family. They can't leave you. Your parents are your parents, your kids are your kids, and your mate is your mate. Once you get married, it's till death do you part. God will use your closest relationships to produce your greatest fruit.

So rather than trying to constantly change them, you may be better off just accepting them for who they are. You will probably enjoy your journey a lot more if you pray for God to change you rather than the people around you. If you are able to produce fruit under trying circumstances, then eventually what bothered you about that person will no longer irritate you. As you die to yourself, you will get victory over those irritating emotions and will be much happier as a result. Always remember, when you are praying for someone else to change, God is looking for you to change. You might as well as die and get it over with.

We can't run from community; we have to embrace it. It's what God uses to perfect us. Doesn't that just make you happy? Well, it should. So, get happy and enjoy the journey. When you think someone else is a "fruit tester," remember you may be the "fruit tester" for someone else!

In Season and Out

I asked God a question: "Why did You curse the fig tree even when it wasn't the season for figs? How could You hold the tree accountable to produce fruit out of season?" It just didn't seem fair to me. Then this scripture came to mind: "Be ready in season and out of season" (2 Tim. 4:2, NKJV).

I realized that no matter what season it is, no matter what our circumstances are, no matter if it's a good day or a bad day, Jesus wants us to be bearing fruit. It will not always be easy to bear good fruit. It requires a death to the desires of the flesh and to the self-life. But God wants us to be ready in season and out of season, and His Spirit gives us the power to do that.

The awesome thing is that when God asks us to do something, it's because He knows He has already made the provision for it! He never asks us to do something on our own without His help.

Jesus is more concerned with our fruit than He is about our gifts or material success. This is revealed in Matthew 7:22–23, where those who operate in great gifts are told to depart from Jesus because He never really knew them. Their lack of fruit caused them to miss the most important thing: relationship with God and acceptance into the kingdom of heaven. Jesus also said in Matthew 21:43, "I tell you, for this reason the kingdom of God will be taken away from you and given to a people who will produce the fruits of it." Fruit is on the top of God's priority list for us.

You Will Be Fruitful

Joel prophesied, "Be not afraid, you wild beasts of the field, for the pastures of the wilderness have sprung up and are green; the tree bears its fruit, and the fig tree and the vine yield their [full] strength" (Joel 2:22). As God continues to work in us, He will cause the wilderness places to become green pastures. He will cause dry, dead places to become alive. He will cause the tree, our lives, to bear fruit and the vine to have full strength. God gives us the strength to bear the fruit He desires us to have. He makes us strong in spirit. This is our destiny.

My heartfelt prayer for you as you read this book is Colossians 1:10: "That you may walk (live and conduct yourselves) in a manner worthy of the Lord, fully pleasing to Him and desiring to please Him in all things, bearing fruit in every good work and steadily growing and increasing in and by the knowledge of God [with fuller, deeper, and clearer insight, acquaintance, and recognition]."

I believe this is the heartbeat of God found within these pages, that we will live in a way that pleases God. As we do, we will bear fruit as His magnificent power is displayed in and through our lives, and in the end we will have grown in our deep, intimate knowledge of God.

PART I

Plugging Into the Power Source

CHAPTER 2

The Power of Intimacy

Hitting the Saturation Point

WHEN GOD FIRST revealed Himself to my family and me, He showed Himself to be a God of miracles and power. I was fourteen years old at the time, and what a year it had been. God stepped into my life, and nothing would ever be the same again. I was raised Catholic. Our family went to church once or twice a year on Christmas and Easter. I used to love lighting the candles in church. The smell of the incense and the peaceful atmosphere were very inviting to me. I still have memories of the midnight mass at Saint Margaret's, looking up into the windows near the ceiling of the church and seeing hundreds of lights flickering back at me as we stood there singing "Hallelujah," holding our little white candles in the dark. I loved it.

I remember asking my parents if we could go to church. For some reason, beyond the influence of man, I was always drawn to church and to spiritual things. I would love to get my hymnal and sing the songs aloud. There was a higher, unseen Force drawing me; I just didn't know it. We were not a super-religious family. I believed in God and in Jesus, but I didn't have a personal relationship with Him. I knew He was the Lamb of God who takes away the sins of the world, but I had not yet had my sins forgiven. To me, God was some distant Being floating in the universe somewhere.

Then it happened, the night that would change my life forever. My mom had been sick for two years. She had spent thousands of dollars on hospital bills. She tried everything she could from modern medicine to homeopathic remedies to alternative spiritual healing techniques. But nothing worked. She only grew worse. I was twelve when she first became sick. Her sickness started with a weird dizzy feeling in her head, but it soon took over to the point where she had constant pins and needles throughout her arms and hands. She couldn't walk straight and eventually had to just lie in bed. By the end of two years, she was bedridden. The doctors diagnosed her with everything in the book from a virus in her spine to a rare blood disorder to strange yeast infections to multiple sclerosis and more. But no matter what medicine she took, she only grew worse.

I still have some of the pages from my journal as a child. "Dear God. I'm really worried about Mom. She is really sick. I don't know what's wrong with her. The doctors don't either. Please help my mom. The medicine isn't working. Nothing is. I don't want her to die." That was from November 9, 1986.

Sometime later that year my grandmother invited her to a Catholic charismatic healing service where the priests were filled with the Holy Spirit. That night she was the worst she had ever been. But she was determined to get to that healing mass. She knew in her heart that God was her only hope. If He didn't somehow intervene, her life was over. As she entered the church that night, she collapsed on the floor in the back of the sanctuary. With tears running down her face, she looked up and saw the cross. She prayed, "Jesus, tonight I am coming to You and You alone." She made her way forward for prayer, and before the priest could even lay his hand on her, the power of the Holy Spirit overshadowed her. The force was so strong that she was knocked back through the air about ten feet across the altar.

As she lay on the floor, she could feel what felt like tons of electricity flowing through her body. She thought she died and went to heaven. The priests helped her off the floor. She could still feel God's power flowing through her. When she stood up, she noticed something. All the pain and sickness was gone from her body! Not only that, but she had given her heart completely to Jesus. In that moment she realized that Jesus was the only way to get to God. She had tried alternative healing methods that dabbled in Hinduism and Buddhist backgrounds, but they only made her worse. She even tried New Age healing techniques. It all failed her. In fact, the more she participated in things such as meditation and yoga, the sicker she became! God was making sure that she understood Jesus was the only way into true relationship with God. She was sincerely seeking to know the truth, and that night she found it!

I still remember when my mom came walking through the front door of our house. She was bright and smiling. I hadn't seen my mom smile in two years. "What happened?" I exclaimed. "You look so different!" She said, "Jesus healed me!"

Here's what I wrote in my journal right after, on January 27, 1987: "I am so happy Jesus healed my mom! He's great!" What a change!

That week my entire family came into a real and true relationship with God. I can remember sitting down with my mom as she shared with me about what Jesus did for us on the cross. Something strange happened on the inside of me. As she spoke to me about Jesus, a sudden awareness of my sins came over me, and I knew I needed forgiveness for them. No one told me I had sinned. I just knew it. We prayed together, and I asked Jesus to forgive me. A new chapter began in my life. I felt clean. Something changed inside of me. It was the beginning of a glorious relationship with God. No longer was He a distant force floating out in the universe somewhere. He had stepped down into my life. He was real!

We soon joined a Full Gospel church that had solid teaching in the Word and lively praise and worship music. The first month of attendance, we all stood against the back wall, my brother and me with our hands in our pockets. It was all so new for us. After a few months something began to break through in my spirit. I found myself being drawn to the front row of the church! So one Sunday, without saying a word to my parents, I walked from the back row to the front row. As I closed my eyes and sang the songs, I could feel a sensation going over my entire body. God was filling me with His presence. It was glorious! God was so close. I could feel Him in me and all around me. His presence was overwhelming.

Reaching the Saturation Point

Each week in church I would close my eyes, lift my hands, and worship God. In those corporate church settings His manifest presence was so real to me. His presence would come like waves over my body. As time went on, I wanted more of God. I wanted to know His presence when I was alone! So I took my tape player (remember, this was 1988, and we didn't have CDs or MP3s yet) and my favorite worship tape and would go into my room, close the door, and worship God for an hour every day in private. I would sing the same songs I had sung a hundred times before in church, but I felt nothing! I felt dry and distant from God. It was nothing like when I worshiped Him in church under the corporate atmosphere of His presence. But I was determined to connect with God.

After about four months of pressing in and seeking God, it happened. I was singing a song I had sung a thousand times before, but this time something happened. I understand now that my spirit reached a saturation point. God's Spirit overflowed from my spirit into my soul and body.

It's a picture frozen in time, a snapshot of glory imprinted in my memory. I was standing in the middle of my bedroom, a young fifteen-year-old boy, my eyes closed and hands lifted up. As I sang, heaven opened up over me. My entire room became filled with the manifest presence of God! My entire body was completely overcome by His presence. God stepped down into my little room. It was just He and I. He was already living in my spirit upon salvation, but now He was overflowing into my soul and body. He was filling all of me. It was a moment of spiritual breakthrough that would transform my personal intimacy with God.

I grew throughout my teen years with the help of a youth group, and God continued to take me deeper and higher in Him. I began to learn a principle from the life of Jesus that would soon begin to release a supernatural power in and through my life. I had such a deep passion to pray and spend time with God. This drive did not come from any human source. It was divinely inspired from within. No one told me to pray. No one told me to worship. It came from the Holy Spirit inside of me.

For years as a teenager and young adult in my twenties, my favorite thing to do was take my guitar and go off into a secluded place for hours and worship God. It was such a special time. This was where I learned to hear God's voice in prophecy. I would go so deep in His presence that God would begin to sing songs back to me prophetically. I would sing spontaneous songs in the Spirit for hours as God revealed His heart to me.

As I learned to live in God's presence, I began to find that even when I was doing nonspiritual things, such as taking a walk or shopping at the supermarket, I would find God's presence right there with me. At times His presence would wash over me in waves. Oh, to live constantly in His presence! This must be our highest pursuit in life.

It was on my first missions trip to Mexico as a teenager that I learned what it meant to be completely saturated and possessed by God. One night I was on the roof of the orphanage where we were working. As a small group of us worshiped God, I began to pray, "Holy Spirit, I want You to possess every fiber of my being. I want every molecule and cell in my body filled with You." As I prayed this, suddenly the manifest presence of God filled every single part of me. It was as if every molecule in my body was electrified with

His presence. In that moment, He had all of me—spirit, soul, and body. It was glorious!

As I studied the Bible, I learned that there was such a deep desire in the heart of Jesus to be in relationship and fellowship with His heavenly Father that His lifestyle reflected His passion. From the time He was a child, Jesus could be found in the temple. He even scared His parents one day when they couldn't find Him because He was in the temple having a deep discussion with the adult teachers over Scripture. His level of understanding amazed the people (Luke 2:44–52).

Jesus was drawn into intimacy with God from a very early age. The same was true for His cousin, John the Baptist. John was a prophetic voice being raised up and prepared by God for a very special purpose. The Bible says in Luke 1:80 concerning John, "And the little boy grew and became strong in spirit; and he was in the deserts (wilderness) until the day of his appearing to Israel [the commencement of his public ministry]."

John was drawn into intimacy with God during his years of preparation and was separated from the voices of this world so he could clearly hear the voice of God. He had an important call and destiny to fulfill. He couldn't fulfill His mandate unless he was alone with God.

As an adult Jesus's lifestyle also continued to reflect a walk of intimacy with God. Before important decisions He would spend much time alone with God, such as when He was to gather the original twelve disciples around Himself. He spent the entire night in prayer (Luke 6:12–13). Out of this place of intimacy His steps were divinely ordered, and the first twelve disciples found their way to Jesus.

Cultivating a Lifestyle of Prayer and Intimacy With God

Jesus set a perfect example and model for us to follow. He showed us what it is to truly walk in supernatural power. He also showed us His source. Jesus was continually being moved with compassion and faith, releasing supernatural virtue everywhere He went. All around Him the sick were being healed and oppressed people being set free. The blind were receiving their sight, the lame were walking, the deaf were hearing, and even the dead were being raised back to life. Now that's supernatural power!

We know Jesus received this power after His forty days in the wilderness. He went in filled with the Spirit, but after a time of testing, He came out under the power of the Spirit (Luke 4:1–2, 13–14). But it didn't end there. Throughout His earthly ministry Jesus was continually withdrawing from the crowds to be alone with God. As He poured out God's power to help people, He was continually being filled Himself. This was the secret to His sustained, unlimited power.

In many portions of Scripture you will see a direct connection between Jesus's secret prayer life and His public display of power. When Jesus taught us how to pray, in Matthew 6:6, He told us to go into a private place and pray to our Father in secret. God who sees in secret will reward us in the open.

A father in the faith, Lou Engle, once shared with me, "Matt, what you do in secret will one day be put on the stage of history." He was telling me how important my private life was before God. How I lived in secret would impact my public ministry. My private prayer life would have a tremendous impact on how God used me publicly. The same is true for all of us.

Kathryn Kuhlman, a woman who moved in tremendous power from God to heal the sick, once shared, "The greatest power that God has given to any individual is the power of prayer."[1]

Another great healing minister, Smith Wigglesworth, said, "I never get out of bed in the morning without having communion with God in the Spirit."[2] He also said, "I don't often spend more than half an hour in prayer at one time, but I never go more than half an hour without praying."[3] Prayer was a lifestyle for him.

An example of Jesus's walk of intimacy and power with God can be seen in Mark 1:32–42. After a night of healing and setting many people free, Jesus went out in the morning before the sun even rose to a deserted place to be alone in prayer. Right after that time of prayer, again He traveled and continued to preach and set more people free. In this instance He also healed a man of leprosy. We see a pattern. Prayer, power, prayer. The power of God will be sandwiched in between our prayer life.

It's a lifestyle. Sometimes Jesus prayed at night. At other times it was in the morning. Since Jesus had to be ready at any moment to minister into a situation, I believe He cultivated a habit of continual communion with God. He had His times of consecrated prayer, but His spirit was always listening for God's voice and guidance. Your relationship with God and times of prayer cannot be put into a box, religious formula, or pattern. Here's a good rule of thumb. Find time to be alone with God in between the times He pours His power through you. Seek to always cultivate His abiding presence in your life. Prayer will become as natural as breathing.

Secret Conversation With God

I love what Brother Lawrence, a lay brother of the Carmelite monastery in Paris in the 1600s, had to say about this.

> I have quitted all forms of devotion and set prayers but those to which my state obliges me. And I make it my business only to persevere in His holy presence, wherein I keep myself by a simple attention, and a general fond regard to God, which I may call an *actual presence of* God; or, to speak better, an habitual, silent, and secret conversation of the soul with God....
>
> In continuing the practice of conversing with God

throughout each day, and quickly seeking His forgiveness when I fell or strayed, His presence has become as easy and natural to me now as it once was difficult to attain....

The time of business...does not with me differ from the time of prayer; and in the noise and clatter of my kitchen, while several persons are at the same time calling for different things, I possess God as if I were upon my knees at the blessed sacrament....

There is not in the world a kind of life more sweet and delightful than that of a continual conversation with God. Those only can comprehend it who practice and experience it.[4]

Is Your Shadow Dangerous?

There is a reason why Jesus's intimacy with God produced power. He was able to hear God's voice and follow His leading and direction as a result of His intimate relationship with God.

Jesus walked in supernatural power because He did and spoke only what He saw and heard His Father doing and speaking (John 5:19). His actions reflected His relationship with God. His sole purpose was to do the will of the Father. His life of intimacy with God produced supernatural results.

And the same is true for us. Well, you may say, "Jesus was God! That's why He had the power He had. I'm just an ordinary person." True, we are just ordinary people, but Jesus was also a man. He came in the form of a person, just like you and me. But He was endued with supernatural power as He submitted His life to God. The same can happen for you and for me.

I love the story of Peter in the Bible. He was one of the more outspoken, strong-willed disciples. He needed a bit more work than the others, but he reached a point in his life where he died to himself and became filled with God's power, so much so that his shadow was dangerous (Acts 5:15–16).

Do you want to have a dangerous shadow? You can carry so much of God on your life that when you walk into a room, God walks in with you. Just like Peter, you can see whole cities impacted and every sick person healed and oppressed person set free! You can carry a level of power on your life that transforms people all around you everywhere you go!

How do you get a shadow? It's very simple. Stand in the light. When you stand in the light of God's presence through a lifestyle of intimacy with Him, His Spirit will overshadow you, creating a glory zone of His power all around you. When you learn to walk with God in an intimate way, His power within you is a natural overflow.

The religious people of Jesus's day discovered this secret of intimacy with God when they observed the extraordinary authority and power displayed through the disciples of Jesus. They were ordinary, uneducated men. Many of them caught fish for a living! No degrees, no college educations, nothing. Just a relationship with God.

> Now when they saw the boldness and unfettered eloquence of Peter and John and perceived that they were unlearned and untrained in the schools [common men with no educational advantages], they marveled; and they recognized that they had been with Jesus.
>
> —Acts 4:13

When you have been with Jesus, remarkable, miraculous things will happen in and through your life.

Surprised by God's Power

I'll never forget the time I was in Bible school ministering at a youth retreat up in Maine. I was asked to preach the message that night. The group of young people there were not very into it. I could hear them popping bubbles as they chewed on their gum. They were talking to one another while I was speaking. Even the youth pastor sat on the front row looking at his watch the entire time I spoke. I finally just asked the piano player to come to the keyboard so we could end the meeting. As I stood there with my eyes closed, I knew it would take more than my speaking skills to touch these young people.

I lifted my hands and invited the Holy Spirit to come into the room. Suddenly, without warning, a strong wind blew down from over my head and past my body. It was the tangible power of God! And the most amazing thing happened. Without me even giving an altar call, the young people simultaneously stood up, ran to the altar, and threw their bodies face first onto the ground. They began weeping and shaking and crying out to God. Tough young teenage boys were crying, and the girl's faces became streaked with makeup. It was quite a scene. I learned that night that one touch of God's presence and power could accomplish more than the greatest oratory skills.

Walking intimately with God must be our lifestyle. Relationship with God will release an overflow of His supernatural power in your life. Not only will God's presence within you enable you to live victoriously yourself, but His power will also overflow out of you to help others receive a touch from God. Your breakthrough into God's presence will become a point of breakthrough for others.

What You Do Today Will Influence Your Tomorrow

As I continued to grow in ministry, God would teach me some very important lessons along the way. After graduating from Bible school, I went on staff at a church as an assistant pastor for five years. Those were very special years. Prayer was very important to me—and still is to this day. I knew if I was ever to be used by God, my relationship with Him must come first. Everything I did for God would flow out of that relationship.

One morning as I came into my office at the church, I walked right into the manifest presence of God. The Holy Spirit was waiting for me in my office! The entire room was engulfed with His presence. As I walked in, God spoke to me and said, "Shut the door. I want to spend this entire day with you." As I spent time with God that day, His presence came so strong upon me that I couldn't even speak a word. At one point I was so overwhelmed with gratitude for God drawing so close to me that I wanted to tell Him thank You. As I opened my mouth to speak, I could sense His presence withdrawing. I suddenly realized that in that moment it was not about the words I could say; it was just about being with Him. My communion with God went far beyond anything words could say.

About halfway through the day I began to feel guilty for spending so much time in prayer. I thought of other things I needed to do. Speaking so clearly to me, God taught me a life lesson that would impact my life and ministry from that day forward. He said, "If you don't have this time with Me now, you will not be able to walk in what I have for you in the future." I suddenly realized that my future ministry was dependent on my current prayer life. With this new perspective, I spent the entire day and night sitting in my office chair engulfed in God's presence.

John Wesley once said, "I have so much to do that I spend several hours in prayer before I am able to do it."[5] He must have realized as well that without the power of intimacy with God, he could never do all God had called him to do.

At that time I had no idea what God had planned for me in just a few years to come. I had no idea I would be sent out in His power to see thousands of sick people healed and thousands brought to faith in Christ around the United States and the world! It all started back in my little bedroom in Long Island, New York, when I would shut the door and worship God for an hour a day. My motive was never to get a big ministry or to even have power. My motive was just to know God and be as close to Him as possible. Everything else was just a natural by-product. Every morning when I am home, I wake up to a little plaque resting on my dresser. It reads, "The man who walks with God will always get to his destination." This is a constant reminder to me that as long as I intimately walk with God and keep my relationship with Him first, He'll take care of everything else.

CHAPTER 3

The Power of Grace

Go With the Flow

O NE OF MY favorite things to do is to go hiking high into the mountains. I love to breathe in the fresh mountain air and feel the brisk wind blowing across my face. I have had many adventures in the great outdoors. I remember one such journey I was on. It was a long and challenging hike. After hours of physical exertion, it was exhilarating to break out of the woods onto a high cliff overlooking the surrounding mountainous terrain. The drop down to the valley below was steep, but I loved getting as close to the edge as possible. I could see the tops of the trees far beneath my feet.

As I looked up into the sunlit sky, I could see a majestic eagle flying high over my head, so free and strong. It was such a sharp contrast to the laborious hike I had just undertaken. I marveled at how it soared with its wings expanded in effortless grace as it glided upon the mountain air currents. Oh, to be like that eagle, soaring high above the earth beneath, free from the labor of having to climb a steep mountainous terrain just to catch a glimpse of the expansive beauty of the world beneath. Would it ever be possible to soar like that eagle, in effortless grace?

Power for life is not about how much self-effort you can put out to make your life better. It's really about spreading your wings and flying, flying on the winds of God's presence and grace.

You plug into God's supernatural power by plugging into His grace. Living a powerful overcoming life cannot be achieved by one's self-efforts alone. You can only go so far in your own ability. Sure, there will be certain things you can change about yourself, but there will be other things that will require the power of God within you to change and transform. That is where grace comes into action.

For years in church I heard teachings about grace. I heard it taught as "God's riches at Christ's expense." That sounds good. But what does it mean? What are God's riches? What expense did Christ pay? I've also heard grace taught as God's unmerited favor and His undeserved mercy. While there is truth in these statements, they still do not get to the true heart of what grace is all about.

God's grace is not there for you just when you make a mistake and need forgiveness for sin. God's grace should not be an afterthought. For years I only sought God's grace after I thought I missed it. I sought His grace when I felt I needed forgiveness, and when you are first learning to walk with God, there will be plenty of times you slip. God's conviction comes, and you humble your heart before Him and ask Him for forgiveness. With that prayer of repentance, you can receive God's forgiveness, have a clean heart again, and keep moving forward. But grace is so much more than that. It is so much more than just receiving forgiveness after we sin.

Grace is there for us before we sin. Yes, that's right. Read it again. Grace is there for us before we slip and fall. So what does that mean? It means that grace is more than just God's mercy and forgiveness when we miss it.

A man was sharing with me this powerful moment where God's grace intervened in his life. It was late one night, and he was very tired. It had been a long week at work, and he was lying on his couch watching TV. Suddenly the thought came to his mind to go on the Internet and look at pornography. A strong desire came over him to do something he knew was wrong. As he lay there, he could feel a strange sensation going over his head. It was the presence of God. Right in the midst of a temptation God's presence washed over him. Moments later the temptation was completely gone! He was able to fall asleep peacefully and woke up refreshed in the morning. This is God's grace in action. Before he fell, God gave him the power to overcome. God knew his heart, and in his weakness God gave him divine strength. God will do the same for you if you set your heart on pursuing and pleasing God.

One of my favorite scriptures in the Bible is Hebrews 4:16: "Let us then fearlessly and confidently and boldly draw near to the throne of grace (the throne of God's unmerited favor to us sinners), that we may receive mercy [for our failures] and find grace to help in good time for every need [appropriate help and well-timed help, coming just when we need it]."

This gives us real insight into what true grace is all about. It's more than receiving mercy when we fail. God's grace is there to help us in our time of need. God's grace is His "well-timed help" just when we need it. When do we need God's grace? Before we miss it. What does this mean for your life? It means that when you are being tempted to do something wrong, something your spirit knows you shouldn't do, you can come boldly to God and ask Him to help you not to fall. You can be confident in His grace. You can be confident that God will hear your prayers for help and give you the ability to say no to ungodliness and yes to His will, plan, and purpose for your life.

This is where true power begins. It does not begin with us; it comes from God in us. Our true source of power to overcome everything negative in life doesn't come from our striving. The ability to make good choices, to be joyful even when there is a whirlwind around us, to be positive even when life wants to pull us into negativity, to be peaceful even when circumstances are chaotic, comes from God's power within us.

My definition of grace is "God's supernatural power within you to help you be all He desires you to be and do all He calls you to do."

His grace truly is amazing. It lifts you above your own earthly limitations and allows you to live and experience God's life in you. In one of my favorite messages by my mom, Veronica Sorger, she defines God's grace as His "divine assistance." He is right there for you when you need Him the most to help you do the right thing. You don't have to wait until you fall to call out to God. Call out to Him before you fall. That's when His grace will begin not only to bring forgiveness but also to transform your life. By His grace, His divine ability within you, you will begin to think differently, talk differently, and act differently. His grace will truly transform every area of your life if you let it.

Overcoming Self-Striving

> But if it is by grace (His unmerited favor and graciousness), it is no longer conditioned on works or anything men have done. Otherwise, grace would no longer be grace [it would be meaningless].
>
> —Romans 11:6

This is what Saint Augustine had to say about God's grace. "Grace is given, not because we have done good works, but in order that we may have power to do them."[1]

The awesome thing about God's grace is that it is not dependent on our works. Popular self-help books may reach people on a natural level and help in some areas, but the reality is we cannot change ourselves. We don't have to be Christians too long to realize that there are many areas of our lives that we know are wrong, but in our own strength we are powerless to do anything about them. Sometimes we get frustrated with ourselves because we do things we know we are not supposed to do. Then we feel guilty and condemned. This is exactly what the enemy wants. He wants to ensnare us in sin and then make us feel guilty for our failures.

But God's grace is there to help us get over ourselves. I know there is a constant battle between our flesh and spirit. That will always be there. But it is possible by God's grace to see our flesh weakened and our spirit strengthened so that it is much easier to live in a way that pleases God. By God's grace we can overcome every sin and weakness in our lives.

Self-striving only makes you frustrated and discouraged. You try to do what's right, but you fail miserably. Paul experienced this in his own life. In Romans 7:15–24 he wrote about the struggle he had with doing the things he knew were wrong and not doing the things he knew were right. But then he discovered God's grace that comes through Jesus Christ. He joyfully declares in Romans 7:25: "O thank God! [He will!] through Jesus Christ (the Anointed One) our Lord! So then indeed I, of myself with the mind and heart, serve the Law of God, but with the flesh the law of sin."

God's grace is a free gift to us. Our salvation in Christ is not a result of our own self-efforts, nor is the transformation that happens in us after we come into relationship with God. The reality is our salvation is instant. The moment we put our faith in Christ we receive eternal life inside of us. However, our transformation is not instant. It happens over time. There are many areas of our minds and souls that need help. There are ingrained attitudes in us. We have patterns of unhealthy emotional responses, and areas of our flesh are addicted to sin. All of these things need to be overcome on a daily basis. And our overcoming won't happen by our striving. Paul experienced this. Even with a new nature from God in his spirit, he still wrestled with the sin principle in his soul and body. But eventually, just as with Paul, personality weaknesses and struggles with our sin nature can be overcome and changed by God's power working in us.

> [Not in your own strength] for it is God Who is all the while effectually at work in you [energizing and creating in you the power and desire], both to will and to work for His good pleasure and satisfaction and delight.
>
> —PHILIPPIANS 2:13

Personality Makeover

God can even help our personalities. That's right. I have found that often our greatest strengths are also our greatest weaknesses. When our personalities can come under the influence of the Holy Spirit, He can help us accentuate our strengths and decrease our weaknesses. For example, people who are strong-willed are great at getting things done. They are movers and shakers. But they also may be prone to anger when they don't get their way. God's grace can help them overcome their anger weakness while still being a productive person. Changing deep-seated personality traits can only happen by God's grace, divine assistance, and supernatural power within.

I want to encourage you that you are not alone in this process. We are all going through it. You can't get discouraged if you haven't been completely perfected yet. You might not have fully arrived, but thank God you are not where you used to be. You are changing, and it is by you cooperating with God's grace within you.

There are a lot of angry Christians in church. Paul teaches us to not sin in our anger. There are times we cannot control an emotion we feel, but we can control the behavior that accompanies it.

One man shared with me his struggle with anger and how God's grace is helping him to overcome it. When he was a teenager, the smallest thing would set him off into a rampage. When asked to do something he didn't want to do, he would get angry. Once when he was asked to do the dishes, he kicked the kitchen door and made a hole in it. Soon every door in his house had a hole in it.

Later in his adult life, he confided in someone that he really struggled with anger. His dad had a bad temper, and he seemed to have inherited this weakness or personality trait from him. After receiving some personal prayer, he obtained a great breakthrough, but he still had his sinful nature to deal with.

A few years later when he read a letter his daughter wrote, saying, "Dad can sometimes get angry," he realized he still needed to work on this area. He realized that in order to receive God's grace not to act out or discipline his kids in anger, he needed to stay close to Jesus. As he spent time with God each day, the Holy Spirit helped to control this weakness in his life.

Being aware of your weaknesses helps to remind you of your dependency on God's grace. Abraham Lincoln once wrote, "We have forgotten the gracious hand which has preserved us in peace and multiplied and enriched and strengthened us, and have vainly imagined in the deceitfulness of our hearts that all these blessings were produced by some superior wisdom and virtue of our own. Intoxicated with unbroken success, we have become too self-sufficient to feel the necessity of redeeming and preserving grace, too proud to pray to the God that made us."[2]

Knowing we need God's empowerment enables us to receive His grace on a daily basis. I'm sure if we forget, it won't be too long until we are reminded. It's a daily dependency and walk with God.

> But He said to me, My grace (My favor and loving-kindness and mercy) is enough for you [sufficient against any danger and enables you to bear the trouble manfully]; for My strength and power are made perfect (fulfilled and completed) and show themselves most effective in [your] weakness. Therefore, I will all the more gladly glory in my weaknesses and infirmities, that the strength and power of Christ (the Messiah) may rest (yes, may pitch a tent over and dwell) upon me!
>
> —2 CORINTHIANS 12:9

It's good news to know that God can strengthen us in our weaknesses. God's grace really is enough. We can't add anything to it. When it comes to living a powerful life filled with God's grace, we have to learn to yield and surrender. It's about yielding, not striving.

Going with the flow of God's power within us is like driving a car. Yielding to God is not a "stop" or "go" sign. It's a yield sign. Near my house in New York is an intersection where I have to merge with oncoming traffic through a yield sign. As I approach the intersection, I have to watch and look to see the flow of traffic that I am coming into. I watch the flow, and I follow and merge into the flow of existing traffic. The same is true with God's Spirit and power within us. His power is flowing. His Spirit is moving. I have to slow down, look to see where His Spirit is moving, and then move into it. As I do, I receive His grace to do all He has called me to do.

In a moment of need I have to slow down, turn my focus on God and His Word, ask for His help, and then receive it right in that moment. The more I have learned to yield to God's help in the moment I need it, the more victorious and joyful I am. Walking in God's grace is really all about walking with God moment by moment. The more I feed my spirit, the stronger I will be to overcome negative things. Whatever you put in is what will come out. If you are feeding your spirit the Word of God, when you need God's help, His power will be right there to strengthen and help you. But if you don't call out to God in your moment of need, you will most likely be operating in your own strength, which will quickly fail.

God's Grace Works in You to Make You Who You Are

> But by the grace (the unmerited favor and blessing) of God I am what I am, and His grace toward me was not [found to be] for nothing (fruitless and without effect). In fact, I worked harder than all of them [the apostles], though it was not really I, but the grace (the unmerited favor and blessing) of God which was with me.
>
> —1 Corinthians 15:10

God's grace makes you right with God (Rom. 3:24), and after you are right with God, you can then become right with yourself and with other people. I want you to really understand how to overcome everything negative in life. God's grace, the presence of the Holy Spirit within you giving you power to reign in life, will empower you to overcome every evil tendency in yourself and every temptation from the enemy. You see, your battle is not just with the devil. Sure he will bring temptation to you, but what you must first get victory over is your own self. You can submit to God, resist the devil, and he will flee from you. But you can't cast yourself out. You have to kill and crucify your old self by God's power within you.

The good news is that your faith in Christ releases His grace within you to help you overcome every evil tendency in your flesh. (See Romans 6:14; James 4:6; Titus 2:11.) His power helps you to overcome every weakness in your own self. All are born with a sinful nature and with weaknesses. Some of these weaknesses are inherited from your family line. They are generational iniquities. They are tendencies within your own self toward sin.

You often see this in families who struggle with alcohol, witchcraft, and sexual perversion. These sinful tendencies are often times passed down from one generation to the next. Sometimes the DNA and soulful makeup of a person causes him or her to struggle with certain things. At times these inherited weaknesses can skip generations. The only way to overcome these things is by the grace of God. His power within you will help you resist your own flesh and live in a way that pleases Him. But there is a choice you must make to receive God's grace and help to overcome what you know is wrong. God's grace does not remove your free will. But if you choose to plug into His grace, He will be right there to help you every step of the way.

Dwight L. Moody once said, "Grace isn't a little prayer you chant before receiving a meal. It's a way to live. The law tells me how crooked I am. Grace comes along and straightens me out."[3]

Grace Removes Every Obstacle in the Way of God's Presence Filling Your Life

I love the story in Zechariah 4 where the prophet is talking about rebuilding the temple. In this portion of Scripture a house is being built for God's presence, but the builders are facing some opposition. Zechariah begins to speak to this opposition: "For who are you, O great mountain [of human obstacles]? Before Zerubbabel [who with Joshua had led the return of the exiles from Babylon and was undertaking the rebuilding of the temple, before him] you shall become a plain [a mere molehill]! And he shall bring forth the finishing gable stone [of the new temple] with loud shoutings of the people, crying, Grace, grace to it!" (Zech. 4:7).

The house of God would be built by God's grace. Just before this the prophet declares the word of the Lord to him, "Not by might, nor by power, but by My Spirit...says the Lord of hosts" (v. 6). In other words, God's house would not be built by man's strength and ability. It would be started and completed by God's grace. He is both the foundation and the finisher. As the Bible says in 1 Corinthians 6:19, we are God's house. He is building us into a dwelling place for His presence. As He builds us, the work is accomplished not by our own strength, but it is accomplished by His grace. The finishing gable stone is put in place with shouts of "grace, grace!" God completes His work in us by His glorious grace.

Everything in your life that would hinder God's presence from filling you will be moved out of the way by His power. Every mountain of opposition is coming down. Every valley is being raised up. God's grace will deal with every hindrance in your life. You are destined to be God's house filled with His presence.

Gifts of Grace

God will use your life in ways that far exceed your wildest dreams. Not only will God give you power to live holy and in a way that pleases Him, but He will also share His marvelous gifts of power, revelation, and utterance with you by that same grace.

The Greek word for the gifts of the Spirit is *charisma*, which *Strong's Concordance* defines as "gifts of grace; a favor which one receives without any merit of his own." You can't work for or earn them. They are given freely by the Holy Spirit, just as salvation is. You can have all of them—and the more you pursue them, the more you will have!

I encourage you to simultaneously pursue both God's fruit and spiritual gifts in your life, all by His grace. First Corinthians 14:1 tells us to earnestly desire spiritual gifts. I often lay my hands on my own belly during times of prayer and ask the Holy Spirit to stir up and manifest the gifts of the Spirit that are within me. As seen in 1 Corinthians 12:8–10, these gifts include word of wisdom, word of knowledge, faith, healing, working of miracles, prophecy, discerning of spirits, different kinds of tongues, and the interpretation of tongues. These spiritual gifts are invaluable manifestations of God's power in our lives. As you ask God to stir them up, He will.

You Will Reign in Life

> For if because of one man's trespass (lapse, offense) death reigned through that one, much more surely will those who receive [God's] overflowing grace (unmerited favor) and the free gift of righteousness [putting them into right standing with Himself] reign as kings in life through the one Man Jesus Christ (the Messiah, the Anointed One).
>
> —ROMANS 5:17

Through God's overflowing grace you will reign as kings in life. His grace is not just enough; it is overflowing. It is more than enough! You can reign in life through this grace. You can overcome every sin, every thought, every attitude, and every action that hinders your life. Yield to His grace in you, and receive all the power you need to live an extraordinary life today.

CHAPTER 4

The Power of Truth

Show Me the Stuff

Flashback—1985. Long Island, NY. We were watching *Back to the Future* in the movies for $2.75 a ticket. Gasoline was $1.09 a gallon. Big hair was hitting an all-time high. My brother was break-dancing. Various music artists were singing "We Are the World" to raise money for famine relief. I was reading my favorite comic books. And my mom was on a journey to find the source of power for healing.

While working in a chiropractor's office, one day my mom got the thought, "In the name of Jesus, be healed." She didn't know where it came from, and she didn't realize what was being revealed to her by the Holy Spirit. Years earlier she had given her heart to Jesus while watching a Billy Graham crusade on a Sunday night at home. My brother and I were just small children, and Sunday night was our family night. As we fell asleep watching TV, Billy Graham would come on. Every week she would cry and give her heart to God, but she had no foundation at all in God's Word. While she had asked Jesus to forgive her sin, she still had some very human-istic beliefs. She thought that all roads led to God, and as long as someone believed in God, they would go to heaven.

While working in the chiropractor's office, she began to meet people who were involved in New Age practices. They wore crystals and practiced meditation, yoga, and psychic healing. They had tapped into a dark power source but were deceived into believing that it was from God. During this time a woman invited my mom over her house to learn a New Age meditation mantra. While my mom was on this journey to find the power source for healing, she stumbled into a deceptive force. As she was leaving this woman's house, a sickness "fell" on her. The very thing she thought would help people opened a door for sickness to enter her life. This began a long two-year journey of searching for the truth.

After exhausting every New Age possibility there was, she began to get a revelation that her sickness started when she strayed away from her Catholic roots, which was Jesus crucified, dead, buried, and then resurrected. It was the night she was at the Catholic healing mass that she renounced every New Age thing she had ventured into and turned her heart totally back to the God of the Bible.

When she put her faith solely in Christ, she was completely healed by God's power and truth. As she spent time in the Bible, God spoke to her very clearly one day: "Why would My Son have to have His beard plucked out, thorns put on His head, a spear in His side, and be crucified and tortured, if there was any other way to come to Me?" She instantly realized by a revelation of truth that Jesus was indeed the only way to God. This was God's blueprint for salvation—Christ alone. That was also the week I gave my heart to the Lord and accepted Jesus as my Savior. Jesus not only healed my mom, but He also revealed to us that He was the only way to get to God. He was the power source she had been searching for all those years. We had finally made our way home.

Coming Into Alignment

I have had several cars throughout my history of driving. My first car was a fifty-dollar special that my dad bought for me when I was first learning to drive. It's white interior looked black! We scrubbed it, trying to make it look "new," but it was anything but new. I loved that car. I nicknamed it the "Blue Bomb." The exterior was navy blue, and it was a bomb!

One day while driving the car, I noticed that it kept swerving off to the left. I had to keep pulling the steering wheel to the right to keep the car on the road. It needed a major alignment. When the wheels are misaligned, they can cause the car to swerve in a wrong direction. This will cause damage to the tires, affecting the traction. If not corrected, the car could have ultimately skidded, causing danger to both myself and other drivers around me. This is why even in our daily lives it is so important to be rightly aligned.

Alignment means "to bring into cooperation or agreement with a particular group, party, or cause; to adjust or improve proper relationship."[1] Just as a car needs to be aligned periodically, we need to have our minds continually aligned with truth, or we can go off course.

What Are You Thinking On?

Where the mind goes, your life will follow. Don't underestimate the power of your own thoughts. They determine how you will live. We have two choices: to walk in the power of the Spirit or to walk in our old sinful nature.

The most powerful law that operates in the life of a Christian is the law of the Spirit of life. Paul teaches in Romans 8:2, "For the law of the Spirit of life [which is] in Christ Jesus [the law of our new being] has freed me from the law of sin and of death." When we accept the sacrifice that Christ made on behalf of our sin, God subdues, overcomes, and completely deprives sin of all of its power. Sin no longer has dominion and control over us because of the law of the Spirit. The Holy Spirit controls our lives. But how does this really happen?

The secret is shared with us in Romans 8:5. "For those who are according to the flesh and are controlled by its unholy desires set their minds on and pursue those things which gratify the flesh, but those who are according to the Spirit and are controlled by the desires of the Spirit set their minds on and seek those things which gratify the [Holy] Spirit."

The secret to living in the power of God and having all of your desires, thoughts, attitudes, and actions controlled by the Spirit is by simply making the choice to set your mind upon things that the Holy Spirit likes. When you set your mind upon the Word of God, your entire life will go in a direction that pleases God. This is why knowing the truth of the Word is so vital to living a life of power.

Knowing the Truth Will Set You Free

Jesus taught us in John 8:31–32, "If you abide in My word [hold fast to My teachings and live in accordance with them], you are truly My disciples. And you will know the Truth, and the Truth will set you free."

God's truth will not only release power into your physical body, but it will also enable you to receive God's power for the full healing and restoration of your mind. Years ago I knew a woman who had been committed into a mental institution. Her mind had become very disturbed. One day she found a Bible and began to read it. No one prayed for her. She just simply spent hours a day reading God's Word. As she did, her mind was completely healed to the point where she was able to get up and just walk right out of that institution. This is the power of truth.

One thing we must all understand is that truth is absolute, and we can know the ultimate source of it. When we have an encounter with the living God, we come to realize that the ultimate truth is found in the Bible. Once we have this foundation, we can then access all the benefits of God's power that come from knowing His Word.

The truth will not only heal your body and mind, but it will also reach down into the deepest areas of your soul, emotions, and identity, bringing total freedom and wholeness into every area of your life. The key to your lasting freedom and deliverance will be God's Word.

The Holy Spirit Is Our Teacher

> But the Comforter (Counselor, Helper, Intercessor, Advocate, Strengthener, Standby), the Holy Spirit, Whom the Father will send in My name [in My place, to represent Me and act on My behalf], He will teach you all things. And He will cause you to recall (will remind you of, bring to your remembrance) everything I have told you.
>
> —JOHN 14:26

Following my mom's healing and my personal salvation, I entered into the "School of the Holy Spirit." God began to so ingrain His truth into my heart that no deception could ever gain access again into my belief system about who God was, about what was right and wrong, and about God's will for people to be whole. The Holy Spirit came as my personal Teacher to lead and guide me into all truth, one scripture at a time.

One thing I have learned is that without the Holy Spirit it is very difficult to fully understand the Bible. I know of people who had not given their hearts to God and read the Bible like a textbook. It was impossible for them to fully understand what it was really saying. Only when the Holy Spirit comes into your heart and life can you fully understand the truth of the Word. The Word of God is spiritual in nature and must be spiritually discerned. Your teacher, the Holy Spirit, is the best power source for truth there is. He will help you interpret Scripture with other Scripture verses and reveal to you the true meaning in its historical and biblical context.

Just Show Me the Stuff

In order to live in true, authentic, holy power, we must wholeheartedly desire to know the truth. When people are seeking after power more than truth, they can fall into deception (Matt. 24:11–12, 24).

In the story of my mom, even though she fell into deception for a season, her heart's motive was to know God's truth. This motive ultimately led her out of darkness.

In my experience as a minister, I have had people approach me, including leaders, whose sole desire was to see signs and wonders without the preaching of the word. Surprisingly, three different leaders said to me in so many words, "You know, if the preaching of the gospel could have gotten the job done, it would have been done a long time ago. What we need are the signs. I just want to see the stuff. I don't want you preaching more than just a few minutes. We want the miracles." There are some who diminish the Word of God in pursuit of the supernatural. This is very dangerous, as it can open the door to deceptive power that is not rooted and grounded in truth. The true source of power is always the gospel of Jesus Christ.

Truth Will Impact Every Area of Your Life

Truth will deeply impact every area of your life. Without truth you can never really plug into God's power and know who you are meant to be. It causes you to soar far beyond the limitations and labels others have put on you. Truth is not what you feel. It's what you know. Feelings can change and fluctuate, but there are absolutes that create healthy God-given boundaries in our lives. If we live within the boundaries of God's truth, we can then experience the limitless power of His presence and grace within us. Truth enables us to live in God's power every day.

Really knowing truth in our hearts will release God's power within us to fully be all He has destined us to be. Without truth we are like waves tossed about in the ocean. Truth is our anchor. It's what holds us when everything else in life is in flux. Truth never changes. Truth is what gives us the power to live an extraordinary life. It keeps us stable during turbulent times. It enables us to rise above every lie we have ever believed about ourselves. Truth empowers. It liberates us to grow to our fullest God-ordained potential.

Since truth is so vital to living a powerful life, we must guard the truth of His Word in our hearts at all cost and let nothing choke its life out of us (Matt. 13:22–23).

As we hear God's Word of truth and allow it to be sown into good soil within our hearts, we will fully grasp and comprehend it, and it will produce in us supernatural fruit. It's this life of truth and fruit that demonstrates God's power within us.

CHAPTER 5

The Power of Identity

Know Who You Really Are

BEFORE YOU CAN truly be who God has called you to be and do what He has called you to do, you must first know who you are. Truth and identity are inseparable. If you don't know the truth, you will be tossed around by everything life throws at you. You will live out of wounded emotions and distorted thinking and will be susceptible to great deception, temptation, and addictive lifestyles. This is why so many people's lives are a mess! They don't know who they really are. They are living like Clark Kent when in reality they are Superman.

Under the Influence

I will never forget that warm, sunny afternoon when I walked out the back door of the retreat house and made my way into the garden area out back. I knew I had to seek God that afternoon. Something very deep was happening inside of me. As I made my way across the lawn, my eye caught a large rock. It was just the perfect size to climb up on and sit and talk to God. It became my prayer place. I was seventeen years old and was on a young adults retreat with a group of friends. God would speak something to me that day that would change my life forever and shake me to the core.

The previous day I had been crammed in the back of a car with four other young adults in their twenties and thirties as we made our way into the countryside. I was the youngest in the group and sat in the back seat. With my head leaning up against the window, I prayed and asked God to have His way in our lives that weekend. Suddenly the voice of the Holy Spirit broke through my own thoughts and said, "My people have idols in their lives." I was taken back by this unexpected interruption. God's inner voice came to me with crystal clarity, but it wasn't at all what I expected Him to say. I knew what an idol was. It's something that is lifted higher and takes the place of God in your life. I quietly began to pray that God would remove and tear down every idol in the hearts and lives of those in attendance that weekend. Truthfully, I wasn't really putting myself in that category. I had no idea what was coming!

The first day was filled with fun, enjoying time with friends, praise and worship, and good Bible teaching. But for the most part it was pretty uneventful. The following day we were given time in the afternoon to either relax or participate in a group activity. Something inside of me was stirring. It was unlike anything I had experienced before. I needed to get alone with God. I needed to wait on Him, but I wasn't sure why. That's when I found myself climbing up on that big ole rock to talk to God. It was in a perfectly isolated location. There was no one around at all. It was just God and me. As the warm sun beat down on my face, I began to pray and worship. Again the voice of the Holy Spirit broke through. It was a divine interruption!

I instantly became aware of my own broken self-image. It was as if a light went on in a dark place. For the first time my eyes were opened to see and understand how I had been viewing myself for so many years. My blind spot was uncovered. A veil was ripped away as God showed me the distorted image I had of myself. I never realized it before. It was just a part of who I was. I didn't know anything different, nor did I know my image was wrong! I realized that not only was the image I had of myself distorted, but also the way I saw God and even the way I perceived other people were distorted. I sat there in a state of shock.

Self-Realization

Self-realization can be a very difficult and painful experience, yet at the same time it can be completely freeing and liberating! Knowing who you really are awakens your spirit to God's unlimited potential. The struggle many people face is that they allow the world, painful experiences, other people, and the lies of the enemy to define them.

Second Corinthians 5:17 teaches us that, "If any person is [ingrafted] in Christ (the Messiah) he is a new creation (a new creature altogether); the old [previous moral and spiritual condition] has passed away. Behold, the fresh and new has come!"

To become the new creation and the amazing person God has destined you to be, you must realize and discern every lie you have been believing about yourself. Coming to a place where you begin to realize the lies you have believed about yourself can shake you to the core of who you are. For years you believed what other people told you. Their words shaped who you were. You never questioned the negative thoughts that ran through your mind about yourself.

The Power of Words

Words are containers of power. They work in both the negative and positive direction. One word of life spoken over someone can have a ripple effect in their life, bringing them to a place of freedom and wholeness. Pablo Picasso, one of the world's greatest artists, experienced the power of words. His mother would say to him, "If you become a soldier, you'll be a general; if you become a monk, you'll end up as pope."[1] Instead he became a painter and ended up being Picasso.

I've seen it go in the negative direction as well. I recently heard a man share his story from his childhood. He was a tall, lanky kid, somewhat clumsy. One day when he was in the ninth grade, a group of older boys cornered him and began to call him names. They told him that he should just go and end his life. He left that encounter bruised inside and out. He left wondering if there was something really wrong with him. The words of these older kids only served to validate the insecurity he already felt inside. Lies that the enemy was telling him were reinforced through the words of others. Thankfully he did not end his life, but till this day he lives under deception about who he is. Lies took root at an early age, shaping the path his life would take. Without Christ and His truth, he fell prey to the plan of the adversary. How many people do we know who fit into this category?

Many people believe lies about who they are because of past traumas and pain. But there is hope at the end of this tunnel! As God's Word, truth, and presence fill your life, suddenly a light goes on, and you realize that what you have been believing about yourself has been a charade, a house of cards, and, with one blow of truth, the house is knocked over.

Knowing Your True Identity

Once you are willing to face the pain of past hurt and you understand your identity has been based on a lie, hope and joy will flood your soul as you realize there is a chance for you to become the person God originally created you to be. You can be the hero you were meant to be. Once the lies are exposed by truth, you begin to experience true self-realization—not who you are in yourself or what other people said about you, but who you are in Him! You must never take on a sinful label as your identity. If you have overcome alcohol or drug addiction, you are not an alcoholic and drug abuser. You are a new creation in Christ! You are a child of God. You are forgiven, loved, accepted, complete, and whole in God. You are holy, and you are free. You are no longer a sinner; you are a saint. You have a brand-new nature, God's nature! Sin no longer has the power to control you. God's life in you empowers you to overcome every sinful, negative thing and to be the person you were created to be. Proverbs 23:7 says, "For as he [a man] thinks in his heart, so is he" (NKJV).

Let me share a story that inspired me about a famous Christian media mogul who under his belt has produced more than twenty theatrical productions, along with films and TV shows. With a history of being brutally beaten by his father, he was also severely physically and sexually abused as a child. Even before the tender age of ten years, he experienced sexual abuse by three men and one female. This abuse brought great confusion into his sexual identity. Speaking of one of the men who sexually abused him, in his own words, he said, "He gave me something to carry that I didn't want, that I didn't desire." Seeing the joy his mother had from God, he desired the same thing. As he grew in relationship with God, he discovered that "what you feed will grow in your life, and what you don't will starve." This cinematic achiever made the choice to be free. He said he was able to be free and "understand that even though these things happened to me, it was not me."[2] He realized that what was done to him didn't have to define him. His identity rested in truth, not a lie.

It's Not My Fault!

As a school kid I didn't always fit in. I had deep convictions as to what was right and wrong and often found myself fighting for the ones who were left out. I remember hanging out with a kid on the schoolyard whom no one else wanted to be friends with. I felt bad for him. I was also imaginative. I loved getting lost in my own world of being a private detective or a superhero. While I had some childhood friends, I became the subject of some intense bullying. I just didn't fit the mold. Many times I became that kid alone on the schoolyard.

I lived my life based on what I thought was right, and at times

I got very persecuted for it. I enjoyed studying and excelled in my schoolwork. I spent hours on homework every night. I would often mess up the grade curve on tests because I would score so high. I also became a very vocal Christian as a young person. I didn't hide my faith. I wanted all the other kids to know God the way I knew Him. Other kids would often ridicule me for my Christian standards. In high school I wouldn't drink at parties, and I knew God wanted me to live pure. While I had friends, I was left out of the popular crowd and was often mocked and ridiculed. Because I am the type of person who takes things to heart, it went very deep in me. While God was developing leadership qualities in me at a young age, I was targeted by the enemy, who was also at work trying to twist things in my mind to make me feel rejected, left out, and like something was wrong with me. Inwardly I suffered deeply from rejection and low self-esteem.

All those memories came flooding in as I stood on that rock at the youth retreat years later. The Lord began to expose lies the enemy had planted in my mind during my childhood years. He spoke to me and said, "These thoughts are an idol. The way you perceive yourself is an idol." My gut reaction was, "God, how can this be an idol? It's not my fault! I didn't choose to think and feel this way about myself. It was because of what other people said and did."

But God gently and firmly responded, "Anything that exalts itself above what I say about you is an idol and needs to be repented of, whether it's your fault or not, even if you were totally innocent in the whole thing. This thought pattern of rejection is an idol because it is established above Me. It's above what My Word says about you. You have to repent of it and break it from your thinking." Even though I wanted to argue, the revelation was too overpowering for me to contend with. I knew God was right. A blinder had been taken off of my mind, and I could see every lie I had believed about myself.

They were lies. My own thoughts had become an idol because they were exalted above what God said was true. Even if I felt it wasn't my fault, I knew I needed to repent for allowing my mind to yield to and believe the lies of the enemy. My moment of breakthrough was at hand! But it was just the beginning.

I repented and asked God to forgive me for seeing myself in a way that did not line up with the way He saw me. I surrendered to Him my sense of rejection and inferiority. I confessed every lie I believed about myself. I finished my prayer time and continued on with the day's activities. That night before I fell asleep, the Lord spoke to me again. Through His inner audible voice He said, "The devil has gotten a foothold in your mind through those thoughts." At this point in my life I had no idea what a foothold or stronghold was. I never even knew I had one! I went to sleep pondering what the Lord was revealing to me.

Tearing Down Strongholds

The following morning I woke up and started to get ready for the day. I was brushing my teeth in the bathroom, and again God spoke. I wasn't even praying! I had toothpaste coming out of my mouth. You know, God can speak to you at the strangest times. You don't even have to be on your knees praying for God to speak. His thoughts and heart can break through to you at any moment—even when you least expect it.

God picked up His conversation from the night before: "That foothold is no longer just a foothold. It's become a stronghold in your life because it has been there for so many years."

In time I came to understand how footholds and strongholds operate. A foothold is simply a little ledge you place your foot on when climbing a rock wall. If the enemy is given a ledge in your thinking to place his foot, over time he will secure his footing on more solid territory and will build a well-fortified place in your mind. This occurs as you give him greater place in your thinking by coming into agreement with what he has to say.

I came to realize that when something gets entrenched in your life for a period of years, the enemy fortifies and strengthens it. He does this by whispering his thoughts into your mind, projecting his feelings and emotions onto your soul, and then he reinforces his lies through the mouths of other people around you. That's his master plan: to ensnare you in as many lies about yourself as possible and keep you bound as a helpless victim. Over time those lies are no longer just a little foothold. They become a stronghold and a fortress built within your mind and soul. You become defined by your thoughts and circumstances.

> For though we walk (live) in the flesh, we are not carrying on our warfare according to the flesh and using mere human weapons. For the weapons of our warfare are not physical [weapons of flesh and blood], but they are mighty before God for the overthrow and destruction of *strongholds*, [inasmuch as we] refute arguments and theories and *reasonings* and every proud and lofty thing that sets itself up against the [true] knowledge of God; and we lead *every thought and purpose* away captive into the obedience of Christ (the Messiah, the Anointed One).
>
> —2 Corinthians 10:3–5, emphasis added

Thoughts and reasonings in the mind that contradict God's Word and purpose for your life can become detrimental strongholds in your thinking if they go unchecked. These strongholds will hold you in a place of bondage if they are not broken by God's power and replaced by strongholds of truth.

Undercover

After God revealed to me that the enemy's foothold had become a stronghold in my life, I left my room, went to the leaders of the group during one of the worship sessions, and asked them to pray for me. I was determined not to leave that retreat with this stronghold still intact. I wanted it broken! The leaders brought me to a private place to pray.

As we began to call on God, the Holy Spirit, by revelation, enabled them to pray. They began to rebuke doubt and unbelief. I could feel literal walls crumbling inside of me. For no logical reason, I began to cry. Their prayers were hitting a place in me much, much deeper than my mind. They were reaching down into my soul and breaking emotional and mental strongholds that had been built by the enemy. I could hear myself thinking, "Why am I crying?" It was beyond what my mind could comprehend. The enemy had built an emotional stronghold of doubt and unbelief in my mind, convincing me I would never fit in. Once that lie was uncovered and exposed, I was released from its grip. The freedom I experienced was glorious. The enemy was losing his ground as God's truth began to break in. When the enemy is able to keep a lie or stronghold undercover, he has you in his grip. But when that lie becomes uncovered, confessed, and renounced, the enemy loses his grip in that area of your life.

The leaders continued to pray, and one by one each wall came down. As the walls came down, floods of emotion came up. Repressed emotions and pain came pouring out of me. There was a cleansing happening in my soul and a renewal taking place in my mind. The enemy's power was being stripped. Brick by brick, his lies were being undone, and in the process I was being gloriously set free. Fear, doubt, rejection, and a low self-image were being banished from my life. The lie that said I was an outcast was being demolished.

Free to Be Your True Self

My identity was being reformed by truth. The truth is, God had His hand on me since I was a little child. He created me with a very sensitive conscience and gave me a heart to please Him and do what was right. As a result I was labeled "different." God also created me with the ability to stand by my convictions even if they were unpopular, causing me to not fit in with the crowd. It was that same sensitive nature that would cause me to have the ability to sense the presence of God so easily and flow with Him in supernatural ways from the moment I received Christ in my life.

What I had seen as bad and different was actually good and different. The truth that began to replace the lie was that I was not a reject; I was a leader. I was not weird or different; I was set apart. I was holy unto God. I was not an outcast; I was lovable and worthy of love. In high school God gave me some great Christian friends who brought more healing to my soul. As I fit in with the "right" crowd, God's crowd, I saw that I was exactly who God made me to be—someone who would change the world!

Over time the truth of God's Word and His abiding presence within me solidified my identity in Christ, giving me much more personal confidence and a healthy sense of self. What the enemy meant for bad, God turned for good. As I learned to stand for my personal convictions and faith as a young person, no matter what names people called me, God would later use me to spread that faith around the world to millions of people. Everything that may have been a magnet for persecution, God has now used for His glory and higher purposes. God's truth forged my identity. My identity forged my purpose. The revelation of my purpose released supernatural power to do the impossible.

If you have ever been the target of childhood rejection or bullying, you are not alone. Dance legend and prolific actor of the 1950s musicals, Gene Kelly, endured bullying on his walks home from school because he took dance lessons.[3] Little did they know he would one day become a movie star with the talents God gave him. Many others who have gone on to do great things also suffered rejection. After his first audition, Sidney Poitier was told by the casting director to not waste people's time and go wash dishes. From that moment on he decided to give his entire life to acting.[4]

Under the Influence of Deception

I want to uncover one of the greatest strategies of the enemy against people. Knowing this one simple truth can completely set you free. A woman once told me a story about something she had experienced. One day she was in her kitchen putting some glasses away when suddenly, out of nowhere, she had this overwhelming desire to drink alcohol. What makes this so unusual is her background. She had come from a family where there was a lot of alcoholism. She grew up in a very dysfunctional home with the police always at her front door as a child. Her father was an alcoholic. Some of her brothers were alcoholics, and they were always stirring up trouble. She grew up detesting alcohol and had never had a drink in her life. She raised her family to feel the same about alcohol. There was never an alcoholic drink in the home. She had never had a desire to drink before. In fact, she hated it. So you can imagine how surprised even she was when this desire to drink came over her.

Later that day she was talking to her husband about it, only to find out that same afternoon he had also experienced a similar thing. While at work he also had a desire to drink alcohol come over him. Neither of them ever drank. So where was this desire coming from? Well, she soon found out not too long after this incident that one of her teenagers was being drawn by alcohol. He had begun to secretly drink with friends at school. The family's generational weakness was now influencing one of her children. When she found out, she realized exactly what was happening. That desire she felt to drink was not her desire at all. It was a projected thought and feeling that was coming from the enemy that was now hanging around her child. The spirit of alcoholism was tempting her teenager, and a door was being opened to it in his life. It was that very spirit that was now trying to project a desire to drink upon her and her husband. But it was laughable, because she would never tolerate such a thought or feeling. Once she realized where it was coming from, she was able to effectively pray for her child and see total freedom come into his life.

This is something you have to know. Not everything you think or feel is you! This is exactly what the enemy does. He talks to you in the first person, making you think the thoughts are yours. But it goes beyond thoughts or images in your mind. He can also try to project feelings onto you—feelings to drink, feelings to smoke, feelings of lust, feelings of fear, feelings of jealousy, feelings of anger, and so much more. Sure, there are times these feelings will be just you. They can come from your old sinful nature that needs to be crucified with Christ. This is where we need to make a decision that we are going to choose to make godly choices and resist our own flesh. But there are times that it is not just you. As you learn to discern when a feeling is being projected onto you from the enemy, you will have total power over it to resist it and cast it away. Your identity is not based on fleeting emotions. It is based on God's Word. And that never changes. You are who you are because of Christ in you. He is your true identity.

Reconnecting With Your True DNA

While Brian was still in his mother's womb, his dad planned to abort him. His dad and mom were in the midst of a divorce, and he did not want another son from her. But by providence of God, Brian's mom decided he would live. From the age of five to eighteen Brian's mom told him constantly that his dad would waive at her stomach, saying, "Get rid of that." Brian reconnected with his dad when he was eighteen. But the words of his mother echoed in his mind, haunting him for years. Was it true? Was he unwanted? Did his dad really feel that way? He was too afraid to really know the truth. The rejection would be too much to bear. He waited for years. Then, when he was thirty-five, he confronted his dad about what he said. It was true. But uncovering this painful place brought healing and restoration as his dad asked for forgiveness.

Growing up, Brian felt an emptiness inside. He missed his connection with an earthly father. But when restoration happened between him and his dad, suddenly he discovered a newfound sense of connection, fulfillment, and identity. Something clicked inside. Something was put back in place as he became aligned with who he was. He saw himself in his dad, and his dad saw himself in Brian. He came out of his dad's DNA. When he reconnected to his original DNA, the emptiness was gone.

The point is not that we all have to reconnect with our earthly parents. Many may not have the opportunity to do that. Know that God is your heavenly Parent. Psalm 27:10 says, "Although my father and my mother have forsaken me, yet the Lord will take me up [adopt me as His child]." When you connect with God through truth, you align yourself with your true spiritual and eternal DNA. When we are adopted by God as His children, we take on His name, His identity, His nature, His character, and His ways of thinking, talking, and acting. Our identity is no longer in our old life. Our identity is in Him.

We are made in God's image and come out of His DNA. When we connect back into relationship with our heavenly Father, we come into correct alignment, fulfillment, and completeness in our identity. Something clicks inside of us. We receive a sense of fulfillment with who we really are. This is where true identity is found. As a result of the reunion between Brian and his father, he also reconnected back with his father's inheritance. The same is true for us. When we connect back into relationship with God, we have full access to God's inheritance and blessing in our lives. Our identity as a true son and daughter of God qualifies us to receive our full inheritance of blessing and power.

CHAPTER 6

The Power of Faith

Tear the Roof Off

L ORD, I DON'T know what You did, but please don't let me lose
it." These were the words my mom, Veronica, uttered to the
Lord the day her symptoms of sickness began to return. It was only
three days after she had received a dramatic power encounter with
God in the Catholic healing mass. As she was on the floor, being
knocked back by God's power, she felt "volts of electricity" flowing
through her body. God's divine power had driven all sickness out of
her body. Though she received this tremendous encounter with the
Lord, she was still very young in her faith and in her relationship
with God. Up until this point in her life she had spent very little
time reading the Bible. So, although she believed in God and had
now entered into a beautiful relationship with Him through faith
in Christ, she knew very little of the truth found in the Bible.

My mom's life had been transformed by God's healing and delivering power. She didn't even fully understand what had happened
to her. All she knew was that Jesus had come in a very personal way
and lifted all her burdens and healed all her infirmities. She was
desperate not to lose the special gift God had given her, her new
life of physical and spiritual wholeness.

As the symptoms of pain began to afflict her body again, she found herself being drawn by the Holy Spirit to read the New Testament. With almost no effort of her own she found herself reading the Bible seven hours a day. This special grace lasted for three full years. After about three months of living in the Word of God for seven hours a day, she had another supernatural encounter with God.

As my mom sat in her room reading the Bible and praying, suddenly it was like a geyser of faith began to rise up on the inside of her. She simultaneously heard the inner audible voice of God speak to her, "Trust Me. By your faith you are healed." With that one statement, a supernatural faith arose in her heart, filling her entire being. She was flooded with God's faith within her. Instantly all the symptoms of pain and affliction left her body, never to return again. Not only was she healed, but now also she had secured and maintained her healing. And it was all connected to faith.

Faith is truly one of the most significant keys to plugging into God's power on a daily basis. Not only will faith enable you to receive healing from God, but it will also empower you to keep your healing. But the power of faith goes way beyond physical healing. It is the divine connector to all of God's promises. It enables you to receive everything God has for you. It's by faith that we receive His grace. It's by faith that we receive answers to our prayers. It's by faith that we receive His righteousness and holiness. It's by faith that we receive freedom and deliverance from all bondage in our lives. It's by faith that we receive peace, joy, protection, guidance, wisdom, and so much more. It's by faith that we are empowered to live the life God intended for us to have. It's by faith that we receive all His benefits and blessings.

Smith Wigglesworth, known as the apostle of faith, moved in tremendous supernatural power. He knew the secret of faith. He once said, "I am not moved by what I see. I am not moved by what I feel. I am moved only by what I believe....I can get more out of

God by believing Him for one minute than by shouting at Him all night."[1]

Understanding the True Source of Faith

If we don't fully understand where faith comes from, it can be easy to fall back into a self-striving mode. Faith is not something you can work up by your own efforts. I have seen people begin to strive to have faith. I have seen them try to manufacture it by their own ability. It doesn't work that way. The moment you begin to strive in your own ability is the moment you step out of His grace and into self. You cannot manufacture God's supernatural faith by your own efforts, but there are things you can do to position yourself to receive His faith.

Let's take a look at my mom's healing. As God enabled her by the Holy Spirit to get the Word of God into her spirit and mind, something began to happen. Not only did the truth of the Word renew her mind, but also, the more it was stored up in her heart, the higher her faith level began to rise. Truth released faith in her heart. Reading and thinking upon the Word gave God something to work with.

As her mind was renewed and her spirit filled with the Word, one day the Holy Spirit took the very Word she had sown inside of her and brought it to life. It became more than just words on a page. The Word became her reality. As the Holy Spirit breathed His life into the Word that was stored up in her, a faith far beyond what she could produce herself rose up from deep within. As God spoke to her spirit and mind, "Trust Me. By your faith you are healed," with the word was released the spirit of faith. Faith engaged the power of God, sealing the miracle God had given her. It was finally finished. Having her mind and heart saturated with the Word was the key to being able to receive God's faith within her own heart, fully manifesting the work God had already completed.

In regard to the power of divine healing, not everyone will

experience the same thing. Some people are healed and never have that healing contested. Others experience a healing touch from God, and a few days later the pain starts to come back again. This is where faith that comes from the Word of God stored up inside of us will empower us to maintain and keep what God has given us.

Ask the Hard Question

If we are not seeing more of the power of God flowing in our lives, we need to ask ourselves a hard question: "What am I sowing into my heart and mind on a daily basis?" If all we are sowing into ourselves are news programs, depressing current events, the opinions and words of others around us, and our own negative confessions, then God doesn't have much to work with. But if we are sowing His life-giving Word into ourselves on a consistent basis, He can breathe His life into those words and release a supernatural faith in our hearts for the impossible. But we have to make sure we understand the source of faith. The source is not us striving to memorize as much Scripture as possible and then somehow we will obtain the faith we desire. It's about sowing truth into our hearts and then allowing the Holy Spirit to breathe on it and make it come alive within us. The source of faith is always God, not us.

The Words of Christ

> So faith comes by hearing [what is told], and what is heard comes by the preaching [of the message that came from the lips] of Christ (the Messiah Himself).
>
> —ROMANS 10:17

Faith comes as a result of meditating on the teachings and words of Christ. We have to make an important distinction here. Faith specifically comes from hearing the words of Christ, not the words of the Law. The Law reveals our inadequacy. The teachings and words of Christ impart faith into our hearts to receive God's promises and blessings. This is why spending time in the New Testament is so vital to living a life of faith.

Once you know the truth of God's Word in your heart, a supernatural faith rises up within you. F. F. Bosworth, an evangelist who had a powerful healing ministry in the 1920s, once said, "The power of God can be claimed only where the will of God is known."[2] As you read God's Word, you learn His will. Knowing God's will is where faith begins.

Jesus is the source of our faith, and He is the finisher of our faith (Heb. 12:2). As we meditate on His Word and abide in Him, He brings our faith to full maturity and completion. Mature faith accesses the unlimited potential of God's power in our lives. Faith removes all the natural boundaries and limitations. Faith makes the impossible possible.

Keep It Simple

Growing in my relationship with God as a young person, I was drawn by the Holy Spirit to read the Bible every day. The Word was so new to me. Each day I discovered something new and amazing about God. I read every word of the New Testament and just simply believed it for exactly what it said. After my mom's healing, our faith was so high as a family that everything we prayed for instantly manifested!

I can remember going into the woods and catching poison oak all over my face. It was terrible! But I read 1 Peter 2:24, which said, "By His wounds you have been healed," and James 5:14–15, "Is anyone among you sick? He should call in the church elders (the spiritual guides). And they should pray over him, anointing him with oil in the Lord's name. And the prayer [that is] of faith will save him who is sick, and the Lord will restore him; and if he has committed sins, he will be forgiven."

We marched right up to the church and had the pastor anoint me with oil and pray over me for healing. The doctor said it would take two to three weeks for it to be healed. I was healed within two days! I was growing in my relationship with God and just simply believed every word in the Bible. I hadn't yet been taught out of my faith by the religious doctrines of man. God and His Word were just so simple. We just believed and received.

I cannot emphasize enough how the simple act of sowing God's Word into your life on a consistent basis can unleash God's faith within you. There was a tremendous forerunner in the healing movement by the name of Dr. Lilian Yeomans who discovered the power source of God's faith in connection with the Word. Due to the heavy stress of practicing medicine, she became addicted to drugs. Her attempts to quit failed, along with the medical help she received. She came to the point of being completely bedridden. In 1898 she went to John Alexander Dowie's healing homes in Chicago, where she spent a lot of time in the Bible.

As she read the Word of God, she realized the truth of God's healing power. With this revelation of truth, her drug addiction vanished, and she was completely healed. She then opened up her own home to the sick where she would read to them scriptures on healing and would tell them to continually speak the Word of God over themselves. As truth entered their hearts and minds, amazing healings took place in their lives. As they lay in their sick beds, after a few days of continually speaking God's Word out of their own mouths, they would jump up completely healed by God. The puttering of feet could be heard from the floor beneath as the infirmed leaped from their beds praising God.[3]

The Faith of God

While many translations write, "Have faith in God," the literal translation found in the Greek New Testament of Mark 11:22 is, "Have you faith of God." The scripture goes on to say, "Truly I tell you, whoever says to this mountain, Be lifted up and thrown into the sea! and does not doubt at all in his heart but believes that what he says will take place, it will be done for him. For this reason I am telling you, whatever you ask for in prayer, believe (trust and be confident) that it is granted to you, and you will [get it]" (Mark 11:23–24).

There is a big difference between having faith in God and having the faith of God. Having faith in God means we believe God is all-powerful and can do anything He wants to do. We all believe God has all the power in the world. The faith of God is very different. This is God's faith within us, not our human faith in God.

After God healed the man at the gate called Beautiful, Peter addressed the people when they thought it was by Peter's and John's own power that the man was healed. He said, "You men of Israel, why are you so surprised and wondering at this? Why do you keep staring at us, as though by our [own individual] power or [active] piety we had made this man [able] to walk?...And His name, through and by faith in His name, has made this man whom you see and recognize well and strong. [Yes] the faith which is through and by Him [Jesus] has given the man this perfect soundness [of body] before all of you" (Acts 3:12, 16).

Peter was very clear about not only the source of the healing but also the source of the faith that produced the healing. It was the faith that comes through Jesus. Jesus was the author and perfecter of Peter's faith and the faith of the man who was healed.

Faith is not intellectual; it is spiritual. It comes from the heart, not the mind. Charles Price was used by God for more than twenty years in healing campaigns. He saw the blind healed; paralyzed and disabled raised from wheelchairs; and clots, cancers, and tumors melt. When talking about his healing services he says, "During those years I've noticed that all great healing services have been preceded by nights of consecration and seasons of prayer. When the crowds have rushed forward seeking healing, the meetings have been hard and difficult. When they have sought the healer rather than the healing, however, the sweetness of His presence has broken the power of the enemy, and the sunshine of His presence has melted the icy feeling that gripped the heart."⁴

Matthew 9:22 says, "Jesus turned around and, seeing her, He said, Take courage, daughter! Your faith has made you well. And at once the woman was restored to health." Again, Matthew 9:29 reads, "Then He touched their eyes, saying, According to your faith and trust and reliance [on the power invested in Me] be it done to you."

It's clear that these individuals received God's power because of their faith. But to get the full picture we must read all Scripture together. While Jesus called it "your faith," we know that it was because of Jesus that this faith was inspired and imparted to them in the first place. The faith that flooded their hearts had its source in God. John 3:27 says, "A man can receive nothing, except it be given him from heaven" (KJV). And 1 Corinthians 4:7 reads, "For who makes you differ from another? And what do you have that you did not receive? Now if you did indeed receive it, why do you boast as if you had not received it?" (NKJV).

Everything we have, including faith, we have received from God. He is always our source for everything.

I want to share a story with you about what happened when a paralyzed woman got her eyes off of man and onto Jesus. This dear woman was so desperate to be healed. She so earnestly desired to receive the power of God in her life. As her husband was wheeling her into a healing meeting, she bumped into the minister. She pleaded with him to heal her. He knew in his heart that at the moment he did not have the faith for her to be healed, and neither did she. He could have just gone through the religious motions of commanding and rebuking, but he didn't. He believed in Jesus and stood on His Word. But he knew he needed an imparted faith that superseded his own ability to believe. She needed it too.

By God's wisdom he encouraged her to draw close to Jesus. He knew Jesus would be the source of the needed faith that would release the healing. Day after day she came to the meetings and sought God. Day after day her husband and friends wheeled her out of the meetings, still paralyzed. But she didn't give up. Days passed, but she kept drawing near to God. On the last night of the meetings her husband carried her to the altar. As she lay on the altar, she got her eyes off of man and completely onto God. During worship she entered into God's deep and holy presence. Jesus came to her and gave her a vision of Himself. She could see Him standing there, smiling and waving at her. Suddenly she became aware of a faith flowing through her heart. At the very moment Jesus imparted His faith into the minister's heart as well. He looked down at the woman and knew she was healed. God's faith flowed through her, and she stood to her feet completely healed. She straightened out, and her shriveled limbs grew![5]

A great general of faith, Lester Sumrall, once said, "The secret behind getting more faith is to get to know God more."[6]

It's wonderful when we can draw close enough to Jesus to clear away all the distractions to hear His voice and receive His divine power and grace. I was praying for a woman once who had a deaf ear. I prayed and could feel God's power surging into her. I knew God's power was present to heal her. As she lay under the tangible power of God, she kept saying, "Lord, I receive it." Each time I helped her to her feet, she was still deaf. Yet I knew God's power was there. By the fourth time I prayed for her, God's voice broke through and silenced her own thoughts. As she was striving to receive, God said, "You already have it." God's word released faith in her heart, connecting her to His power. Guess what happened? When she got off the floor, her ear was completely healed, even better than her good ear!

The Role of Prayer and Fasting

Understanding the role of prayer and fasting will also help you to receive God's faith. Matthew 17:14–21 gives an account of the healing of an epileptic boy. The disciples couldn't cure him, but

Jesus did. When Jesus was asked why the disciples had no success, He said it was because of their unbelief. It wasn't a question of God's will. Nor did Jesus focus on the boy's faith. It was the level of faith in the disciples' hearts. Yet He also pointed out that "this kind does not go out except by prayer and fasting" (v. 21, NKJV). Prayer and fasting help to release God's faith within us. It's the faith that produces the miracle, not the fasting. Fasting and prayer in this instance serve as the passageway into the fullness of faith that exists in God's heart. Again, it isn't by our works but by His faith and grace extended toward us.

Inherit the Promises Through Faith and Patience

In Hebrews 6:12–15 we see two keys that will propel us into God's power and His glorious future for us: faith and patience. We need both if we are to receive His power and accomplish what God has set before us.

Abraham was given a promise by God at the age of seventy-five in Genesis 12. God promised that he would become a great nation and that through him all the nations of the earth would be blessed. If many of us received such a promise from God at age seventy-five, we would probably say, "But God, I am too old now. If You wanted to do something with me, You should have used me when I was younger." No matter how old you are, it's never too late for God to do something spectacular through your life.

Then Abraham had to wait another twenty-five years before this promise would begin to come to pass through the birth of his son Isaac. Even then Abraham had to trust God to keep Isaac safe so that a great nation could be born from him. It would be many more years before God's word would fully manifest itself. So, Abraham was now one hundred years old when Isaac, the son of promise, was born. That's twenty-five long years of waiting, persevering, trusting, and believing.

The one thing that kept Abraham going all those years was faith. Faith produced the endurance Abraham needed to walk out God's promises. Faith is essential if we are to endure to the end. Faith believes no matter what we see. Faith sees the promise while everything else looks hopeless. Faith gives us an inner assurance that God will bring His word to pass. Our faith is not based in what we can see or feel. We are not moved by momentary circumstances. Our reality is God's Word. This is what our faith is established upon. As we meditate on His truth, everything else will line up accordingly. But we have to be willing to persevere in our faith. It's through the combination of faith and patience that we walk and live in God's power and manifested Word.

> For we walk by faith [we regulate our lives and conduct ourselves by our conviction or belief respecting man's relationship to God and divine things, with trust and holy fervor; thus we walk] not by sight or appearance.
>
> —2 CORINTHIANS 5:7

Faith gives you power for the impossible (Rom. 4:20). When you choose to believe God and consider that His character is trustworthy and truthful, even though you may be as good as dead, God can birth His purpose, will, and promise through your life, so that multitudes of others can be blessed as well. Remember, what God wants to do through you is way bigger than just you! His plans are always bigger than just one person. God wants to do something extraordinary through you for the sake of others.

Faith Has Action

Lastly, I want you to understand that faith is more than words. Faith has action. The story of Charles Blondin, a famous French tightrope walker, teaches us a powerful lesson on true faith.

> Blondin's greatest fame came in June of 1859 when he attempted to become the first person to cross a tightrope

stretched over a quarter of a mile across the mighty Niagara Falls. He walked across 160 feet above the falls several times, each time with a different daring feat—once in a sack, on stilts, on a bicycle, in the dark, and once he even carried a stove and cooked an omelet!

On one occasion, though, he asked for the participation of a volunteer. A large crowd gathered, and a buzz of excitement ran along both sides of the riverbank. The crowd oohed and aahed as Blondin carefully walked across one dangerous step after another—blindfolded and pushing a wheelbarrow. Upon reaching the other side, the crowd's applause was louder than the roar of the falls! Blondin suddenly stopped and addressed his audience: "Do you believe I can carry a person across in this wheelbarrow?" The crowd enthusiastically shouted, "Yes, yes, yes. You are the greatest tightrope walker in the world. You can do anything!" "OK," said Blondin, "Get in the wheelbarrow..." No one did.[7]

So also faith, if it does not have works (deeds and actions of obedience to back it up), by itself is destitute of power (inoperative, dead).

—JAMES 2:17

Never forget, when you make the choice to add action to your faith, you release the power of God into operation. True faith will always be accompanied by an action. It's easy to say, "I believe." But true faith will be willing to get into the wheelbarrow and onto the tightrope. True faith releases a corresponding action.

This is exemplified in the story of the men who tore the roof off to get their paralyzed friend to Jesus. Luke 5:18–19 tells us, "Some men were bringing on a stretcher a man who was paralyzed, and they tried to carry him in and lay him before [Jesus]. But finding no way to bring him in because of the crowd, they went up on the roof and lowered him with his stretcher through the tiles into the midst, in front of Jesus." When Jesus saw their faith, He not only forgave the man's sins, but He also completely healed him as well. Their faith caused them to press through every obstacle to the point of physically tearing a hole in the roof to get to Jesus. Now that's faith with action!

Choose to fill your heart and mind with God's truth and keep your focus on Jesus, drawing near to Him in worship, and He will cause His faith to flood your heart and mind, opening up to you God's limitless possibilities for your life. God's faith in you will enable you to receive the fullness of His blessings, grace, power, and purpose. Faith will connect you fully and completely to His unlimited supply of power for every area of your life.

PART TWO

Harnessing the Power

CHAPTER 7

The Power of Integrity

Issues of the Heart

DR. BENJAMIN CRANDALL, the president of my Bible college, once shared a story when I was a student. He told us of a popular television evangelist who had fallen into the sin of adultery. As a result he lost much of what God had given him. This minister shared a dream he had before he fell. In the dream he saw a snake as big as he was. Then the snake became three stories tall. The minister interpreted this dream to mean that what was opposing him was too strong for him to overcome. Since he was such a high-profile minister, he felt he had no one he could go to for help.

Dr. Crandall had a very keen insight. He said, "He had the right dream but the wrong interpretation. The correct interpretation is this: kill the snake while it is still small so that it doesn't become bigger than you." In other words, he was saying to deal with the sin issues and struggles in your life early on before they get too strong and you are taken down by them.

We are born with the potential to be heroes, to be champions. But there is an issue of the heart that will be key to seeing us finish our race. Power is an amazing thing. It can be both productive and destructive, depending on how it is used and how it is cultivated and harnessed. I recently heard a true story about a racehorse. The owner wanted the horse to excel to its maximum potential, so she hired the best trainer and the best jockey she could find to ride the horse. This jockey was known for his willingness to push his horses to their extreme potential.

During his races this horse would come out of the starting gate in last place. He was the underdog. At first it looked like he would come in last, trailing far behind all the other horses. But then, in a burst of inspiration and adrenaline, he would charge around the outside, passing all the other horses, and finish first. He was gaining a reputation of being the best short-distance runner, but it was still a mystery whether he would succeed in running long-distance races.

As he continued to win races, soon the horse qualified for the US Triple Crown. The last race was to prove the most challenging as it was a long-distance race. Would he have the stamina and endurance to not only run fast but also to sustain that speed over a long distance? Would the horse be pushed too hard and have its heart burst in the process? Would victory end in tragic defeat? As the gates were opened, he came out running full speed, charging right to the front! The strategy of the opponent was to get the horse to start out strong so it would be worn down in the length of the race and lose.

As the race continued, the horse maintained its speed. Neck and neck with his opponent, everyone held their breath, waiting for the horse to lose its stamina. But to everyone's surprise the horse gained in speed all the way to the finish line, finishing first! His heart didn't burst under the pressure of the race. Under the extreme pressure and physical exertion, the horse's heart was strong and valiant, able to carry him all the way to the finish line in triumphant victory. He surprised everyone!

This is the amazing and inspirational true story of Secretariat. He was an American Thoroughbred racehorse who, in 1973, became the first US Triple Crown champion in twenty-five years, setting records at the Kentucky Derby and Belmont Stakes that still stand. He appeared on the covers of *Time*, *Newsweek*, and *Sports Illustrated* in the same week, and he was the only nonhuman chosen by ESPN as one of the "50 Greatest Athletes of the Century," coming in at No. 35, ahead of legends like Mickey Mantle.[1]

The horse had extreme potential to be a champion. Not only did he need the right training and the right rider for that potential to be maximized, but also his heart had to be strong and large enough to endure the exertion put on it during the race. When Secretariat died years later, a shocking discovery was made during his autopsy. All of Secretariat's organs were of normal size except his heart. Dr. Thomas Swerczek, a professor of veterinary science who performed the autopsy, is quoted as saying, "We were all shocked. I've seen and done thousands of autopsies on horses, and nothing I'd ever seen compared to it. The heart of the average horse weighs about nine pounds. This was almost twice the average size, and a third larger than any equine heart I'd ever seen. And it wasn't pathologically enlarged. All the chambers and the valves were normal. It was just larger. I think it told us why he was able to do what he did."[2]

Issues of the Heart

Just as Secretariat's heart was robust, so must our hearts be, with the nature and qualities of God. An enlarged heart is the keeping power of integrity. Integrity is what will harness God's power in our lives to its maximum potential. God may give us special gifts, abilities, and graces that cause us to surge ahead to the front of the pack. Such was Secretariat; he was born with certain qualities that made him a champion. He had strong muscles and the ability to run fast. But it was also the strength of his heart that enabled him to win the race.

The quality of our heart's integrity is what will enable us to finish the race strong. Derek Prince once said, "God is more concerned with our character than with our achievements. Achievements have importance only in the realm of time. Character is eternal. It determines what we will be through eternity."[3]

Integrity Through Brokenness

We are not born with integrity. Integrity is something that is developed in our lives through the choices we make every day. It is very similar to the process a horse goes through to harness its tremendous strength and power. Integrity involves a process of brokenness. But when we yield to this process, God's power within us is able to reach its fullest and highest potential.

During its training a horse must undergo a breaking process. During this period of time the horse's strength is harnessed so that it can be correctly channeled and directed. Without this breaking the horse will remain a wild, untrained animal with its strength being exerted in unproductive and dangerous ways. An unbroken horse can cause a lot of damage and pain to the people around it. But once a breaking takes place, the extreme power of this magnificent creature can be harnessed to make it a thoroughbred champion! Its strength and power can be completely used toward a goal and purpose, which is winning the race.

To understand the power of integrity that comes through brokenness, I would like to look at how the power within a horse is properly harnessed. Horse breaking refers to the process used by humans to get horses to let themselves be ridden or harnessed. "Breaking in" is the term used when mounting the horse for the first time.

When a horse is broken in, a horse's spirit doesn't need to be broken with it. Many people tend to believe that horse whispering is some kind of mysterious art, which is unachievable by a common person. There is absolutely no mystery to this unique practice. It is all about understanding the behaviors of a horse and being able to read the horse you are working with. A horse is a herd animal and has a basic fight-or-flight instinct. Understanding these basic things enables a good relationship to be formed between the horse and its rider. It is vital that a rider builds a bond of trust between him and his horse. This makes the horse much easier to train.[4]

Just as a rider and a horse establish a relationship of trust, enabling the horse to be trained without breaking its spirit, in the same way our relationship with God enables Him to train us by His Spirit in the most productive and life-giving way. When we submit to God's dealings in our lives, He gently breaks the areas of our stubborn wills that need to come under submission, and He empowers us to reach our maximum potential. As areas of self are broken, God's power within us becomes harnessed to produce the greatest results through our lives.

In her book *Brokenness*, Nancy DeMoss states, "Brokenness is the shattering of my self-will—the absolute surrender of my will to the will of God. It is saying, 'Yes, Lord!'—no resistance, no chafing, no stubbornness—simply submitting myself to His direction and will in my life."[5]

The key is having a heart that can endure the test of extreme pressure and time. For many, they are born with God-given strengths and abilities. They are graced and gifted by God with certain capabilities. They start out strong. They are sprinters. They appear to be finishing first. But when the test of time sets in and the pressure builds up from a long-distance race, their hearts burst. Their triumph ends in tragedy, taking many other people out in the process. "Whether life grinds a man down or polishes him depends on what he's made of," said Kathryn Kuhlman.[6]

Harnessing God's Power for the Long Haul

God doesn't want us to just start strong. He doesn't just want us to be champions at short races. He wants to create in us the ability to run fast and hard for the long haul. He wants to undergird His power in our lives so that it will carry us all the way through to the end. We can have the right trainer and the right rider, but only we can decide the condition of our heart. The heart that can endure pressure over the long haul is a heart of character and integrity. Integrity is what will keep your heart strong and enduring. Integrity is what will ultimately qualify you to be a thoroughbred champion. It's what will empower you to run your race and win.

We have been created to be vessels of God's power. Developing a life of integrity is crucial to harnessing, maintaining, and increasing God's power in our lives. When we only focus on the gifts God gives us and neglect the process of cultivating a life of integrity, we can become disqualified in the process. Integrity will be our keeping grace! Integrity will enable us to carry God's power for the long haul in our lives. Integrity is produced through brokenness.

Smith Wigglesworth, a man powerfully used by God in the healing ministry, testified, "Before God could bring me to this place, He has broken me a thousand times."[7]

Brokenness Brings Complete Victory

Let's look at how power is released through brokenness in a strategy the Lord gave to Gideon in Judges 7:16–22. In this portion of Scripture Gideon divides three hundred men into three companies. He puts into their hands trumpets and empty pitchers with torches of fire inside of them. When they get to the edge of the enemy's camp, they blow the trumpets and shout, "The sword of the Lord and of Gideon!" (v. 18, nkjv). When they blow the trumpets, they also break the pitchers in their hands, releasing the fire that's hidden inside. In their left hand they hold the fire; in their right hand they hold the trumpets. When the sound of the Lord is released through their shout, the Midianite army turns on itself and flees before Gideon and his men! The battle and victory are won.

It's interesting to note that both hands were occupied with a torch and trumpet. There was no hand to hold a sword. Why?

Because the sword was in God's hand. The principle here is simple. When the vessel is broken, the fire is released. Combined with the sound of the trumpet, the enemy is sent into confusion and defeated. When we are broken and release a sound of praise to God, our enemy is defeated. God's power is released on our behalf through this divine strategy.

True brokenness releases the power of God in our lives. It enables God to fight our battles for us, so the enemy is completely defeated. True heart integrity comes as a result of godly brokenness. There is a big difference between godly brokenness and worldly brokenness. There is a godly sorrow and a worldly sorrow. One leads to increase. The other leads to decrease. One produces power; the other causes us to lose God's power. One leads to life. The other brings forth death. Ungodly cracks will leak the power of God. Godly brokenness will sustain and increase it. Godly brokenness releases the fire. Ungodly brokenness quenches it and puts it out.

There are two men in the Bible who clearly demonstrate the power of brokenness and integrity. They are Saul and David. Both men were imperfect. Both made mistakes. Both sinned. One had his power taken from him. The other was able to maintain it in his life. One had integrity. The other did not. What was the difference?

Saul made a lot of mistakes as king. He fell into insecurity, jealousy, anger, hatred, pride, rebellion, fear of man, and witchcraft. He was an imperfect vessel. Yet when he was first called by God, he was humble and lowly in his own eyes. But soon pride took over his heart.

When the prophet Samuel confronted his sin, Saul freely admitted it (1 Sam. 15:30). But in his next breath he asks to be honored before the people. Saul was not truly broken or repentant before God. He had a worldly sorrow. He was sorry that he got caught. He was sorry for the consequences he now had to face. But he still cared more about his own reputation than he did about hurting God's heart. His heart was not pure. It was not truly broken or repentant. He was still seeking honor before men.

A fellow minister whose ministry has substantially grown, now reaching the masses, shared with me about how his first pastor publicly shared from the pulpit that he was sorry for how he had been in the past. He shared that he wanted people to know that he had changed and was not the same person any more. Under his years of ministry there was a wake of wounded and hurt people left on the sidelines, including my friend. For years his pastor had used control, fear, and anger to manipulate the people he was called to serve. After losing a lot of people from his church, he came to a place of brokenness. He wanted people publicly to know he had changed.

Then my friend received a private e-mail from the pastor. In the e-mail he wanted to know why he hadn't received more public recognition and honor from my friend. This e-mail came at the same time he was publicly sharing his supposed brokenness from the pulpit.

Like Saul, this leader had a type of brokenness, but he was still desiring public honor and recognition in his heart. It was not true, godly brokenness. We have to be careful we don't deceive ourselves about the sorrow we feel. Are we sorry for the things we have lost? Or are we sorry because we have hurt God's heart along with those of other people? Godly sorrow produces a change and transformation in our heart. Worldly sorrow does not. This carnal sorrow only feels bad for itself.

> The sorrow of true repentance is sorrow for offense against a holy God, not simply regret over the personal consequences of our sin. Sorrow over being found out or over suffering hardship or discipline because of our sin is not godly sorrow, and has nothing to do with repentance. That sort of sorrow is but selfish regret, concern for self rather than for God. It merely adds to the original sin.[8]
>
> —John MacArthur

Let's look at David's brokenness. Like Saul, David made mistakes when he was king—some pretty bad ones. He committed adultery as well as murder. Yet God called David a man after His own heart. How can this be? How can a man who commits such horrible things be after God's heart? When David was confronted for his sin, we see his response in Psalm 51.

David was not concerned about his reputation before people. He was concerned about grieving God's heart and losing God's presence in his life. His relationship with God was the most important thing to him. It was because of his godly brokenness that he did not lose the kingdom, nor did he lose God's power in his life. He sinned, but he received forgiveness through godly repentance. Even though he still faced consequences for his bad choices and actions, he didn't lose his relationship with God or his authority and power. Godly brokenness brought restoration in his life. The integrity produced in David's heart through his testings, including both the ones he passed and failed, caused God's power to be harnessed, maintained, and sustained in his life, maintaining his kingship. David's heart's response meant everything to God. Even though he failed at times, he won in the end because he really had a heart after God. He allowed God to work integrity into his life.

Overcoming Hardness of Heart

He said to them, Because of the hardness (stubbornness and perversity) of your hearts Moses permitted you to dismiss and repudiate and divorce your wives; but from the beginning it has not been so [ordained].

—Matthew 19:8

Modern-day marriage missionaries Clint and Penny went through a painful divorce with an overshadowing of adultery in the final stages of their marriage. After the breakup Clint buried his emotions and moved on. Their relationship, for all intents and purposes, seemed dead. After eleven years of not talking or seeing each other, one day a package arrived on Clint's doorstep with a note from his ex-wife asking for forgiveness. Shortly after that they met for coffee, and Clint realized he still loved her. He asked her to remarry him, and their relationship and marriage covenant have been completely restored. The secret to their success is the fact that they got on their faces before God in a place of brokenness and sought Him for His divine assistance. They also intentionally set time aside to effectively communicate with one another on everything. Now they travel helping other married couples experience this same restoration.[9]

In a day where it seems that the marriage and family unit is disintegrating, even in the lives of Christians and ministers, God is calling us into a place of brokenness before Him so our hearts can be softened. Only through this place of brokenness can God truly restore what is being stolen. We must yield and surrender our hardness of heart to Him. This is the only answer. This is our hope.

Cultivating a repentant heart is the essential key to living a life of integrity. A broken and contrite heart will fully turn to God in weakness and receive God's strength to change. Godly sorrow brings a deep change within us. It causes us to hate what God hates and love what He loves. It causes us to turn away from old patterns and behaviors that we know grieve God's heart. It sets us free to truly live our lives by the power of the Holy Spirit within us. Integrity is an internal conviction that no one else can give you. It has to come from within your own heart. True repentance will produce great fruit in your life. John the Baptist proclaimed this in Luke 3:8: "Bear fruits that are deserving and consistent with [your] repentance [that is, conduct worthy of a heart changed, a heart abhorring sin]."

> God uses broken things: broken soil to produce a crop, broken clouds to give rain, broken grain to give bread, broken bread to give strength. It is the broken alabaster box that gives forth

perfume. It is Peter, weeping bitterly, who returns to greater power than ever.[10]

—VANCE HAVNER

Living by an Internal Standard

Integrity is an internal standard and conviction. It is having a sensitive conscience before God. The more sensitive your conscience is, the more in tune with the Holy Spirit you will be. You will know instantly when you are treading on dangerous ground. You will know when God's heart is being grieved. As you follow your conscience, you will develop integrity in your life. True character and integrity are revealed in the choices you make when no one else is around. Integrity will cause you to live a fully transparent life. Oh, how wonderful that is! When people see you, they can look right through you and see the nature and character of God inside of you. Integrity will cause God's purity and light to shine in and through you with no hindrances.

I remember the day I entered an arena for a healing meeting. I was standing near the altar area, and a man came walking over to me with his eyes wide in wonder. He stood in front of me, lip quivering and tears running down his face, and told me he could see the glory and presence of God on me. I will never forget that moment, a moment when someone was impacted through God's life in me, shining through me.

Dave, an Arizona homeless man, came across a bag with more than three thousand dollars in it. He had a decision to make. Would he keep it for his own needs or return it to the owner? His sense of conviction told him he had to return it. The owner of the bag was amazed when the bag filled with money showed up five days after he lost it. He never thought he would see it again.[11]

This story illustrates that you can exercise character no matter what the circumstances are. It's these unforeseen moments of decision that really mark the kind of person you are.

I love what Dwight L. Moody said about character: "Character is what a man is in the dark. God doesn't seek for golden vessels, and does not ask for silver ones, but He must have clean ones. A man ought to live so that everybody knows he is a Christian and most of all, his family ought to know."[12]

My own personal goal in life is to be as transparent as possible so that the person I am in front of people is the same person I am in private. When I was a child, I had a very sensitive conscience. I couldn't do anything wrong without telling on myself! This may sound funny to some, but it's true. If I felt I did something wrong, I had to confess. I am the same today. I can keep no secrets. My life is an open book. If I ever feel I have grieved God's heart in some way, I have to get before God and pray until I feel my heart is clean. This constant sense of repentance and brokenness before God keeps me in His presence. It's how I cultivate His presence and power in my life. If I feel something has come into my heart that is separating me from His presence, I have to pray it through until I feel restored. I believe this is a mark of true repentance.

> Repentance is not a merely intellectual change of mind or mere grief, still less doing penance, but a radical transformation of the entire person, a fundamental turnaround involving mind and action and including overtones of grief, which result in [spiritual] fruit.[13]
>
> —D. A. Carson

The Little Things Count

The little things in life really do count. It's usually the small decisions we make that can have the biggest impact. God wants us to have integrity in every area of our lives.

> Genesis 1 logs God's commitment to excellence when it says, "God saw all that he had made, and it was very good" (v. 31). Christians should always do good work. Christians ought to be the best workers wherever they are. They ought to have the

best attitude, the best integrity, and be the best in dependability. Integrity characterizes the entire person, not just part of him. He is righteous and honest through and through. He is not only that inside, but also in outer action.[14]

—R. KENT HUGHES

If you want to live in God's extraordinary power, taking responsibility for personal integrity in your daily life really makes a big difference. This comes down to the little things like cleaning the house, taking out the trash, and having good personal hygiene. Or being on time for work, going the extra mile for your boss, being honest in your relationships, treating people with kindness and respect. Or having a humble attitude of yourself, not stealing things from your workplace that you know aren't yours, such as paper and pens. Not abusing your lunch break at work when you know you have a certain allotted time. All of these things might seem like small things to you, but it's the small things that, when added up, make us who we are as people. You would be surprised who is watching you. If you are caught not telling the truth, not following your employer's guidelines, not submitting to company policies, you will gain a reputation for being a person without honor. People won't trust you, and you will never advance forward in life.

This even affects things like our personal health. Diane was struggling with being 305 pounds and couldn't see the value or the danger of those little decisions she made all day long. For example, she didn't really consider that every time she ate an extra brownie, she was pushing herself further into obesity. All she saw was the "whole" problem. She thought she was fat, unhappy, and powerless. But she wasn't powerless at all. It was within her power to make those little decisions that would put her on the right path. For example, if she had not eaten a 200-calorie candy bar every day, she would have saved 6,000 calories in a month, enough to lose about a pound. If she had taken a short walk, she would have burned a few calories—and probably felt better about herself.[15]

I have found this to be true in my own life. I know that just by removing a few unhealthy things from my eating habits, such as french fries and soda, I was able to lose enough weight to fit into my clothes again. I was healthier inside and out just by making a few adjustments. These small choices are part of my overall integrity as a person.

According to blogger Diane:

> The decisions you make now can have a huge impact on your health. According to the CDC, losing 10 percent of your body weight reduces your risk of heart disease and can help bring your blood pressure lower. If you weigh 200 pounds, 10 percent is just 20 pounds. Definitely possible—especially when you think about making one small decision after another until you reach your goals. Losing weight, just like other things in life, is about decisions. We don't always make perfect decisions, but if you make more good ones than not, you can reach your goals. Having integrity in the small things impacts your overall life.[16]

Setting Healthy Boundaries

Part of living a life of integrity is setting healthy boundaries. As I have learned to walk in God's power, I have found it a very necessary thing to choose to set right boundaries. I will be honest. This is not always an easy thing to do. Sure, God gives us the grace to make right choices, but that doesn't mean your old nature is not going to want to fight. Living a powerful Christian life is not always easy, but Jesus never said it would be easy. In fact, He told us that we would need to crucify our flesh with its passions and desires. This can be a painful process as we fight against our old nature to allow God's new nature to reign in us (1 Pet. 4:1). But the benefits of living with integrity are amazing.

Paul teaches in Ephesians 5:10 that we should "learn [in your experience] what is pleasing to the Lord [let your lives be constant proofs of what is most acceptable to Him]."

One of the healing generals that I have great respect for lived a highly consecrated life. Smith Wigglesworth connected this lifestyle of holiness to the power that flowed through him. He was known to have such high convictions that he wouldn't even let a secular newspaper pass through the front door of his house. He was a consecrated vessel that moved in a tremendous power of the Holy Spirit. He once shared regarding his convictions:

> You must every day make higher ground. You must deny yourself to make progress with God. You must refuse everything that is not pure and holy. God wants you pure in heart. He wants you to have an intense desire after holiness. Two things will get you to leap out of yourselves into the promises of God today. One is purity, and the other is faith, which is kindled more and more by purity. The moment a man falls into sin, divine life ceases to flow, and his life becomes one of helplessness.[17]

I remember a story where Smith Wigglesworth was staying at the home of a minister whose church he was preaching at. The man whom he was staying with had no feet, only stumps. Smith said to the man, "Go and buy a new pair of shoes in the morning." This was an astounding thing to say to someone with no feet! So the man responded in faith and got up the next morning and went to the shoe shop. Upon entering the store, he was approached by the assistant, who asked if he could help him. The minister replied he would like a pair of shoes. The assistant, realizing the condition of the man, hesitated before replying that they could not help him. The minister, seeing his dilemma, said, "I would like a pair of black shoes, size eight please." The assistant returned with the shoes, and as the minister put his one stump into the shoe, a foot and leg instantly formed. The same thing happened with his other leg. He walked out of the store with two new shoes and two new feet![18] A life of consecration and integrity is crucial to stewarding God's power in our lives.

In Exodus 19:12–23 God instructs Moses to set boundaries around the base of the mountain so no wild beast or person can break through while Moses is with God on top of the mountain. God didn't want anything unholy to break through and defile the place of communion He was having with Moses. Just as Moses set boundaries, you need to set boundaries. When you learn that something in your life separates you from God's presence, you must surrender it to God in prayer and ask Him for the grace to let it go. There can be a battle within your own heart at times. There may be things you don't want to give up, but they are having a negative impact on your relationship with God. The closer you want to walk with God and the more genuine power you want to live in, the more you may need to give up. But if your heart is after His presence, in the end it is worth it. These boundaries also protect you from falling into unnecessary temptation.

There is some temptation you can't avoid. Sometimes it will be outside of your control. But there are other times we open the door to increased temptation and sin by what we allow ourselves to see and listen to. If we make the choice to watch things or listen to things that we know are not in agreement with God's Word, we allow ourselves to be susceptible to increased temptation and attack. We make ourselves more vulnerable than we should be.

When you are walking with God, you are hidden in His secret place of protection and safety (Ps. 91). Making choices of integrity keeps you safe and secure in God's presence. If you know there are things in your life that can potentially grieve God and make you weak to wrong choices, then you need to set boundaries. That may be choosing to turn off certain TV programs. It may be setting up Internet blocks, filters, and accountability programs to keep yourself from falling into sexual immorality. Whatever boundaries you need to set to cultivate your personal integrity, this is vital if you want to have a life filled with God's ever-increasing power.

Choosing Right Associations

I learned very quickly in my walk with God that directly connected to a life of integrity is the power of association. Association brings transference. Whatever you spend time with is what you become.

> He who walks [as a companion] with wise men is wise, but he who associates with [self-confident] fools is [a fool himself and] shall smart for it.
>
> —PROVERBS 13:20

The more sensitive you are in the spirit, the more you will have to guard your associations. I know this from personal experience. I am like a sponge. I absorb whatever I spend time with. When I was younger, I got the nickname "the Sponge" because I would so easily soak up God's presence and power. If I just got near the anointing of God, I would instantly soak it up. The same happened with spiritual gifts. If I got around people who would prophesy, I would prophesy. My prophetic gift would go off the charts. If I got around people who had tremendous faith for healing and miracles, I would absorb that faith and anointing, and the miracles I would see exponentially multiplied. It's true. I have the capacity to absorb anointings. It's wonderful!

> Associate yourself with men of good quality if you esteem your own reputation. It is better to be alone than in bad company.[19]
>
> —GEORGE WASHINGTON

But because of this capacity, I have had to really guard what I let into my life. My extra sensitivities at times have caused me to absorb some very negative things too. I have learned through experience that my closest associations must be with people who really have a heart after God and are walking in faith and power. I have had to draw boundaries when it comes to relationships with people who have a lot of emotional baggage and issues that haven't been dealt with. Hanging around angry, negative people can drain the life of God out of you. It's one thing for God to use you to minister life to others; it's another thing to open up your spirit to those who can drag you down. We have to choose our close friendships wisely. We also have to be wise in every area of association, including what we watch on TV, in the movies, and on the Internet. It's a different world today. To maintain personal internal integrity, we must choose to associate with the anointing and presence of God as much as possible.

As we cultivate a life of integrity through godly repentance, brokenness, and good associations, we will harness God's power in our lives for the long haul, enabling us to finish our race strong all the way to the finish line.

CHAPTER 8

The Power of Perspective

A Bird's-Eye View

HAVE YOU EVER wondered what it's like to see life through the eyes of an eagle?

Sitting high above the earth, majestically perched on a treetop, you look down and see the world from heaven's perspective. Big things look small. There are no walls to confine you. No limitations whatsoever. All predators are far beneath you.

If you are truly going to soar and accomplish phenomenal things in your life, you will need to shift to see life through the eyes of an eagle. The power to persevere and live in God's power during the difficult moments of life comes when you are able to see your life from God's vantage point. This ability to see beyond the natural limitations will give you what you need to run your race to the end and obtain every blessing God has for you. It's the power of perspective.

Genesis 37–50 contains the incredible story of Joseph. Joseph was a man given an amazing vision and dream from God. He saw greatness in his future. He saw a day where he would be lifted up above his father and brothers. When he shared his dream with his brothers, they were overcome by jealousy, rage, and hatred, and they conspired to kill him. Joseph was thrown into a waterless pit. In a moment of greed, they realized they could get more out of selling him than by killing him, so they sold him into slavery. He was sold to the Midianites, who then brought him to Egypt. In Egypt he was sold to Potiphar, the captain of the royal guard under Pharaoh.

After enduring this deep pain of betrayal, Joseph was then falsely accused by Potiphar's wife of making advances toward her, and he had to run for his life. He finally found himself locked in a dungeon. He couldn't go any lower. How did this happen? How could he go from having such an amazing dream to this dark, cold, and lonely place? Where was God in all of this? I'm sure Joseph was tempted many times to think God had completely forgotten about him or had played a cruel joke.

After many years of enduring one painful trial after another, a *suddenly* happened in Joseph's life, bringing everything into proper perspective. One day the chief of the butlers and the chief of the bakers were thrown into prison with Joseph. They both dreamed dreams that were interpreted by Joseph correctly. Soon the chief butler was released and restored back under Pharaoh, but he forgot about Joseph. The day came when Pharaoh had a dream and needed it interpreted. But no one in the land could interpret it. Then the chief butler remembered how Joseph interpreted his dream, so he told Pharaoh about it. The moment of destiny had arrived. The king called upon Joseph to interpret the dream. This was the result.

> You shall have charge over my house, and all my people shall be governed according to your word [with reverence, submission, and obedience]. Only in matters of the throne will I be greater than you are. Then Pharaoh said to Joseph, See, I have set you over all the land of Egypt. And Pharaoh took off his [signet] ring from his hand and put it on Joseph's hand, and arrayed him in [official] vestments of fine linen and put a gold chain about his neck.
>
> —Genesis 41:40–42

What an amazing ending! Well, almost. The end had not yet come. There was still more God had planned for Joseph. We'll get there in a minute. I want to pause and ponder the power of perspective and what it will do in your life.

Walls, Walls, Walls

For years Joseph was surrounded by walls—walls on every side and at every turn. First it was the walls of the pit his brothers threw him into. These walls were not only physical but also emotional. They were walls of betrayal, anger, bitterness, and pain that his brothers built around him. Then it was the walls of false accusation. Then finally it was the walls of a dungeon. And it was all out of Joseph's control. These were circumstances that surrounded him due to the sinfulness in the hearts of other people.

There will be times you find yourself behind walls—walls that have been built by the actions and attitudes of other people, walls that you have no control over, walls that seem to hinder you and keep you from fulfilling God's will and plan for your life, walls that have the potential to bring utter defeat and depression.

But I have really good news for you. You will be fruitful and will be everything God has called you to be despite any wall that seems to limit you. Get ready. You are about to break out of every wall, boundary, border, and limitation that tries to hold you back. How do I know this? Well, let's take a look at the prophetic word Joseph's father, Jacob, had over him at the end of his life.

In Genesis 49:22–24, 26, Jacob declares that Joseph is a fruitful bough planted by a well whose branches run over the wall. Despite the bitter attacks that came against Joseph's life, despite the walls that surrounded him, he was fruitful in the midst of limitation and eventually grew right over the walls that surrounded him.

Many times we pray for God to change our circumstances. We think that if the apparent walls that surrounded us would just be removed, then we could move forward and have the life God intended us to have. Then we could be happy. Then we could have the joy, peace, and prosperity Jesus died to give us. Then we could fulfill that vision God has put in our heart. We wait and wait and wait, not realizing that in the midst of our limiting circumstances we are not limited at all.

When Everything Goes Wrong

My own life has not been an easy road. Much like the case with Joseph, when God's promise came to me that I would see stadiums filled and numerous miracles performed, it seemed everything went in the opposite direction. I was a premed student with plans to become a doctor. When God called me, I left it all behind and went to Bible school to prepare for full-time vocational ministry. From there I graduated and went into pastoral ministry. Although my salary wasn't high, I was happy because I was serving God.

After several years of pastoring, it became apparent through the anointing that was flowing through me that it was somewhere in God's plan for me to travel. I began to get a desire to see people healed. One day God spoke to me that it was His desire to heal people. I knew in my heart that He wanted to use me in the area of healing. When I shared my vision to travel and see people healed with my church leaders and peers, at first it was met with joy. They could see that call on my life and agreed it was God's plan. We rejoiced over the vision of how I could lead missions teams overseas and travel while still pastoring on staff. They witnessed the evangelistic call on my life and shared with me that it was God's will for me to travel. Each time I was given the pulpit to minister, God's power would show up and move in a mighty way.

But that joy quickly faded, and my ministry went in a different direction. Rather than teaching an adult Bible study class, I found myself with twenty kids, teaching them how to camp and tie knots. This was not my anointing at all. I couldn't care less about how to tie a knot. Things that I thought were going to happen in ministry didn't, and I had to walk through a very painful stripping process. Part of this was losing my pulpit ministry. But I knew what God had promised. I knew He had a higher calling for me. I was in the dungeon, but I could see the palace.

Not only did it look like I was surrounded by natural walls that limited my ministry, but also at times I was surrounded by spiritual and emotional walls. At times I felt like I was on an emotional roller-coaster ride. I even had to go for heart tests because of the emotional stress I was under. There I was, a twenty-five-year-old minister in the doctor's office strapped up to all sorts of machines trying to figure out why I had so much pain in my chest. It wasn't my heart. It was the stress.

While it looked like I was going backward in ministry, I was actually being positioned for a divine promotion from God. I just couldn't see it yet. I was to learn some very valuable life lessons that would stay with me forever.

I'll never forget the day I was in a leadership meeting with several other pastors and leaders. A minister introduced me to everyone as a "gopher." I felt demeaned because at the time I was serving in leadership. In that moment I simply looked down and held my peace. Then suddenly, the president of my Bible college, Dr. Benjamin Crandall, a senior man in leadership who had led one of the greatest churches in New York City, said, "Let me tell you all about Matt. Matt was president of his Bible college class for four years. He graduated with highest honors and is an exceptional young man after God." This was one of those many moments where God was vindicating me, yet working humility in me.

My father would always tell me, "Hindsight is 20/20." It's easy after you have been through something to later see what God was doing. I remember my very first days in ministry. I was bright-eyed and bushy-tailed. I had such a glorified vision of ministry. I was so excited to get my first pastor's office. My first week on staff I was told, "Well, Matt, we don't have any extra office space for you, but you can have the storage closet." The closet became my first office.

It had no windows except a small one to the hallway. But I fixed that room up to be the best office I could. I took the blind down that was on the window just to open it up a bit.

The following Sunday morning I was in church, and the head usher came up to me in a panic. "Matt, where is the blind?"

I said, "I took it down."

He said, "You can't. That's the nursing mothers' room!"

I was in shock. "No, it's not. It's my office."

"Well, it may be your office," he said, "but it's the nursing mothers' room on Sunday."

Week after week I would come into my office to find it filled with an aroma. And it wasn't the aroma of Christ. It was the dirty diapers left there from the day before!

Then each Sunday after church I ministered at the local nursing home. I preached to the same five elderly people week after week. Some of them told me the same stories over and over. I had to get them saved every week because they couldn't remember getting saved the week before! I had a vision for nations, and God had me sharing the gospel with five people. Nursing home ministry is wonderful. I never want to diminish anything we do for God. But in perspective, it didn't fit where I saw myself going. Yet God was teaching me a valuable lesson. Along the way He was giving me His divine perspective.

The Power of Humility

True humility can't be taught to you in a sermon. It's something that must be walked out through experience. God will allow painful and limiting circumstances in our lives to work a deeper level of humility and servanthood in us. While I thought I was being limited, God was busy working humility and servanthood in my heart. It was painful at times. But the work done in me during those years has stayed with me and marks everything I do now.

Sometimes I hear people blaming leaders over them for more

doors not opening for them. We must understand that God is our source, not man. He is the one who opens doors that no man can shut. He also shuts doors no man can open. God will allow us to go through seasons of frustration where we find ourselves doing things we don't even want to do. But there is a divine purpose in it all.

Let's face it, not everyone is built for manual labor. There are some people who love to be active doing things and others who prefer to be behind a desk working with their mind. But I have learned a very valuable lesson in life: none of us graduate from the kitchen. In other words, no matter what God entrusts us to do, we always have to be willing to stuff envelopes, empty the trash, and clean the bathroom. While these may not be our favorite things to do, nothing is beneath us. We have this kind of servant attitude worked in us, many times, by those in authority over us who ask us to do things we don't want to do. If we get a diva mind-set that says, "That is beneath me," then pride sneaks into our hearts, and we can disqualify ourselves from a promotion God wants to give us.

With God's perspective, I can now rejoice and thank God for every painful experience that worked greater humility in me. There have been so many times even in recent years where God has taken a painful moment and worked a deeper humility in my heart. Humility is not something we arrive at. It is an attitude of the heart that we must continually cultivate and develop. We are servants called to carry the image of Jesus on our lives for all the world to see. God gives us power so we can serve and help others. We must never forget that we are servants first, no matter what our title or position may be.

It's amazing when you get to experience this level of humility in the lives of people who have great influence. I had the privilege of accompanying Reinhard Bonnke, one of the Lord's leading evangelists, on a mass crusade outreach in Nigeria. This general has led millions of people to faith in Christ all across Africa. I'll never forget the time I spent with him. Each morning around ten of us would gather together for devotions and prayer. Reinhard would share the word with us and eat breakfast with us at the table. At night, after standing before hundreds of thousands of people, he would sit with us in his undershirt and just talk and laugh. He has a great sense of humor. I asked him if he travels with ministry bodyguards. He laughed and said, "No. I don't have any bodyguards. I just travel with my team." There were about five people from his team with him.

One night, just before he was to preach at the crusade, he turned to the young man he was raising up as an evangelist and said, "Daniel, you take the meeting tonight. I am going to go back to my room." He handed his platform over to this young man—a platform that took him years to build, not to mention the million dollars invested in putting such an outreach together. He later told us, "I have to pass the baton. I have to raise up the next generation to take my place." I was semi-stunned by his statement. I had heard a lot of ministers talk about how it's important to raise others up, but rarely have I ever seen one give his platform to a younger, less experienced leader to help empower and release them into their call. This was true humility at its finest—no fear, no insecurity, no competition. I believe it's this very heart attitude that has enabled Reinhard Bonnke to reach and sustain what God has given him. But even more than that, it has empowered him to multiply himself in others, leaving a legacy behind him that will far outlast even his own life. What a testimony to the power of humility!

The Release of God's Favor

Not everyone gets to experience leaders with this heart. But God uses the difficult moments for a purpose. The painful circumstances and surroundings that I experienced as a young minister soon positioned me in places where God's favor opened up new doors of opportunity leading me into my destiny. With each step of faith God unraveled His divine plan for me. No matter what happened,

I never allowed bitterness or resentment into my heart. I kept my heart clear. I remained humble. I took every beating with a smile. Sure, I had to work through the pain, but I never let it taint my attitude or spirit. This was vital if I was to fulfill my assignment from God. The only thing that can disqualify you from God's blessing is if you allow anger or resentment to defile your heart and short-circuit God's higher plan.

The secret is staying planted by the well, as Joseph did. The well is our secret source of power. It's God's presence and anointing. As long as we stay connected to our source, no matter what surrounds our life, our branches will keep growing until we go right over the walls that are around us! In other words, you will be fruitful in your call, fruitful in your purpose no matter what man tries to do. Nothing can hold you back when God's hand is upon you. You will be fruitful and experience the life of power God has for you no matter what other people say or do. In fact, it may just be the negative things they do to you that propel you right into God's blessings! "What? Did I just read that?" Yes, you did. The very things people do to hurt you will be the very things that God uses to maneuver you into your life's purpose. But in order for that to happen, you have to really grasp the power of having the right perspective.

Getting a Higher Perspective

> It is important to live each day with a positive perspective. It is not wise to pretend problems do not exist, but it is wise to look beyond the problem to the possibilities that are in it. When Goliath came against the Israelites, the soldiers all thought, "He's so big, we can never kill him." But David looked at the same giant and thought, "He's so big, I can't miss him."[1]
>
> —Dr. Dale E. Turner

Psalm 105 talks about what Joseph had to walk through. It shows us that God's perspective can be completely opposite to man's perspective. The circumstances may be the same, but God knows the end result.

Psalm 105:17–22 states, "He sent a man before them, even Joseph, who was sold as a servant. His feet they hurt with fetters; he was laid in chains of iron and his soul entered into the iron, until his word [to his cruel brothers] came true, until the word of the Lord tried and tested him. The king sent and loosed him, even the ruler of the peoples, and let him go free. He made Joseph lord of his house and ruler of all his substance, to bind his princes at his pleasure and teach his elders wisdom."

Verse 17 explains it all. "He sent a man…who was sold as a servant." From the earthly perspective Joseph was sold into slavery. He was abused and mistreated by his brothers. They were so jealous they wanted to kill him. They sold him as a slave so his destiny could never be fulfilled. They tried to destroy him. This was man's perspective. It seemed as if the actions of Joseph's brothers were causing the exact opposite thing to happen than what God had spoken. From the earthly perspective man was destroying Joseph's dreams and destiny.

God saw things very differently. Joseph was not just a man being sold into slavery. He was a man being sent by God. Man's viewpoint said, "Sold"; God's viewpoint said, "Sent"—same situation, different interpretation. The problem is, God does not always send us the way we think He should. But Joseph needed to be divinely positioned by God so that at the right moment he could be promoted to his place of destiny. God knew that the best way for Joseph to get near the king was to be placed in the dungeon where he would meet the chief butler. It would be this one connection that would bring Joseph from the dungeon to the palace. But Joseph had to be in the dungeon to make this connection!

The entire time, even when man couldn't see it, God's hand was at work to position Joseph exactly where he needed to be to fulfill the dream. God even used Joseph's brothers' ungodliness to fulfill His purposes. Each painful experience pushed Joseph closer to his divine assignment. Each act of betrayal and accusation caused Joseph to be divinely positioned by God. Then when the right moment had arrived, God shut off all the revelation in the land. No one could interpret Pharaoh's dream—no one but Joseph, that is. This is what God was doing all along. Then in one single moment of breakthrough, Joseph was promoted to the top!

Bird's-Eye Perspective of Training

As a new baby eaglet grows in size, at some point it becomes time to fly. The parents encourage the eaglet by flapping their wings above the nest. If that doesn't work, the parents entice the young eagle to fly by holding food just out of reach. While these young eagles have a natural-born instinct to fly, they must still practice to gain strength. While in the nest young eagles will flap their wings and at times become slightly airborne. They learn how to fly by watching their parents. Soon baby fat turns into muscle, and they become more agile. With a need to fulfill their hunger, eventually they will catch an updraft of wind and take their first soaring flight.[2]

We really learn from this that God will allow our circumstances to get uncomfortable so we become motivated to fly. In the same way a baby eagle is motivated to fly due to the discomfort of hunger, God will use uncomfortable circumstances to encourage us into our destiny, even if it is the scariest thing in the world. Before I launched out into evangelistic ministry, God had given me a vision of an eagle getting launched out of the nest like a rocket. I knew my time was coming. But I was still scared to make the transition into the unknown. God had to make my surroundings uncomfortable in order to propel me into a greater destiny. As they say in Jamaica, "No problem, mon!" It's all perspective.

Somewhere along his journey Joseph obtained the bird's-eye view for his life. In Genesis 50:20, he said to his brothers who had tried to destroy him, "As for you, you thought evil against me, but

God meant it for good, to bring about that many people should be kept alive, as they are this day."

Somewhere along his painful journey Joseph got a glimpse of God's higher perspective. (See Genesis 45:5–8.) He realized that every bad thing that happened to him along the way served the purposes of God in getting him where he needed to be to fulfill his divine assignment.

You must realize that every trial you have had to face, every time you were mistreated by others, falsely accused, rejected, abused, pushed down, criticized, all of these things have served to maneuver you into the proper position to get you to where God needed you to be so you could fulfill His will for your life. Often during the process it's difficult to see God's hand at work. It's usually not until afterward that you realize what God was up to.

I want to encourage you to stay planted by the well even before you can fully see God's purposes. As you worship and wait on God, He can reveal to you His hidden plan. But even if you can't see the full picture, keeping a good attitude and a pure heart will be essential if you want to fulfill your kingdom assignment.

Joseph had obtained God's perspective. That's why he could love, forgive, and bless those who mistreated him. He was able to turn around and thank them for what they did because he realized it had to happen to bring him to his destiny. That's why you also can rejoice when you fall into various trials. That's why you can get happy when people mistreat you. God is using them to get you somewhere. Don't let your pain destroy you. Let it propel you!

Life After Death

Brandi's father was an abusive and violent man. With a criminal record and more than twenty DWIs/DUIs, he would violently abuse Brandi's mother, verbally and physically. In an effort to cause her to miscarry while pregnant with Brandi, her stomach became his punching bag. Brandi was aborted by her mother and father on

September 12, 1983. She was given the ultimate stamp of rejection as a sentence of death was imposed upon her in the womb. She was burned alive by a saline abortion at twenty-one weeks in the womb. As she lay there lifeless, to everyone's shock her arm shot up. She was still alive! She survived and was further spared from infanticide.

As a result of what she went through while in the womb, she struggles with physical handicaps today. In school she was teased and picked on by the other kids because of her differences. She never received love or support from either her mom or dad. Brandi's mom would tell her that she wished the abortion had been successful.

But Brandi made a choice. She chose to forgive and not let shame, embarrassment, or her physical disabilities silence the voice God had given her. What was intended for her destruction had only served to make her stronger. God has enabled her to rise above her physical challenges and overcome them with her testimony. She lives not only as a survivor but also as a hero, championing the cause for the unborn and those with physical handicaps.

On May 19, 2010, as a result of Brandi's testimony, a law was passed by the Louisiana state senate requiring doctors performing abortions to do a pre-abortion ultrasound and give the mother the choice to see the ultrasound image or a printout. Now pregnant women can make an informed "choice." Brandi's life is having a profound effect on natural laws, and as a result, lives are being saved. Make the choice, like Brandi, to turn your stumbling blocks into stepping-stones of purpose and destiny.[3]

The Perfect Storm

The eagle uses the winds of a storm to propel itself higher and higher. As it effortlessly soars, it can rest its wings and preserve energy. While other birds are hiding in the trees, the eagle is soaring to a new height. In the same way, you can never waste a good trial. Don't hide; fly!

> Consider it wholly joyful, my brethren, whenever you are enveloped in or encounter trials of any sort or fall into various temptations. Be assured and understand that the trial and proving of your faith bring out endurance and steadfastness and patience. But let endurance and steadfastness and patience have full play and do a thorough work, so that you may be [people] perfectly and fully developed [with no defects], lacking in nothing.
>
> —James 1:2–4

When you endure through trials, God is working in you to remove all your defects. He's bringing you to a place of spiritual maturity so you can have the best life possible. So when it looks like everything is going wrong, get happy! Rejoice! Not only is God working out His amazing plan for you, but also in the process He is refining you so that when you get to where you are going, you will have the heart you need to stay there. God's ultimate goal isn't just what you will do for Him. It's who you will become. His goal is to make you fruitful. Having the right perspective will give you the power to produce abundant fruit. It's this fruit that will empower you to fulfill your purpose.

Joseph fulfilled his assignment from God and saved a nation. Man sold him, but God sent him. The same happened with Jesus. He was betrayed for thirty pieces of silver and sold by Judas to the Pharisees. Jesus was sold by man but sent by God—sent to save the world from their sin. Joseph was sent to save his nation from famine. As a result Joseph was able to preserve a remnant in the earth called Israel through which the Savior would be born to ultimately save the world, which actually makes the story of Joseph much bigger than Joseph and his brothers. God's plan for you is much bigger than you realize.

Fulfilling Your Ultimate Destiny

When you read about the life of Joseph, you see that success is not just about what we accomplish for God during the time He gives us. It's not just about what we do. The true mark of success is actually who we become in the process of walking out our journey.

In Genesis 49:22–26, not only did Jacob talk about Joseph's trials and sufferings that he had to endure and the blessings he would receive from God, but he also talked about Joseph's fruitfulness. Joseph was not one who could be contained. He would expand and multiply under the blessings of God. In the process of everything he had to walk through, he became fruitful. What does that mean? Did it mean he liked to eat fruit? No. It meant that his life produced the nature, character, and heart of God. It meant that he did what was right even when it was hard. He believed God when things looked hopeless. He refused to let bitterness and resentment rob his destiny. He refused to let his pain and wounds defeat him. He refused to take vengeance on his enemies even when he had the power to.

You see, God's destiny was to entrust Joseph with great power and influence. But God needed to know that he could trust Joseph with that power and that it would be used correctly. So He allowed Joseph to be tested to see how he would react and respond. God's Word tested Joseph. Joseph kept his heart clean and free. When God's perfect timing came, Joseph in a moment was catapulted into God's blessing and purpose. And his heart was in the right place at the right time so nothing could hinder what God wanted to do through him. He was a fruitful bough. Joseph was able to fulfill his divine assignment and use his power correctly because he had God's perspective. This perspective empowered Joseph to love and forgive, realizing God was working everything for his good.

One thing I want you to understand. No matter what man does to you or doesn't do for you…no matter what your circumstances say to you…absolutely nothing can keep you from the abundant

life God has for you as long as you choose to walk in love and forgiveness because you see your life from God's perspective. Not only
did Joseph succeed in accomplishing great things, saving the nation
during a time of famine, and rescuing his own family from peril,
but he also fulfilled God's ultimate destiny for him and became
fruitful. He walked in perseverance, love, forgiveness, grace, and
mercy. This is what God was looking for the whole time. Joseph
finished his race strong and became all God destined him to be.

You will realize one day, if you haven't already, that many of life's
pains are blessings in disguise. I remember when I could no longer
remain on staff as a pastor because God was calling me into travel
ministry. While I wanted to do both, God had other plans—better
plans. I remember when another minister said to me, "Matt, one
day you will be really thankful for this." I thought to myself at that
time, "Yeah, right. I'm losing everything—my church family, spiritual home, and ministry." I was actually semi-traumatized by the
whole thing and had to fight off depression for about six months
after my transition. I didn't feel too thankful at the time. But
looking back now, I realize that was exactly what needed to happen
for me to have the freedom to run the race God had set before me.
Anything less would not have been God's perfect will for me. And
because I kept my heart free from any trace of offense and honored
God's authorities and those He placed in my life, nothing could
stop God's blessings.

Always remember this. Though the enemy may have a plan and
an assignment to bring pain and destruction into your life, God's
assignment is always greater. When you submit to God, keep a
pure heart, and worship Him even in your brokenness, God will
grant to you His heavenly perspective, allowing you to enjoy your
journey a whole lot more and experience His resurrection power
every day of your life. Just as Joseph was released from the prison,
you too will be released into every good thing God has for you.
Don't waste a good trial, and never let the enemy steal your praise!

CHAPTER 9

The Power of Perseverance

Mission Possible

I REMEMBER WATCHING THE television show *Get Smart* as a kid. It was my favorite detective show. Agent 86 was always faced with insurmountable challenges that he had to overcome.

Much like Agent 86, you are God's secret agent, and your assignment is to save the world from chaos. Should you choose to accept this assignment, you may face some of the hardest challenges of your life. But God will provide you with the secret weapon you need to accomplish this task.

Living an extraordinary life filled with God's power does not mean life will always be easy and trial free. Life is filled with its ups and downs. The up times are great, but it's what we do with the down times that will really determine our ultimate destination. If we can learn the power found within our secret weapon, perseverance, nothing will be able to hold us down or keep us back from fulfilling God's assignments for us.

Jane lay there stunned as her husband strained for his last few breaths of air. Just hours before everything was picture perfect. She was in the house relaxing from her day at work. Dan was in the garage working on some odd jobs. It was a warm summer day. The sun was shining, and the birds were chirping. The kids could be heard playing in the sprinklers on the side of the house. Laughter filled the air. Then suddenly, an uneasy feeling hit Jane in the pit of her stomach. She didn't know why. She stood up from the couch and walked to the window to check on the kids. They were laughing and playing without a care in the world. She took a deep breath and sat back down on the couch, but the feeling wouldn't leave her. Some time passed. Suddenly, the thought of Dan popped into her mind. She walked out the front door toward the garage area. All seemed quiet and serene. When she turned the corner toward the garage, she called out his name. "Dan?" Nothing. Just silence. Then her eye caught a glimpse of Dan's arm. As her eyes came into focus, she realized Dan was lying on the garage floor. She ran over to him, calling out his name. As she knelt down next to him, she picked up his head and held him in her arms. With tears streaming down her face, Dan gasped his last few breaths of air. Then he was gone. Gone. Leaving a wife and two small children behind. Leaving a gaping hole of loss and pain. This scenario of loss can be played out many different ways. Life does not always go the way we plan. What do we do when life throws us a curve ball? We must keep on swinging. It's only over if you quit and give up. I found out early on that you cannot always control your circumstances. Unfortunately, however, you can let your circumstances control you—and many people do. They are driven by the fleeting emotions of their soul based on what life dictates to them to feel.

But when God gives us His strength and power, He enables us to rise above the greatest adversity. Rather than being helpless victims, we become fearless warriors who can rise successfully to every challenge. Perseverance is one of the greatest keys to living an incredible, super-abounding life. Perseverance is what will get you to your ultimate life's goals and enable you to release the hero within.

Never Give Up!

"Never give up! Never, never, never, never give up!" These words resound in my heart and mind to this very day. Quoting the timeless words of Winston Churchill, Dr. Benjamin Crandall, the president of the Bible college I attended, thundered these words during my ordination service into ministry. They have been a light to my path ever since. I have found along the way that life is dotted with many tempting parking places. It's easy to settle down in a comfort zone. It takes courage and strength of spirit to keep going.

A dear friend, spiritual father, mentor, and champion of the faith, James Goll, had to walk through an extremely difficult trial. Sometimes we think that if we are living right and serving God, life will always be perfect. Well, we quickly discover that life is not perfect, and at times the Lord allows us to walk through some very difficult things. But one thing is for sure; God will always turn it for our good and work His perfect plan in the process.

James and his wife, Michal Ann, persevered through a fierce battle with cancer. They were both afflicted at the same time. She never stopped believing or trusting God, and neither did he. During worship at a conference someone walked up to him and handed him a card in a blue envelope and said, "This is a word to you from your wife." He opened it up real quick and read the outside of the card. "Never, never, never, never give up. Winston Churchill." He put it back inside the envelope, never reading the note on the inside, and stuck it into his Bible.

By the time he returned home from his meetings, his wife had already fallen into a very deep sleep on the verge of death. He had one last night to spend with his beloved. Their health-care giver stepped outside their room, and he got to spend the night alone with his wife. In the middle of the night, at 3:30 a.m., he got up and knelt by her bedside. He laid his head on her chest and said, "Honey, if you've got one last word for me, I really want to hear it." He prayed for her and gave her to Jesus. As he wept over her and gave her back to the Lord, he watched over the next four hours as her body just slowly unwound. He was there as she left her body to be with the Lord in heaven.

After walking through all the funeral services with friends and family, three weeks later he found himself ministering in Korea. Although it was a very difficult time, he was fulfilling a commitment he had made to minister. While he was there, one night he dreamed about the card someone had given him before she passed and relived the moment. He realized that he never read the inside of the card. What did it say?

The outside of the card was a word to all of us. The inside was her word to him and their four children. The outside read, "Never, never, never, never give up." The inside read, "I'll never, never, never stop cheering for you." Those were her last words to her beloved husband. No matter whether she was here on earth or in heaven, she would always be cheering for him. He would never forget those last words of encouragement.

Soon after James's wife passed, he was declared cancer free. He was healed on this side of eternity; Michal Ann was healed on the other.[1]

No matter what our circumstances are...no matter what difficulties we face...God wants to help us finish our race to the end. We must never give up! Just as Michal Ann would always cheer for her husband, God is always cheering for us. You are on the winning side, and you must never forget that.

I love what Franklin D. Roosevelt once said: "When you come to the end of your rope, tie a knot and hang on."[2]

Many great men and women in history faced extreme trials, setbacks, and disappointments along their life's journeys. They endured the hurtful criticisms of others. They had to hold on to their faith and trust their heart even when others said they would be nothing and would go nowhere. Some of the most seemingly insignificant people accomplished the most amazing things because of one thing: perseverance! They refused to give up no matter how hard it got. No matter how many times they failed, failure didn't defeat them. Mistakes didn't stop them. The quality of perseverance they possessed enabled them to turn life's negatives into stepping-stones of radical achievement.

When, God? When?

When you are a person with a big vision, it can be challenging when things don't move as quickly as you want them to. My first five years of ministry were spent as an assistant pastor. I had various functions, including counting the offerings, doing hospital visitations, and watching over the children's programs, among other things. As time went on God began to give me a vision of stadiums filled with people being healed by the miraculous power of God. But the outlets where I was were very limited for this vision. I had rare opportunities to preach, and my full potential remained in a very confined place, much like David in the cave of Adullam.

Life can feel that way when you have a vision with no expression or outlet. This is where perseverance becomes crucial to get you through the in-between times. The in-between time is the time between the inception of your vision and its fulfillment. It's where all the testing and trials happen along the way. A lot can happen during that time, both good and bad. But one thing is for certain, God will use it all for your good to fulfill His purposes for your life.

One day I heard of a young evangelist being used by God in spectacular ways. He had a flourishing ministry of miracles, and his name was everywhere. I can remember reading a report of what God was doing through him. It's not always an encouragement to your flesh when you are believing God for great things in your own life and you see someone else being extravagantly blessed while you apparently have nothing. It's really just one big test.

I flopped my body on the couch and sat there having a party, a pity party. Why, God? Why? When, God? When? I was so discouraged. Why was God blessing him and not me? It didn't seem fair. Well, life is not always fair, and we don't always get what we want when we want it. But if we can learn to rejoice when others are blessed, our time will come. I have really learned this through experience. We waste so much time getting discouraged over other people's success and blessing, we can't enjoy our own journey in God. It really is true. When God sees us getting happy for someone else, He eventually pours out His blessings on us.

I soon got a grip of myself and began to thank God that He had a plan for me. I had a vision from God and was determined to see it happen. As I persevered and walked step by step in obedience to God, He began to open the right doors for me, put me in the right place at the right time, and made a way where there was no way. Now, years later, God has given me a thriving ministry that was birthed by a vision and walked out with perseverance. I learned a valuable lesson. Refuse to compare yourself with what is happening to others. Rejoice in their blessing, and your time will come.

The key? When things looked hard, I never quit. When doors didn't open fast enough, I kept knocking. When crowds were small, I kept preaching. When people didn't get healed, I kept praying. My perseverance paid off. Now, we have seen thousands healed by God's power. God gives us the power to persevere, and it's that perseverance that sees the power of God released and the promises of God brought to fulfillment.

I've learned this simple lesson while trying to open the front door of my house in the dark. It's often the last key on the key ring that opens the lock. Sometimes you can't completely see how to open the door that's in front of you, but if you keep trying, eventually your perseverance will pay off.

Cross Your Mountain One Pebble at a Time

You don't have to be perfect all the time to reach your destiny. You just have to persevere. No matter what comes your way, you can never give up.

Somebody once said, "Nobody trips over mountains. It is the small pebble that causes you to stumble. Pass all the pebbles in your path, and you will find you have crossed the mountain." It's the little things that can try to discourage you along the way.

Paul said at the end of his life in 2 Timothy 4:7, "I have fought the good (worthy, honorable, and noble) fight, I have finished the race, I have kept (firmly held) the faith."

Sometimes life is a fight. If you simply make the choice to not give up when it gets hard, you will make it through to your finish line. Remember the source of your strength. In yourself at times you will feel weak and tired. You may even feel worn out on the inside. The best thing to do when you feel this way is to get before God in prayer and allow Him to strengthen you with His Word and His presence. This is how we make it day by day. This is how you finish your race, one prayer at a time.

Perseverance will enable you to finish strong. It's not just about how you start. It's also about how you finish. A lot of people have no problem starting something. But show me someone who has seen it through to the finish, and I will show you someone who understands what it means to be a champion.

After Fred Astaire's first screen test, the memo from the testing director of MGM, dated 1933, read, "Can't act. Can't sing. Slightly bald. Can dance a little." He kept that memo over the fireplace in his Beverly Hills home. Astaire once observed, "When you're experimenting, you have to try so many things before you choose what you want, that you may go days getting nothing but exhaustion." And here is the reward for perseverance: "The higher up you go, the more mistakes you are allowed. Right at the top, if you make enough of them, it's considered to be your style."[3]

Many people start well, but somewhere along the way they lose sight of God and sight of their goal. They lose sight of themselves and of the values and principles that got them to where they are today. When you lose sight of what's right and you let your convictions slip, it's easy to walk down a detoured path that will miss God's final destination for your life. Don't get detoured. Finish what you start.

One of the activities I remember the most growing up was our family hiking excursions. My dad would take my mom and me out into the wilderness for days with just a backpack on our backs and canteens on our sides. We would hike deep into the mountain forest and traverse up and down over rugged terrain. Usually it was a fun and exciting adventure, but there was one trip I will never forget. I should have known better when I saw the name of the trail: SUFFRIN. Sounds a lot like suffering, doesn't it? Well, that's exactly what I thought just a day into it.

It was mid-July in New York, and it was hot and humid—not the ideal time to carry a fifty-pound pack on your back for eight hours a day, walking miles in the blistering heat. But thankfully my dad had a map! And on that map were the markings of where all the water wells were supposed to be, so we could refill our canteens. Each time we came to a water well, it was dried up from the summer heat. No water! Two days into the hike, there was no way we could turn around. We had to keep moving forward.

Leading out in the hike, I was following the little blue marks laid out for us on the trees, when suddenly the markers disappeared. Where did they go? I looked left, right, forward, backward. No markers. I was sure we didn't take a detour. I was being very careful to stay on course. The only way left to look was up. We looked on the map and noticed that the trail my dad had brought us on was an advanced trail for serious hikers. We did not fit that category! No ropes and cables here, folks; just hiking boots and backpacks. Heavy backpacks.

Realizing the only way to go was up, we started on our climb with fifty pounds on our backs pulling us away from the wall. About halfway up I decided I would check out our progress. I don't recommend this to anyone at home. The second I saw the tops of the trees below my feet, I was struck with panic and fear. I froze, clinging to the side of the mountain. As terror seized my heart, I let out a guttural scream. My mom became so nervous she went hysterical laughing. We have this little problem in our family. Nervousness makes us laugh. I inherited this wonderful trait from my mother. My dad, on the other hand, definitely does not possess this trait. He let out a few choice words. The more he yelled, the more we laughed. There we were clinging to the side of the mountain, my mom and me laughing hysterically, and my dad yelling beneath us. I began to plead the blood of Jesus and call on the angels to surround us. My mom said, "Matt, I'm sticking with you!"

I soon overcame my fear and dread and slowly continued to climb upward. We made it all the way to the top ledge. One by one we managed to hoist our bodies over the ledge to the flat ground above. I literally kissed the ground. I will never forget that journey. In fact, I don't think we went back to the Suffrin trail ever again! My motto is, "If suffering can be avoided, then avoid it!"

We know in life we don't always have the luxury of choosing what path we walk on. Sometimes we find ourselves climbing a mountain precipice wondering if we have what it takes to make it to the top. Other times we find ourselves in a deep ravine. This is where the power of perseverance comes into play. Without perseverance we'll never make it successfully to the end of our journey. We might not like where those little blue markers take us, but here are some important lessons we can learn from my journey through Suffrin.

1. Never look back over your shoulder. Keep looking in the direction you are supposed to be going. This will decrease your chances of falling (Gen. 19:26).

2. Calm yourself, and remember that you are covered by God (Ps. 91:4).

3. No matter how bleak a situation may look, there is always hope if you persevere and refuse to give up (Prov. 23:18).

4. God will give you wisdom and the tools you need to overcome in every situation (Acts 17:11).

5. You must make up your mind that you are never going back to where you came from. You must choose to continue to press on to high mark and prize of God (Phil. 3:14).

6. There may be moments of testing and trial you go through, but there is always an end in sight. Your situation is temporary (Ps. 30:5).

7. Never let fear stop you. Fix your mind on things above, and God will give you the courage to keep pressing forward to your final destination (Col. 3:2–3).

8. Life may go in directions you never expected, and you might feel you don't have the strength to go on. Remember, when you are weak, He is strong in you (2 Cor. 12:10).

9. Never forget to laugh. Even in the most perilous of circumstances, the joy of the Lord is your strength. If I fell laughing, at least I would have died happy (Neh. 8:10).

Passing Through the Place of Contention

It is possible for you to press through to a place of breakthrough, if you don't give up. I call this passing through the place of contention. Usually right before your greatest breakthrough is the greatest battle. I saw this in the life of our family just before my mom received her healing. On her way to the church for a healing service, she could hardly get out of bed, but she forced herself to do so. And that night she was healed!

If you feel spiritual pressure on every side, and if you feel like you are facing the greatest warfare of your life, hold on! Your breakthrough is just ahead of you. It's right at the door.

We see this principle throughout the Bible. Before Isaac could go to a new level of fruitfulness in his land of inheritance, he faced this place of contention. In Genesis 26 we see that when Isaac sowed into his land of inheritance, God greatly blessed and increased him. Yet even with all of the blessing and increase he had, God still had more for him. God wanted to make him even more fruitful. And God wants to do the same for you. He wants to bring you from glory, to glory, to glory!

The enemy contested Isaac's increase. When you are about to go to your next level of promotion, you will have to face this spiritual contest head-on. The enemy is not going to roll out the red carpet for you to come in and take over. As Isaac continued to dig wells in his land, the Philistines contested it. The first well was called Esek, meaning contention. The second well was called Sitnah, meaning enmity. But Isaac refused to give up. He knew the land was his. The third well they called Rehoboth, meaning room. God helped Isaac break through the contention and made room for him to be fruitful in the land. As he pressed through and didn't give up, his fruitfulness increased. And so will yours.

Use Your Secret Weapon Wisely

So, you made it through to the end, and this chapter has not self-destructed! You are well on your way.

As you continue on with your mission to fulfill your future assignments from God, use your secret weapon wisely. Perseverance is your key to overcome the obstacles that may lie ahead. You can do it. I believe you can, and so does God. He's the best partner in crime fighting there is. Together, you can save the world.

CHAPTER 10

The Power of Vision

Pulling Your Future Into Your Now

A s God empowers you by His grace to deal with the issues of your past and to persevere through every difficult and trying situation, He doesn't just bring you out of something, but He brings you into something. He brings you out of your past so you can enter into your future. You enter into your destiny through the power of vision. Vision will cause you to move beyond every label someone has put on you, every pain you have had to endure, and every injustice you have had to face. Vision will empower you to accelerate through your now moment into your future purpose and calling.

Get ready to dream big! God wants you to have a vision way bigger than yourself. It should be something impossible for you to achieve on your own. He really wants to be glorified through what He accomplishes in and through your life. The more impossible it is, the more glory He will get.

Michelangelo, an Italian Renaissance painter, among other things, created two of the most influential paintings in the history of Western art. These included scenes from Genesis on the ceiling and images of the Last Judgment on the wall of the Sistine Chapel in Rome. Michelangelo once said, "The greatest danger for most of us is not that our aim is too high and we miss it, but that it is too low and we reach it."[1] He understood something about having vision that lifted you above your own abilities.

Vision is so vital for you to fully move into all God has for you. The direction you look in will determine your path in life. Some people get stuck in the quagmire of their past. They only focus on the negative things in life. They focus on everything they don't like and on what everyone else is doing wrong. They focus on their own limitations, weaknesses, and inabilities. Their focus is more on the actions of others, their own natural circumstances, or why they can't move forward into the place God is wanting to bring them. They always have an excuse for why their life is going in circles repeating the same old patterns.

To really live every day to the fullest, life must be filled with vision, God's vision. Vision produces a sense of purpose. It is the driving force behind what we do. Without a vision, people perish (Prov. 29:18). Vision causes you to advance forward and accomplish God's will for your life. Vision is all about how you see your future. All great accomplishments and achievements start with a vision and a dream. Vision will empower you to be a world changer and nation shaker. Vision enables you to see beyond the limitations and empowers you to achieve the impossible.

Vision is having the ability to see what God sees for your life. When you see beyond the obvious, your eyes are open to see the potential of who you can be and what you can accomplish.

Vision Comes in Stages

Many times vision comes in stages. God often reveals His plan to us one step at a time. When I was in college studying to become a doctor, God revealed His will to me that He had called me to vocational ministry, but I had no details. He gave me a vision that would lead my life in a certain direction, but like Abram, I didn't fully know where I was going. As I obeyed Him each step of the way, His vision continued to unfold.

From that place of revelation God showed me to go to Bible school to be prepared and trained for ministry and to get a strong foundation in God's Word. After four years of intensive Bible study, God then revealed to me that I would become a pastor on staff at my local church. After four years of pastoring and gaining more knowledge and experience in ministry, God then began to give me a vision for miracles and salvation for the lost. With this vision came a new desire to travel and preach God's Word and see His power released on the masses. It was this vision that brought direction to my steps and led me right into my future.

Vision Requires Risk

Vision is a great thing to have. But if all you have is vision, then at best what you may have is a glorified daydream. Thomas Edison, the inventor of the lightbulb, said it this way: "Vision without execution is hallucination."[2]

Vision cannot remain alone. It must be accompanied by action. The greatest vision killer is procrastination. How many times does God place something in our hearts, only for us to just sit on it? There comes a time in every great visionary's life that action must be added to their vision. I have always found that when I take steps of faith in response to what God has placed in my heart, my action releases the hand of God to begin to open doors for me that would have otherwise remained shut.

When God spoke to me to launch out into traveling ministry, I had no open doors at all. I just had a vision from God. But God was faithful to confirm His will to me in several significant ways. This gave me the courage I needed to take the necessary risks. I had to make the choice to leave my comfort zone. In order to begin traveling in ministry, I had to lay down my position as an assistant pastor. I had to leave everything behind, including my paycheck.

That can be a very scary thing. My vision propelled me forward into my destiny, but along the way I had to be willing to take risks.

I was able to take those risks for several reasons. First, God had clearly spoken to me and confirmed His word through the counsel of several other leaders in my life. So my steps were not in presumption; they were in obedience and faith. I could also take these risks because of my firm confidence and trust in God. I knew God had always taken care of me and that if I was in His will, everything would work out according to His perfect plan.

During my last week of pastoring, I still had no open doors to preach on the road. I was at the hospital doing my last hospital visitation as a pastor. As I was walking through the foyer on my way out to my car, I walked right into another local pastor from the area. I had only met him once three years earlier, but he remembered me. He greeted me and asked, "So, Brother Matt, how are you doing? What's new?" After a little small talk I shared with him, "Well, pastor, I am traveling on the road now in ministry." It was my confession of faith. He looked straight at me and said, "I would like for you to come and preach at my church. Please call my secretary, and we will set a date. When are you available?" I said, "Next week." That was my first open door as an evangelist. God has continued to open doors for me ever since.

I have learned that when one door closes, God always has a better door waiting for you. Alexander Graham Bell once said, "When one door closes, another opens, but we so often look upon the closed door that we do not see the one that has opened for us."[3] It's so important that we don't miss God's opportunities by focusing too much on what we feel we have lost.

What is so wonderful about vision is that it will empower you to endure the process you have to walk through to get to where God is bringing you. The road is not always easy, and vision will keep you moving when it gets difficult. Even with Jesus, it was for the joy set before Him that He could endure the cross. The vision within His heart for humanity being reconciled back to God gave Him the strength He needed to fulfill God's purpose for His life. Vision will keep you moving in the right direction and will give you the passion to make needed sacrifices along the way.

Where Are You Looking?

There will be seasons in your life where you have to look back in order to move forward. There will be times you will have to face your past with all of its pain and ugliness, but you can't stay there forever. God doesn't want you to get stuck. As God was harnessing His power in my own life and preparing me to be a vessel that would touch the world, I went through some very intense seasons of introspection where God was dealing with some painful issues from my past. But I couldn't stay there forever. I couldn't dwell on those negative things forever. This is the difference between a victim and an overcomer. A victim constantly dwells on what's been done to them and why their life is messed up as a result. An overcomer faces pain head-on, works through it, and then moves on. A victor eventually refocuses their vision not on where they were or even on where they are right now. An overcomer begins to look forward to where they are going and how God is going to gloriously use everything for good in their life.

In Genesis 13:14–15 God instructed Abraham, "Lift up now your eyes and look from the place where you are, northward and southward and eastward and westward; for all the land which you see I will give to you and to your posterity forever."

Abraham had to look from where he was to where God was bringing him. He had to get his eyes off his present moment, location, and circumstance, and he had to see where he was going. Your destiny is determined by what you can see. My question to you is, what do you see?

Abraham would be reminded every night of his destiny in God. In Genesis 15 God brought Abraham outside and told him to count the stars. He said, "So shall your descendants be" (v. 5). Abraham believed and trusted God's words. He had a continual reminder that no matter what his present moment looked like, this was where he was going. He would be the father of multitudes. Every time he looked up and saw the stars, he saw his future.

You Multiply What You Look At

We find a phenomenal illustration from the life of Jacob that shows what you focus on will multiply in your life. In Genesis 30:25–43, we read the story of how Jacob is ready to move away from his father-in-law, Laban, and start his own life. But Laban resists his going and asks Jacob what he can pay him. Jacob asks for Laban to give him the speckled and spotted animals from his flock as his wages. Laban agrees, but later that same day he removes all the spotted animals from his flocks so Jacob couldn't get them.

But God gives Jacob supernatural wisdom. This is what he does. "But Jacob took fresh rods of poplar and almond and plane trees and peeled white streaks in them, exposing the white in the rods. Then he set the rods which he had peeled in front of the flocks in the watering troughs where the flocks came to drink. And since they bred and conceived when they came to drink, the flocks bred and conceived in sight of the rods and brought forth lambs and kids streaked, speckled, and spotted" (Gen. 30:37–39).

The story goes on to say, in Genesis 30:41–43, "And whenever the stronger animals were breeding, Jacob laid the rods in the watering troughs before the eyes of the flock, that they might breed and con-ceive among the rods. But when the sheep and goats were feeble, he omitted putting the rods there; so the feebler animals were Laban's and the stronger Jacob's. Thus the man increased and became exceedingly rich, and had many sheep and goats, and maidservants, menservants, camels, and donkeys."

The flocks birthed and multiplied what they looked at. When they looked at the speckled tree branches, they gave birth to spotted lambs. The principle is simple. We multiply in our lives what we set our vision on. If we set our eyes on the good promises and purposes of God, that is what will be multiplied in our lives. If we focus on the negative, we will multiply the negative. It really is true. The more you dwell on the negative things in life, the more depressed you become and the more you move in a negative direction. Dwelling on your own weaknesses magnifies them. Dwelling on the wrong things others have done to you magnifies and multiplies offense and anger in your heart. Dwelling too long on your wounded past multiplies a victim mentality and feelings of defeat. As you choose to focus on God's vision, you will see His promises multiplied in your life.

> When I was young, I said to God, "God, tell me the mystery of the universe." But God answered, "That knowledge is for Me alone." So I said, "God, tell me the mystery of the peanut." Then God said, "Well, George, that's more nearly your size."[4]
>
> —George Washington Carver

George Washington Carver, a devoted Christian, grew up as a slave in Missouri in 1864. His life exemplifies the power of God-given vision. I remember reading a story about Dr. Carver being locked away for six days and nights in his office. When one of his students inquired about what he was doing, he replied, "We found the answer." "We?" the student questioned. Then Carver continued to explain that he was never alone in that lab for a moment. God was with him the whole time. God had revealed over three hundred products from within the small peanut, including ink, ice cream, cosmetics, bread, dyes, soap, candy, sausage, oils, and so much more. Carver's God-given vision for the peanut brought great multiplication and jobs for many in the South during a difficult time. Just like with the patriarch Jacob, God multiplied Carver's vision.[5]

Pull Your Future Into Your Now

I have heard a lot of teaching on God's timing. And for sure, there are some things that are sovereignly set in God's timetable. But there are other things that aren't. Many times we settle for less than what God has for us because we believe it's just not God's time for us to be blessed. Did you know that your vision can actually pull your future into your now—even something that has a set appointed time by God for your future? Vision not only moves you forward, but it also pulls your future into your now moment.

We see this happen when Jesus is at the wedding in Cana of Galilee. While He is there, they run out of wine. Mary, Jesus's mother, hears this news and turns to Jesus and says, "They have no more wine."

Why did Mary bother to tell Jesus this, as if He could do anything about it? Jesus's response to her is almost comical. "Woman, what does your concern have to do with Me? My hour has not yet come" (John 2:4, NKJV).

Basically, what Jesus was saying to her was, "Shh. Why are you telling Me this? It's not yet My time to do a miracle. My power is not supposed to be shown yet."

Mary's response is even funnier: "Whatever He says to you, do it" (v. 5, NKJV).

She completely ignored Him, just as a good mom would. Mary had vision that the others did not. She saw what Jesus could do, and she could not contain it. Her vision pulled Jesus right into the manifestation of a miracle, even though it was not God's chosen time for it.

Mary's vision pulled something that was set for a future date right into her now moment. That is what vision will do for you. If you see it, you can have it. Vision releases faith in your heart that gives you supernatural access to God's amazing power, now. Vision can cause you to accelerate God's timing, bringing your future into your now. Get ready to see what God sees, releasing His power, purpose, and destiny into your life.

Releasing the Power

CHAPTER 11

The Power of Blessing

The Favor Factor

DURING ONE OF our MSM-hosted conferences, a prophetic minister shared with me that the Lord showed him that money was being stolen from our ministry. I was surprised when he shared this with me because I was not aware of any missing money. I honestly thought that maybe he had missed it. Shortly after that our board of directors made some adjustments to our offering policies as a ministry so that whenever possible, offerings would be given directly to our ministry. It was something placed in their hearts to do. I was never aware of any issues with our offerings. Certainly money was never the reason I went into the ministry. When I first started in ministry, my weekly salary was less than three hundred dollars a week. I had that salary for years.

But something very unusual happened when we started to receive our own offerings. They doubled, tripled, and even quadrupled! I was amazed. I couldn't understand why there was such a dramatic increase. Then it dawned on me. Could it be possible that some of the churches I had ministered at were keeping some of the offerings that had come in for our ministry? Maybe. Only God will fully know. I know many of the pastors we have become friends with over the years are men of character and integrity, and I do not believe they would ever do that. But it's possible that at times our offerings were being skimmed.

Stolen Money

I was ministering at a church where the power of God moved in a mighty way. There was a great blessing of God's glory and presence released in the meetings. The pastor had shared with me that during the meetings an offering would first be received for the church, and later in the meeting an offering would be received for our ministry. Normally we receive the offerings directly, but the pastor preferred processing them through the church. Since it is my heart to serve, I submitted to the pastor's preference. I was happy with the arrangements and was glad the church would be able to cover expenses for the meeting out of the first offering. Our heart is to serve and be a blessing in every way possible.

After the meetings were over, the church gave us a check for what came in the offerings for our ministry. When I saw the amount, I thought possibly a mistake had been made or that the offerings just hadn't been fully processed yet. I knew in my heart that probably much more had actually come in for our ministry. I was hurt and felt like my trust had been betrayed. I never imagined that the pastor would take money out of our offerings, especially since it was announced to the people that everything being given in the offering was for our ministry. My initial reaction was one of hurt and disappointment. Had I not taken control of my soul and brought it under submission to the Holy Spirit, those feelings would have soon turned to offense and possibly anger and resentment. I knew I couldn't let my heart go there.

I had a choice to make. As I prayed and sought the Lord, He brought me to 1 Peter 3:9–11:

> Never return evil for evil or insult for insult (scolding, tongue-lashing, berating), but on the contrary blessing [praying for

their welfare, happiness, and protection, and truly pitying and loving them]. For know that to this you have been called, that you may yourselves inherit a blessing [from God—that you may obtain a blessing as heirs, bringing welfare and happiness and protection]. For let him who wants to enjoy life and see good days [good—whether apparent or not] keep his tongue free from evil and his lips from guile (treachery, deceit). Let him turn away from wickedness and shun it, and let him do right. Let him search for peace (harmony; undisturbedness from fears, agitating passions, and moral conflicts) and seek it eagerly. [Do not merely desire peaceful relations with God, with your fellowmen, and with yourself, but pursue, go after them!]

The revelation that God is a just and fair God hit my spirit. I realized that if I would pray and release a blessing over this pastor, it would only increase God's blessing in my own life. I couldn't lose.

But in order for me to be able to genuinely release God's blessing, I had to first pray through my hurt and make the choice to forgive. I would not be able to bless if I harbored resentment in my heart.

Inherit God's Blessings

First Peter 3:9–11 gives us a blueprint for living in the power and blessings of God. When you are scolded, tongue-lashed, insulted, and berated, don't respond in the same evil way. Respond with blessing! How do you do that? You pray for the person's welfare, happiness, and protection, even when they don't deserve it. Rather than reacting in your flesh, step back, leave the room, walk away, and do whatever you have to do to remain in the Spirit so you can release blessing.

John 10:10 declares, "The thief comes only in order to steal and kill and destroy. I came that they may have and enjoy life, and have it in abundance (to the full, till it overflows)." Jesus came to give us an abundant, overflowing life that is filled with His blessings and goodness. Jesus died so that we can really live, not just exist. True life starts when we surrender to Christ, forgive those who have hurt us, and bless those who mistreat us. The more you bless, the more you will be blessed.

To enjoy the abundant life Christ died to give you, you must be mindful of three things.

1. Always release and pray blessing over people, especially the ones hurting you the most.

2. Keep your tongue from evil. Refuse to agree with what the enemy is doing. Avoid at all cost angry, hurtful, bitter, negative, fearful, and reactionary words. Choose to line your mouth up with the Holy Spirit and with God's Word.

3. Aggressively pursue peace. Go after peace with God, with other people, and with yourself.

Release the Power of God

One of the greatest ways we can release the power of God in our own lives and into the lives of others is through the release of blessings. When you come to faith in Christ, you are granted His power and authority to release blessings over yourself and others. What does this mean?

The word *blessing* can be defined as "a special favor, gift or benefit bestowed by God, thereby bringing happiness." It also means "to protect or guard from evil, the act of invoking divine protection or aid." Another definition is "to grant approval."[1]

When we release blessings over someone, we invoke God's supernatural favor in their lives. This authority and power to release blessing empowers us to release from God special gifts, favors, benefits, protection, and provision into the lives of those around us, as well as in our own lives.

Why Should I Bless My Enemies?

God doesn't call us to just bless our friends or those who are good to us. He also calls us to bless our enemies. Luke 6:28 says, "Invoke blessings upon and pray for the happiness of those who curse you, implore God's blessing (favor) upon those who abuse you [who revile, reproach, disparage, and high-handedly misuse you]."

Why would God call us to do this? Well, mainly because it represents His heart. God loves everyone, even those who hate Him. He asks us to do the same. But He is a very fair and just God. When we live in a way that pleases Him, we are rewarded for this godly behavior, both in this life and in the one to come. There are benefits to blessing those who abuse and mistreat us.

Jesus taught His disciples, "Whatever house you enter, first say, Peace be to this household! [Freedom from all the distresses that result from sin be with this family]. And if anyone [worthy] of peace and blessedness is there, the peace and blessedness you wish shall come upon him; but if not, it shall come back to you" (Luke 10:5–6).

When you release blessing over an undeserving person, it comes back upon you! Every time you do good to one of your enemies or pronounce a blessing over someone who has hurt you, you are actually releasing God's blessings—including His favor, benefits, protection, and provision—back into your own life. God blesses those who accurately represent His nature, character, and heart.

Authority to Decree Restoration

As I was praying over the situation of money being taken out of our offering, God brought me to Proverbs 6:31: "But if he is found out, he must restore seven times [what he stole]; he must give the whole substance of his house [if necessary—to meet his fine]."

I suddenly realized that not only did I have the responsibility to forgive and the opportunity to bless, but I also had the authority to decree a sevenfold return of everything that was taken from me!

As I went into prayer, I released my hurt to God, prayed a blessing over the pastor, and declared that whatever was taken out of our offering must be returned with a sevenfold increase. I knew God was bigger than my circumstances and bigger than the actions of any person. Rather than demanding that my offering be given to me, I trusted God to bring a sevenfold financial blessing into my ministry.

In my heart I chose to trust God as my ultimate provider. I realized that He sees everything, will work it all for my good, and is just and fair, but I needed to exercise my authority and lay hold of the blessing that was rightfully mine because of Christ's finished work on the cross and because of the authority of Scripture.

As I made the sevenfold decree, that very week checks began to show up in the mail. Large donations for the ministry came in from several unexpected places. Our online resource orders shot through the roof, and that following week we received one of the largest offerings our ministry has ever experienced at the next church we ministered at. The thief had to give back seven times—and then some! The provision came from God as He moved upon the hearts of pure-hearted people to give and sow into the ministry. God provided as people heard the voice of God and partnered with His will to sow into what God was doing.

When you choose to bless, you will reap blessing! When you choose to love even when it is hard, God will turn all things for your good and override the sinful choices of other people that affect your life.

Setting Favor Into Motion

And the Lord said to Moses, Say to Aaron and his sons, This is the way you shall bless the Israelites. Say to them, The Lord bless you and watch, guard, and keep you; the Lord make His face to shine upon and enlighten you and be gracious (kind, merciful, and giving favor) to you; the Lord lift up His [approving] countenance upon you and give you peace

(tranquility of heart and life continually). And they shall put
My name upon the Israelites, and I will bless them.

—NUMBERS 6:22–27

You release blessing over someone through the power of your
words. As you decree God's Word over them, a blessing is dispatched. Numbers 6:22–27 is a good guideline for a blessing.
Through the spoken words of your mouth you release God's watch,
guard, keeping power, enlightenment, grace, kindness, mercy,
favor, approval, and peace.

When you bless someone under the direction and unction of the
Holy Spirit, divine favor is set in motion in their life. This favor
will open doors of opportunity for them, release supernatural provision for the vision God has given them, and also maneuver them
into the right place, at the right time, to meet the right people
whom God wants to use in their lives. You can be a dispenser of
God's divine blessing for another person. And remember, what you
do for others, God will do for you!

Let's not forget the words of James Allen, a New Zealander
statesman and Minister of Defense from 1912–1920: "The man who
sows wrong thoughts and deeds and prays that God will bless him
is in the position of a farmer who, having sown tares, asks God to
bring forth for him a harvest of wheat."[2]

There is tremendous power released through blessing. You may
be familiar with the movie *Bella*, a feature film about a woman
considering having an abortion. *Bella* was produced by Metanoia
Film, and the word *metanoia* is Greek for "conversion." The film's
producer and actor, Eduardo Verastegui, experienced the miraculous power of a blessing. His vision was to start his own production
company that would produce films that would "entertain, uplift,
heal and above all, respect human dignity."[3] In an interview for the
Holy See, a Catholic newspaper, he said, "We want people to leave
the movie theaters wanting to love more, forgive more and complain less; we want them to leave with a candle in their hearts, full

of hope and faith. I want to have…our Lord Jesus Christ on the set and not have to cover [His] eyes. And I don't want any actors to have to compromise their values."[4]

Metanoia's first film, *Bella*, written in two months, almost didn't make it to the big screen. Verastegui had no money to produce it. Upon meeting with Pope John Paul II in Rome, he explained his mission to him and asked the pope to pray for him. He received a special prayer of blessing. Ten days later Verastegui met a family who literally gave him the money he needed without even reading the script or signing a contract. They shot the entire film in twenty-three days and sent it to the Toronto International Film Festival, where they won. *Bella* became a box office hit and was rated #1 by the *New York Times*, *Readers Poll*, Yahoo, and Fandango. But the film's producer says these awards aren't their greatest success. It's the "letters and e-mails and phone calls we received from young pregnant women who were scheduled to have an abortion and after seeing the film—by the grace of God—changed their minds and decided to keep their babies."[5]

This is the power of blessing! Not only did it release the hand and favor of God to bring a miracle financial provision, but also with the success of the movie, the lives of countless women have been eternally impacted. Blessing released favor, and with that favor came transformed lives.

The Power of a Spiritual Leader's Blessing

I remember when I was stepping out of pastoral ministry into the evangelistic field, the one thing I wanted from my spiritual leaders was their blessing. I can remember sitting down with my pastor when he asked, "Matt, what would you like me to do for you?" My response was, "I would love to have your blessing."

I feel it is very important to be submitted to spiritual authority. I had always believed that if I was to correctly walk things out, I needed to do things the right way. That included submitting to the counsel of my authorities and receiving their blessing in what God was doing in my life.

I realize that not everyone will have the luxury of serving under healthy spiritual leadership that can recognize what God is doing in their lives and have the heart to bless them. But I can tell you this: God is well able to direct your steps and bring healthy spiritual leaders into your life who will genuinely bless what God is doing in and through you. God did this for me, and He can do it for you.

As I submitted myself to God and His plan, He brought amazing men and women of God into my life who could see and recognize the call of God that was upon me. I am eternally grateful to each one of them for their amazing hearts for God and for me. Each time I have received a prayer of blessing from one of God's generals, I have seen dramatic increases of God's favor, anointing, open doors, and financial blessing in my life. Not only will God do this for you, but He will also use you to bless what He is doing in the lives of others. Not only will you be a spiritual son or daughter to someone, but you can also be a spiritual father or mother and see what God has done in you multiplied in others.

Honor Brings Blessing

I also want to share a secret with you that not only blesses God's heart and makes Him happy but will attract blessing to you as well. Something that God has put in me from a very early age is the understanding and conviction that we must honor our spiritual authorities. Our spiritual leaders are gifts from God.

> Honor (esteem and value as precious) your father and your mother—this is the first commandment with a promise—that all may be well with you and that you may live long on the earth.
>
> —Ephesians 6:2–3

I believe this scripture not only applies to our natural birth parents but to our spiritual fathers and mothers as well. When you honor the authorities God has placed in your life, you are honoring God. You receive from whatever you honor and value. When you honor a leader by treating them right, showing them proper respect, praying for them, and finding ways to bless them with your words, attitudes, and actions, you open your spirit to receiving the anointing, power, and gifts that God has placed within them. You attract to yourself what you value and esteem. So it's not just about receiving a blessing from our authorities. We must also find ways that we can be a blessing to them as we honor and esteem them in our hearts.

Activate and Release God's Blessings

Make the choice today to be a blesser. As you release blessings through the words of your mouth, God's power will be unleashed through you in amazing ways in the lives of others. Through the simplicity of the spoken word, you can impact lives for the good and see people released into their destinies.

> Words are both better and worse than thoughts; they express them, and add to them; they give them power for good or evil; they start them on an endless flight, for instruction and comfort and blessing, or for injury and sorrow and ruin.[6]
> —Tryon Edwards, American Theologian (1809–1894)

Here are some blessings you can release today:

1. Think of the people who have hurt you the most; then spend time in prayer releasing them into God's hands, forgiving them of any perceived injustice, and praying for them as Job prayed for his friends.

2. Bless your family, friends, and leaders daily by praying the Aaronic blessing over them found in Numbers 6:22–27.

3. Pray for and bless Israel today. Genesis 12:3 promises that as we bless Israel, we will be blessed.

4. Pray for God to show you any areas where the thief has stolen from you. Then after you have forgiven the people involved and prayed a blessing over them, decree for a sevenfold return to come forth as seen in Proverbs 6:31.

5. Pray for God to give you healthy spiritual fathers and mothers who will bless you. Also look for others whom you can pour those same blessings into.

CHAPTER 12

The Power of Joy

Be Contagious

I WAS A YOUNG minister at the time. While I desired to live in God's joy, there was one day where it was stolen from me. I can't even remember why, but I know I was miserable and depressed. I will never forget how another older minister said to me that day, "Matt, I am so glad to see you maturing in the Lord. I can see how sober you are becoming." I thought to myself, "Dude, I am depressed!" I wondered, since when did depression equal spiritual maturity? I knew Galatians 5 said that one of the fruit of the Spirit is joy. That means the more mature you are, the more joy you should have. Usually everyone asked me why I smiled so much. It was because I had joy. But this day I was depressed, and this older minister thought I was maturing. It was the opposite! The sign of a truly powerful life in the Spirit is not how sober and miserable you are. It's how joyful you are, no matter what's going on around you.

The greatest honor we can give Almighty God is to live gladly because of the knowledge of his love.[1]

—BLESSED JULIAN OF NORWICH

A legalistic, religious mind-set will tell you that you have to be sober, miserable, and depressed to be a mature Christian. You don't have to look like you have been sucking on sour lemons all your life to radiate the image of Christ. That doesn't work. Try telling someone, "Oh, come to church with me, follow God, and you can be as miserable as I am!" They will run in the opposite direction. Why do you think there are so many self-help books out there? The main reason is because people don't want to be miserable and depressed. They want to be happy! And they can be.

Do You Have a Flat Tire?

You want to be happy. You want to enjoy your life. This is one of the biggest needs and desires within each one of us. You can possess all the wealth in the world and have access to every material possession there is, but if you don't have joy, it's worth nothing. If you want to live a wonderful life filled with power to be and do all God has called you to be and do, then you must know how to have joy. Without joy you will be miserable and depressed. It's like riding a car with flat tires. Everything will be a struggle. When you lack joy, it can be a struggle just to get up in the morning. Who wants to live like that? I don't, and I know you don't either. So let's learn how to live an exceptional life in the power of joy.

I want to be as real and transparent as I can be with you. We are all human. No matter how much power we experience in our lives, no matter how close we are to God, we still have a soul and live in a body. We all have emotions that we need to learn to deal with and overcome. Everyone, no matter how anointed and used of God they are, will have moments where discouragement and depression try to get them down. Some will struggle with this more than others, depending on their personality. People who are highly sensitive will be more susceptible to discouragement. If you have a tendency to get discouraged easily, you will have to press in more after God and allow the Holy Spirit to produce His fruit of joy in you.

To a degree, joy is a choice just like anything else. You may say, "Well, I want to be happy, but I just can't be. I'm miserable, and I can't help it!" That may be true. You may have gotten into such a low place and are so under the pressure that you just don't see a way out. You may even have a serious medical condition that causes depression in your life, or maybe there is a tendency or weakness toward depression in your family line. There are times people may need to seek medical help if they have a genuine chemical imbalance in their body. This is an extreme case. If you think you may fit into the category of having a medical condition, you should seek out help. Even if it is a medical condition, God has the desire and power to heal anything that may be off in your brain or body.

For others, it's not a medical condition. It's a choice. There will always be circumstances that can upset you and discourage you. It's up to you whether you let them drag you down or not. No matter how hard it may seem, when discouragement wants to paralyze you and drain all the life and motivation out of you, you will need to make the choice to get up and live your life. You must start by refusing to come into agreement with your feelings. You can't let your feelings control you. This is where you mature in your faith. You don't have to live out of your fleeting emotions. You can live out of your spirit and bring your emotions into check, but it starts by making the decision to do so. God will empower your free will to stand up, shake the dust off of yourself, and get a grip. Once you make the decision to not let an emotion rule you, God's power in you goes into action to enable you to then shake depression off and rise above it.

It's like the snake that tried to attach itself to Paul in Act 28:3. He shook it off into the fire. That's exactly what you have to do. You have to shake it off! It goes back to knowing the power of truth and agreement. No matter what you feel, you have to come into agreement with God's power in you, choose to speak God's Word over yourself and to yourself, and refuse to let anything dominate you.

One of the hardest things can be living with a miserable person.

An even harder thing is if you are that person. You can at least escape and get away from miserable people, but you cannot escape yourself. No matter where you go, you are always there. Life can be very difficult when you are riding on the coattails of someone else's emotions, especially if they are bipolar or emotionally unstable. You cannot let the emotions of others get onto you. You don't have to live that way. This is why you have to be very careful whom you yoke yourself with. If you are in a situation where it's a close family member, God will give you the grace and strength you need to overcome and not be dragged down.

This is a good rule for us all to live by. Mother Teresa said, "Spread love everywhere you go. Let no one ever come to you without leaving happier."[2]

Grappling With Depression and Anxiety

I'm sure you have found out by now that there are a lot of things that happen in life that are beyond your control. At times it may feel like your circumstances are swirling like a whirlwind around you. If you sit and watch the news long enough, you'll want to pull the covers over your head and not come out.

Many people are grappling with circumstances that seem to have them running in circles. They are being driven by their environment and knocked around by their emotional reactions. They're earthbound. Their minds are gripped with fear, worry, concern, and anxiety. Just in the last decade the number of Americans using antidepressant drugs has doubled.[3]

> In 2006, Americans, who make up approximately 6 percent of the world's population, consumed 66 percent of the world's supply of antidepressants. In 2002, more than 13 percent of Americans were taking Prozac alone. Prozac is one of thirty available antidepressants. Anti-anxiety drugs, such as Zoloft, are so widely prescribed that in the year 2005, the $3.1 billion sales of Zoloft exceeded the sales for Tide detergent.[4]

USA Today reports:

> About 10% of Americans—or 27 million people—were taking
> antidepressants in 2005, the last year for which data were
> available at the time the study was written. That's about twice
> the number in 1996, according to the study of nearly 50,000
> children and adults in today's *Archives of General Psychiatry.*[5]

In another article posted in August 2009, it was reported that:

> …one in 10 Americans is now taking antidepressants within
> the course of a year, making antidepressants the most pre-
> scribed kind of medication in the country. The number of
> Americans on antidepressants doubled between 1996 and
> 2005, and the number of prescriptions written for these drugs
> has increased each year between 2005 and 2008.[6]

People are consumed with thoughts of terrorism, global warming,
nuclear war, poor government decisions, swine flu, the economy, not
to mention strife in their families, rebellious teenagers, struggles in
marriage, financial pressures, as well as their own inner struggles
with things like discouragement, negative thought patterns, poor
self-image, weight struggles, identity crises, and so much more. No
wonder so many are living far below the abundant life Jesus came
to give us!

The Divine Exchange

When I sense discouragement coming upon me, sometimes it helps
to share it with someone else, but often times this just magnifies
what I am feeling. It doesn't remove it. I have learned about the
divine exchange. Prayer really works! When I feel my soul starting
to dominate my spirit, I get into a place of prayer, and sometimes
fasting, where I can talk to God. I tell Him everything I am feeling;
I give it all to Him. I ask Him to help me overcome it. I just keep
praying until I start to feel a release. I choose to give it to God and
focus on the good things in my life.

> You will show me the path of life; in Your presence is fullness of joy.
>
> —Psalm 16:11

When you learn to practice God's presence in your life through daily prayer, worship, and spending time in His Word, you will experience the fullness of God's joy in your life. This is one of the reasons I spend so much time in prayer! It keeps me in His presence, which keeps me in the Spirit.

It's obvious St. Augustine knew this secret. He said, "There is a joy which is not given to the ungodly, but to those who love Thee for Thine own sake, whose joy Thou Thyself art. And this is the happy life, to rejoice to Thee, of Thee, for Thee; this is it, and there is no other."[7]

There is nothing that will discourage you more quickly and make you a miserable person than by focusing on the negative. If you focus on the negative things in your circumstances and in other people around you, of course you are going to be miserable. If the only things coming out of your mouth are negative things, you are not even going to like hanging around yourself—and no one else will either.

Some of you reading this need a major overhaul in this area. You need the negative thought patterns in your mind renewed with the positive things in God's Word, and you need to learn how to just close your mouth if you have nothing positive to say. You need someone to tell you these things. Stop speaking negatively. Stop complaining and being miserable. Stop gossiping. Stop focusing on everything that's wrong and start focusing on what's right—even if the only thing you can find positive is the fact that God loves you and your sins are forgiven and you are not going to hell. Thank God for that. Making the choice to be thankful will really help you get over being negative and depressed. No one can do that for you. You just have to make the choice.

Get Your Mind Off Yourself

I was flying on an airplane going to speak at a conference when I pulled out the magazine in the seat pocket in front of me. As I began to peruse it, my eye was caught by an article, "Buying Happiness." In the article the author shares that "grateful people report feeling 25 percent more happiness and energy and 20 percent less envy and resentment in several recent studies at the University of California. They also slept 10 percent longer each night and exercised 33 percent more if they wrote down what they felt thankful for." The author shares the truth that "gratitude is an antidote to negative emotions."[8]

> Be happy [in your faith] and rejoice and be glad-hearted continually (always); be unceasing in prayer [praying perseveringly]; thank [God] in everything [no matter what the circumstances may be, be thankful and give thanks], for this is the will of God for you [who are] in Christ Jesus [the Revealer and Mediator of that will]. Do not quench (suppress or subdue) the [Holy] Spirit.
>
> —1 THESSALONIANS 5:16–19

When you choose to be a thankful person no matter what is happening, you will be a continually happy person. Your joy will not end.

Sometimes you just have to get your mind off yourself and your problems. One of the best ways to do this is by making the choice to help someone else. Get your mind off yourself and onto someone else. Find ways to be a blessing to someone. Find ways to help other people. It will really turn things around in your own life. Perspective is so important. When you realize there are people who are way worse off than you are, it makes your own problems seem smaller.

In that same article I read on the airplane, the author was sharing how you could put a smile on your face with the pennies in your pocket. I was intrigued. The article shared that "people who give charitably rank themselves as happier people than people who don't, according to a 2008 study by the University of British Columbia." She writes that anonymous acts of kindness make us feel like a better person creating feelings of happiness. Being generous boosts positive emotions, making you feel better about yourself and those around you. She encourages people to "drop change into an expired parking meter. Pick up a friend's lunch check. And give a generous charitable donation."[9] You see, God was right. He loves a cheerful giver! He knows that thinking about others above yourself and that giving generously make us happier people! If you want to be happy, start doing something for someone else.

Paul shares in Acts 20:33–35, "I coveted no man's silver or gold or [costly] garments. You yourselves know personally that these hands ministered to my own needs and those [of the persons] who were with me. In everything I have pointed out to you [by example] that, by working diligently in this manner, we ought to assist the weak, being mindful of the words of the Lord Jesus, how He Himself said, It is more blessed (makes one happier and more to be envied) to give than to receive."

When we think about and give to others, we are more blessed. We become happier people when we give.

The Duct-Tape Anointing

The enemy always likes to magnify a negative situation. He will make something so big in your own mind that it just makes you distraught until all you can think about and talk about is that problem. When you only focus on your problem, it makes it bigger and worse, until you are so worked up about it you end up doing something you regret later on. Some of you need to apply the "duct-tape anointing." What is that? Well, the next time you are tempted to talk negative and just focus on what's wrong in your conversation, pull out a piece of duct tape and put it over your mouth! It's the key to your breakthrough.

One woman kept calling our office every day with the same problem and prayer request. She would go over it again and again. Eventually we had to use tough love with her. We encouraged her to simply get her mind off herself and do something to help someone else. People who enjoy their pity party don't want to hear this. They want you to join in the party with them. And at times I have fallen into this trap. Sometimes out of sympathy you want to just stroke someone's wounds while they sit in their miserable state. You can do that for a while for someone, but that person can't stay there forever. Eventually they have to get up, forgive the person who hurt them, and move on with their life.

If you find people trying to avoid you or you feel rejection coming from others around you, it may be that you are living in such a negative state and are exuding this onto everyone around you that they simply can't take any more of it. You need to make adjustments, and fast, before you drive everyone away. It starts with the small things. Make the choice to get out of bed in the morning. Don't keep hitting the snooze button. Some people live their life hitting the snooze button. It's time to wake up and really live the life God has for you, a life of joy. Develop a pattern where you spend time in worship and meditating on God's promises in His Word. Choose to speak positive, uplifting things, and focus on the good in your life and in the lives of those around you. Just by making those few changes you will find your entire outlook on life changing, and soon your soul will line up with your spirit and you will begin to experience God's joy and exude it.

Are You Happy or Joyful?

There is a big difference between happiness and joy. Joy goes much deeper than happiness. Temporal things can make you happy for a while. Your emotions can get a temporary boost from things like shopping, going to a movie, or playing or watching sports. But when those activities are over, your soul goes back down again.

They're really just temporary escapes. You don't want a temporary escape or a quick fix. You want a lasting state of joy. Joy doesn't come from your soul. It comes from your spirit by the Holy Spirit. Joy is a fruit of the Spirit that is not dependent on your outward circumstances. It really comes from the presence of God inside of you. This is why prayer, worship, and spending time in the Word are so important in cultivating joy in your life. The more you focus on God's perspective and His truth, the more you will emanate the spirit of joy.

The Kingdom of God Is Within You

Joy is actually the result of God's kingdom within you. Joy at times may involve an extreme emotion, but in your day-to-day life, it can manifest as a calm, peaceful resolve. Joy and peace are very much related to one another. Let's see how this works.

Romans 14:17 defines God's kingdom as "righteousness and peace and joy in the Holy Spirit" (NKJV). There is a very specific order here that cannot be ignored. First comes righteousness, then peace, and then joy. If you are missing joy, then you need to check in on the first two, righteousness and peace. It all starts with righteousness.

Righteousness is the state of being right with God. It's knowing you have a clean conscience. When your heart is right with God, you will be right with yourself and with others. A clean heart before God that is free from sin then experiences peace. Peace with God leads to peace with yourself and then peace with others around you. When you enter into this place of peace, the natural result and overflow will be God's joy. You will be filled with joy when you know you have turned away from all sin, gotten things completely right between you and God, entered into His peace within yourself, and are walking in a way that pleases God. This is really the ultimate source of our joy. Everything else comes and goes. Joy that comes out of being right with God and at peace with yourself and others does not fade. It can be a constant in our lives, depending on how close we are walking with God. The more the Holy Spirit fills every area of your life, the more righteousness, peace, and joy you will have.

There's an old saying: "If momma's not happy, no one's happy." How true that is. Well, the same is true for the Holy Spirit. If the Holy Spirit is not happy, you will not be happy. If there is something in your life grieving God, He will not be happy inside of you. The most miserable people on the face of the earth are Christians living in compromise. They know the right thing to do, but they are doing the wrong thing, and the Holy Spirit is grieved on the inside of them. God will allow you to be miserable until you get it right with Him. This is part of His loving discipline.

Sin may be enjoyable for a moment, but that soon turns to misery, especially in the life of a believer because God does not want you going down a road that will eventually hurt you. He will make you miserable as quickly as possible so that you turn away from negative things and back to God's best for your life. Some people find this out too late, and their lives are destroyed by the momentary pleasure they once found in sin. But in the end it leads to death. True joy is found when living in a right place with God. That is why fame, fortune, and all the sin in the world cannot fulfill the vacuum inside. It's like a black hole. The only thing that can fully fill that place is God.

Dealing With the Roots

The fruit of constant depression is a sign that there are deeper roots that need to be dealt with. These roots can range from negative thinking patterns, to wounded emotions, to deep inner struggles with sin and addiction, to undealt-with anger, offense, and unforgiveness. These things can be open doors to spiritual oppression. There will be times the ministry of both inner healing and deliverance is needed. But as we apply the Word of God to our lives and walk it out on a daily basis, God heals us everywhere we hurt and brings us through a process of self-deliverance known as sanctification.

In order to maintain our joy, we must follow the advice found on a sign that hangs in my living room: "Love deeply, listen patiently, forgive freely." We must love unconditionally, forgive quickly, maintain our peace, and refuse to let offense and anger take root in our hearts. This is where the power of choice comes in. Deal with stuff quickly to keep your heart free and your life filled with joy. The truth is, you can't afford to allow a moment of offense in your heart. The joy of the Lord is our strength. Without joy, we get weak: "And be not grieved and depressed, for the joy of the Lord is your strength and stronghold" (Neh. 8:10).

Joy in Unexpected Places

S. D. Gordon once shared, "Happiness is the result of what happens of an agreeable sort. Joy has its springs deep down inside. And that spring never runs dry, no matter what happens. Only Jesus gives that joy. He had joy, singing its music within, even under the shadow of the cross."[10]

Every time I travel to a third-world country, I am amazed at the little children. Whether it's Africa, India, China, or somewhere else, I have seen a common thread. It's no wonder Jesus said we need to become like little children. I watch little African children running around barefoot in the dirt, no earthly possessions, not much food, not even shoes for their feet. Yet there they are, running all around me with big smiles on their faces, seemingly oblivious to the poverty that surrounds them. This is life for them. Yet in the midst of great lack there is the joy of life that can be seen in their smiling eyes and in the sounds of laughter.

I love what Robert Schuller has shared regarding this: "Joy is not the absence of suffering. It is the presence of God."[11] This is exactly right. We can never fully escape suffering. And some people have a lot more of it than others. But when our joy comes from the presence of God, it's unshakable.

Brother Lawrence, a Parisian monk from the fifteenth century, also deeply believed that our joy is connected to our relationship with God. He believed that it was a great deception to think that times of prayer were different from other times. Brother Lawrence maintained a constant connection to the presence of God in his daily activities. He accomplished this by simply staying in an endless conversation with God. This gave him access to continual joy.

I experienced this very thing when I traveled to the mountains of China into the earthquake region of Chengdu. Over 4.8 million people were left homeless from this natural calamity, and more than 80,000 lost their lives. I witnessed an entire city buried under rubble as the surrounding mountains and hills avalanched in on it. It was a burial ground. Yet high in the mountains was a small school with about one hundred children who were left orphaned in the earthquake. With no more earthly parents, they came to this school to be cared for. As I traversed up this mountain path to visit the children, I was met by so many little faces who had been left all alone in the world. During their school recess, we all went outside. Surrounded by rubble and debris, we played a game of tag. I will never forget the laughter that filled the air among so much pain and loss. Those little smiling faces beamed with joy as these kids ran into my arms for me to swing them around. Joy in the midst of pain and loss. Joy that had nothing to do with their natural surroundings. Joy that superseded the natural luxuries of life.

The Anointing Destroys the Yoke

There is a supernatural element to the joy we can experience in God. There may be times that God, in His infinite love and mercy, will see the pit we find ourselves in and will overwhelm us with His joy in order to bring a breakthrough, deliverance, or healing.

This is the special anointing of joy that not only breaks the yoke but also demolishes it.

> You have loved righteousness [You have delighted in integrity, virtue, and uprightness in purpose, thought, and action] and You have hated lawlessness (injustice and iniquity). Therefore God, [even] Your God (Godhead), has anointed You with the oil of exultant joy and gladness above and beyond Your companions.
>
> —HEBREWS 1:9

The anointing is a very powerful gift from God that we cannot overlook. Some may try to live life without it, but they will only get so far. Self-will and discipline may be able to achieve some things, but God's anointing goes much further than what any person can achieve in the natural. God's anointing adds His "super" to our "natural." One touch of the manifest presence and power of God can change everything in your life. That is why I place such a high value on the tangible anointing of the Holy Spirit. I've seen God work emotional miracles through His presence.

Sometimes the greatest miracles are not physical; they are spiritual and emotional. It's a horrible thing to walk around with a physical sickness. It's equally horrible to walk around with an emotional and spiritual sickness, an internal affliction that keeps people bound in depression, hopelessness, fear, and self-pity. This emotional sickness can be tormenting and completely disabling, causing people to not be able to leave their homes, interact with other people, or move forward with their lives. Even in church, where everything is supposed to be good, people suffer very deeply with things. Because we feel it's wrong to have problems, we hide our battles in secrecy. But it's that very secrecy that keeps us in bondage and pain.

Confess to one another therefore your faults (your slips, your false steps, your offenses, your sins) and pray [also] for one another, that you may be healed and restored.

—JAMES 5:16

Sharing your struggles with a trusted friend, leader, or family member who can pray with you brings in the light and exposes any hidden darkness. This brings tremendous freedom. Church must be a safe place where we unconditionally love one another to wholeness and freedom.

Supernatural Joy

I personally have benefited from the supernatural power of joy. I remember my first time was when I was a young teenager. I had just recently come into a relationship with God. I can remember sharing with my mom that I felt so discouraged about something. I felt so down and depressed. My mom began to pray for me. As I lay on my bed, suddenly I began to laugh. I said, "Mom, why am I laughing?" I didn't understand it at all. I went from feeling depressed one moment to laughing the next. I laughed that depression of soul right out of myself. It was a supernatural joy that was stronger than my soulish emotions.

For those who may wonder if God would ever make us laugh, let's look at Job. If there was one person who needed to laugh, it was Job! Job 8:21 says, "He will yet fill your mouth with laughter [Job] and your lips with joyful shouting."

I experienced this again a few years later. I was still in my teen years. Teen years can be full of drama. Teenagers are going through so many changes, inside and out, that everything can become a big thing to them. I was having one of those days, and I was seriously troubled and depressed about something. Generally, I am a happy person, but throughout my life I have had moments of some pretty deep darkness. I was attending a Christmas program in a church one night during Christmastime. The lady was singing "Mary, Did

You Know?" on stage about Mary giving birth to Jesus, and I was thinking, "I don't care if Mary knew." I was so depressed. I couldn't smile or even enjoy the show. They gave an altar call at the end for people to come to know God. I just sat in my seat depressed.

After the altar call, my friends got up to leave. As I sat in my seat, something wonderfully supernatural happened to me. Suddenly, for no natural reason whatsoever, I began to laugh. I laughed and laughed and laughed. The service was over. No one was praying for me. I had never seen anyone "laugh in the Spirit" before. I really didn't know what was happening. As I got up to leave, I staggered down the aisle in the church and could barely walk. I then just fell sideways into one of the rows of chairs and lay there laughing! I laughed for about twenty minutes. My friends had left the building. I couldn't help myself. The joy that I was experiencing was truly beyond me. It was God's joy being released in me. When I got up, all my depression was completely gone! I was free. God's anointing had liberated my emotions so that I could be free in His joy. Oh, how wonderful is the joy of God that breaks off the junk that tries to weigh our souls and emotions down!

This kind of supernatural joy is beyond our ability to produce or even choose it. There are times God's power will touch your life and just break through where you are. It is beyond the realm of human control. It is God stepping in and saying no more to the pain and depression you feel. I have never been able to manufacture or produce this kind of joy at will. God knows what we need when we need it and at times will choose to touch us this way. It is a very special anointing from the Holy Spirit.

Ten Thousand Pounds Lifted!

I have conducted meetings where almost entire rooms of people have received this holy laughter. It's an amazing thing to watch. But there are times God will minister to select individuals this way. I remember one meeting where I was preaching in Canada. During my message a woman began to laugh. It was as if she could not help herself. Others may have thought, "She shouldn't be laughing. That's rude. It's distracting the preacher." Well, I knew that it was the Holy Spirit and that something glorious was happening. I just let her laugh. She laughed through the entire message.

She came back the next night and shared her experience with us. She told me that when she was a child, she had been bounced around between nine foster homes and had been sexually abused for years. She could never even remember smiling, let alone laughing. This meeting was the first time she ever laughed. She was so full of pain, hurt, anger, and rage that she was held captive by her own pain and despair. When she went home that night, she still couldn't stop laughing. She woke her children and husband up with it. She giggled all night long. She told me that when she woke up the next day she felt like "ten thousand pounds had lifted off her life." She felt joy for the first time, and all the anger and bitterness were gone. She laughed it right out!

We see this powerful anointing of joy in Isaiah 61:3: "...the oil of joy instead of mourning, the garment [expressive] of praise instead of a heavy, burdened, and failing spirit."

The Power of Laughter

Don't underestimate the power of God's joy in your life through laughter. Laughter is a powerful God-given force that brings freedom, healing, and restoration spiritually, emotionally, and physically. Laughter is good like medicine. That's why I love when God enables me to bring laughter to people when I preach. One time a man exclaimed out loud as the room was erupting in laughter, "This is medicine!" It is. The world is full of so much pain and sorrow. We need a good laugh every now and then. The more you can laugh at yourself and at life, the happier you will be. Sometimes you just can't be so serious. Be contagious with joy!

> A happy heart is good medicine and a cheerful mind works healing, but a broken spirit dries up the bones.
>
> —Proverbs 17:22

Not only does God seem to have this perspective, but also there has been scientific research done as well on how laughter affects our lives. It actually keeps our bodies strong and resistant to disease. Hospital Corpsman 2nd Class James Botkin of the behavioral health unit in Naval Hospital Yokosuka in Japan has found in his research that "humor is equally helpful to our mental health and the way we deal with stress and worry. A good laugh exercises many muscles of the body and causes the brain to release endorphins. These 'feel good' brain chemicals raise both our mood and our coping abilities. Sometimes things don't seem as bad when looked through the eyes of humor."[12]

Everything in Balance

While we are talking about the positive affect of laughter, joy, and exercise in our lives, I want to encourage you to live a balanced life. This includes getting proper sleep and rest. In a recent *Time* article on sleep, the American Academy of Sleep Medicine revealed that the optimum sleep time per night is seven to eight hours.[13] When you miss your sleep, it's much easier to get cranky and irritable. It's hard to be happy when you are always dragging and tired. It's also very important that you balance work and play. Make sure to schedule in down time to relax and have some time for yourself and with your family. This can be a challenge for people who are very vision motivated. But proper rest helps you to refuel and increases your levels of joy.

Everything must stay balanced for you to experience God's ultimate joy in your daily life. These are built-in principles that cannot be ignored. And never forget your true and ultimate source of joy—God! He's with you every moment of every day.

Activate and Release Your Joy

Why not start today and release the power of God's joy within you. Here are some ways you can be contagious.

1. Smile at ten people.

2. Share a funny joke with a friend.

3. Compliment and encourage three people.

4. Spread a positive uplifting word about someone.

5. Write an encouraging note to someone who needs it.

As you spread the joy of God, you can kill the germs of depression, loneliness, isolation, rejection, and so much more. So go ahead; spread it to as many people as you can. Be contagious!

CHAPTER 13

The Power of Generosity

Pay It Forward

J ANET WAS ON her way to a friend's house when she drove by a man digging through a Dumpster looking for food. She thought to herself, "If he is still there on my way home, I am going to go to McDonald's and get a gift certificate for him to get some hot food." As she drove home an hour later, he was still there sitting out in the cold. She immediately went to McDonald's and got him a ten-dollar gift certificate. She gave it to him, and he told her that no one had ever really cared about him and that because of her, he believed there was still good in the world. He told her that his name was John and that just a few years earlier he was living a "normal" life, but he lost everything after he got a divorce. As she was leaving, he asked what payment she wanted for the gift certificate. She said, "Nothing. Just keep the chain going!" She got back in her car and cried, not because she was sad, but because she was so overwhelmed with joy.

Based on a novel written by Catherine Ryan Hyde, "pay it forward" is a selfless action plan that has sparked a worldwide social movement,[1] but Jesus taught this concept of selfless giving much earlier than that. In Matthew 25:34–40, Jesus revealed that every

167

time you do something for someone who can never repay you on the earth, you are doing it for Him. When you clothe the naked, you are clothing Christ. When you visit the sick or those in prison, you are visiting Him.

It's time to start a new movement of selfless giving. We can set off a chain reaction that will spread from one person to another like a domino effect. One of the greatest ways to release not only God's power but also His genuine heart to the world is through giving. Generosity is what enables us to fully release God's influence through our lives, making a paramount difference in our world and leaving a legacy behind us. Generosity will cause you to freely give what God has freely given to you. It is through this act of giving that multitudes can be impacted through your life.

One of the greatest joys of my life is the Girls Home we have been able to build as a ministry in Chennai, India. I know that after my earthly journey is over and I have completed God's will, that Girls Home will continue on, reaching further and longer than my own earthly years ever could. Generosity empowers you to leave a lasting legacy! Thanks to the generous and loving seeds of friends and partners of our ministry, we have been able to successfully rescue girls off the street and save them from a life of hopelessness, abuse, and despair. Each year we also rally our friends and partners to send Christmas gifts and donations to these precious, beautiful children. There is no greater joy than seeing someone's life completely transformed because of a heart that loves to give.

I will never forget my very first evangelistic meeting on the road. I had just made the transition from pastoral to evangelistic ministry. God had so clearly confirmed to me His direction and will that it made it easier to take this radical step of faith. As in every step of faith, there was a big risk involved. Stepping out in obedience to God's call cost me everything. When God began to call me to a traveling miracle ministry, I had to leave everything that was familiar and comfortable behind. There were many risks and fears I had to face head-on. There was the risk of not succeeding in what

I felt God was calling me to do. I had so many questions: Would doors open for me to travel? Would I have enough money to live? Was my ministry going to succeed? My step of faith was a sink-or-swim situation. Thankfully as I obeyed God, He was right there with me each step of the way! I learned an important principle early on that set the course for my life and ministry and moved me into a supernatural dimension of God's provision for all He had called me to do.

The Power of Firstfruits

It was in my first evangelistic meeting that God taught me about the power of generosity. During the meeting God began to release physical healing and miracles. I still remember that service where God gave me a word of knowledge for a woman with an ovarian cyst. As I called it out, the fire of God went into her belly, completely dissolving the cyst! I was young, and my faith for miracles was high. I was very childlike in my faith before God.

He spoke to me that day. I felt a very distinct impression from God to take the offering I would receive in that service and sow it into another mission's ministry. I knew exactly whom to sow it to. I loved what Heidi Baker was doing for Jesus in Mozambique, Africa. God spoke to me, "I have called you to go to the nations. You are going to need supernatural provision for this ministry." I knew in my heart that by planting a seed into Heidi's ministry, I could believe God for a harvest of provision for my own missions works that would unfold in the months and years to come. God gave me a specific amount. He told me five hundred dollars. I know that might not sound like a lot, but in those days to me it was.

After the service I counted the offering. It came to two hundred fifty dollars! I said, "God, you told me five hundred dollars. There is only two hundred fifty dollars here!" Then I heard, "Well, you have a bank account, don't you? Use that money." My mind responded, "Well, yes, I have a bank account, but I also don't have a job. That's my only money to live on!" God said, "Give it." So I gave it. God told me it would be a firstfruits offering for my ministry. I had no idea what a firstfruits offering was, so I looked it up in Proverbs 3:9.

I was honoring God with my very first increase as a ministry. I knew that as I honored God with this portion, He would always take care of me financially. This giving was not legalistic. It was birthed out of a revelation of God's heart and Word, which gave me His faith to trust Him as my source. Sure enough, just a few months later, God opened our first door to go to India on our first missions crusade. On that crusade we saw thousands of Hindus and Muslims give their hearts to Jesus. And God provided every penny we needed for it. I sowed into missions, and God provided for our missions. This would become the pattern of our life of faith in ministry.

God loves a cheerful giver (2 Cor. 9:7). You can be so happy when you give because you can expect by faith that what you sow will come back to you in exponential ways. Our joy in giving reveals our heart of faith and trust in God. People who get offended about money don't have this revelation. They are stuck in their natural thinking, and as a result, they will be limited to their own natural provision. When our generosity is a result of true heart faith, there is so much joy in it. It's exciting to give to God. When I give, faith comes alive in my heart that God is going to release supernatural blessings in my life.

More Than Enough!

Everything Jesus did in His earthly ministry He did for a reason. Every word, every action revealed an aspect of God's nature and ways. When Jesus fed the five thousand, a very powerful truth about the heart of God was revealed to us: God doesn't want to just meet our needs. He is a God of more than enough.

Then He ordered the crowds to recline on the grass; and He took the five loaves and the two fish, and, looking up to heaven, He gave thanks and blessed and broke the loaves and handed the pieces to the disciples, and the disciples gave them to the people. And they all ate and were satisfied. And they picked up twelve [small hand] baskets full of the broken pieces left over. And those who ate were about 5,000 men, not including women and children.

—MATTHEW 14:19–21

The need was so great. Imagine having to feed five thousand men, not including women and children. That number could have easily been fifteen thousand people. Talk about a massive feeding program! The disciples knew that in themselves there was no way they could meet this need. They said, "Jesus, send them all away." And Jesus responded, "No. You give them something to eat." The statement was almost hysterical given the current situation. How on earth would they do that?

Jesus looked around. The disciples could only find one boy who had five loaves of bread and two fish. The power of generosity was set into motion by this young boy. It figures a child would lead the way. It takes the faith of a child to access the supernatural and extraordinary. As this boy generously gave his lunch that day, a miracle was set into motion. It all started with the generous heart of a young boy—a young boy who so trusted Jesus that he was willing to give the little he had rather than hold on to it for himself. This is the kind of heart God can work with. Bob Hope once said, "If you haven't got any charity in your heart, you have the worst kind of heart trouble."[2] How true this is.

It's very important what Jesus does with this small provision. First, He gives thanks for it. If you are to be a happy and generous person, then you have to start where you are and begin to express thanks to God for what you have, no matter how small it seems. You see, when it comes to giving, it's not always the size of the gift but the level of sacrifice attached to it. God sees the heart. For some, ten dollars is a huge seed, because it may literally be all they have. For others, a thousand dollars may be a small seed because they would never even miss it.

The point is this. That little boy gave five loaves and two fish; while it seemed insignificant, Jesus could do a lot with it. The truth is, cultivating a generous heart starts when we have little, not when we have much. Harold Nye once said, "If you are not generous with a meager income, you will never be generous with abundance."[3]

In order to be a thankful and generous person, you must focus on the positive and not on the negative. You have to choose to have a thankful attitude for every little thing God blesses you with. A complaining negative attitude short-circuits God's power. A thankful heart and attitude release God's blessing.

After Jesus gave thanks and blessed the provision, He then broke the bread and the fish. But He didn't stop there. After He broke it, then He gave a piece to each disciple. The miracle didn't happen in Jesus's hands. The miracle happened in the hands of the disciples. As long as the bread and fish stayed in Jesus's hands, it was limited to five loaves and two fish. The moment it left Jesus's hand, a power was unleashed, setting a miracle into motion.

I'm sure the disciples were tempted to think, "Hmm, lunch. Just enough for me." It probably looked like just enough to satisfy their own need and hunger pangs. This is where the test was. Would they eat it themselves, or would they give it away?

The disciples chose to "pay it forward." As they obeyed Jesus and began to give the bread and fish away, a miracle happened right before their eyes! The bread and fish multiplied in their palms. As they gave it, more appeared.

Could you imagine the excitement and joy they must have experienced in that moment? Somewhere along the way as it multiplied, it began to spill over so that they could no longer contain the increase in their hands. They had to get baskets. Well, as the baskets were passed, every person was fed to the full! At the end of it all, there were twelve baskets left over, full of fish and bread. This was more than enough to feed each disciple. In fact, it was a feast.

Jesus could have had the food multiply to just meet the needs of the people. He didn't have to give anything extra. But He did, and each disciple got one full basket each. Jesus revealed something to us here about the heart of God. God is a God of more than enough! He didn't just meet the need. He showed His own disciples that if they generously serve and give to others, at the end of the day He will always take care of them and provide for their needs—and not just barely enough, more than enough!

We also see this principle taught in Proverbs 11:24: "There are those who [generously] scatter abroad, and yet increase more; there are those who withhold more than is fitting or what is justly due, but it results only in want."

God's heart for you and me is that as we become generous people and give to help others, God will always be there to take care of us. And what an adventure it is along the way! When you step out of your circle of need into someone else's circle of need, God steps into your circle of need. While you are actively helping someone else, God is actively helping you. You can never out-give God. Never! That's His heart and nature. He's a God of more than enough for you. He's your source. Once you know that, being generous is fun. You understand there is great joy in giving to people who can never repay you. This is true giving, with no strings attached. It's not giving to get back. It's giving out of a heart of love, knowing God will supply your every need and take care of you as you take care of others. Author Adam Mayers said, "You have never really lived until you've done something for somebody who can never repay you."[4]

Give to Those Who Can't Give Back

Stacy had a vision to see her city transformed by God's power. God had placed His heart of love and compassion inside of her for the poor. Stacy and her husband started a Christmas outreach in the heart of Asbury Park, New Jersey, and invited all the children in the city to attend a Christmas dinner. They shared the story of Jesus and led each child to faith in Christ. They served hundreds of people dinner and gave a present to each child. For some of them, this would be the only celebration of Christmas they would have and the only toy they would receive.

Each year as the outreach continued, the attendance doubled. They desperately needed a larger venue but didn't know where to go. They couldn't bear to turn more people away. One day Stacy was walking around the property of the Paramount Theater, which seated fifteen hundred. It was the perfect place for their outreach. As she was walking, she ran into a man who was the friend of the manager for all the events at the theater. She asked him, "Who do I see to talk about using the theater?" He said, "What do you want to use it for?" She told him. But she had no money, no real funding, just a vision. He gave her the contact information for the events manager, and she called the man the following day. He was very interested in talking with her. Not only did he give them the theater to use, which normally rented for thousands of dollars a day, but he also arranged to collect toys for them and supply refreshments, a sound man, a lighting man, security, and more. All at no cost! Over the last several years thousands of people have attended the outreach. Each year God continues to supply thousands of toys so that His precious children experience His unfailing love. Stacy's story shows that when you touch the ones who can never give back, God supernaturally releases divine favor to supply all you need to build His kingdom.

The Power of Kingdom Prosperity

In order to step into the power of a prosperous life of generosity, you have to overcome the need for self-preservation. Self-preservation wants to just protect what you have. This attitude restricts God's blessings and actually will cause you to lose out on what God has for you. It keeps everyone separate out of fear of loss. This is what motivates some pastors to restrict the people in their church from supporting regional events. They are afraid another church is going to "steal" their sheep or their sheep's money, bringing loss to their own church and ministry. In the process, they miss out on corporate unity and the blessings God brings with that. If we would choose to follow God's heart, we can overcome these fears and begin to experience the full blessings of God. Rather than feeling like people are taking from us, we can freely give to one another, helping to advance God's kingdom in the earth. (See 2 Corinthians 9:6–12.)

Dr. Bree Keyton was in the Congo, and the Lord said, "I want you to go up to Snake Mountain." She told her interpreter, "We need to go up Snake Mountain." He severely warned her, "People who go up Snake Mountain don't return." Despite the ominous danger, Bree went up via the Lord's command. She found many Africans starving to death. So she went back down the mountain and bought supplies of rice, beans, and blankets. Then she returned and shared the gospel with the dying people. Many were saved and very thankful.

A few weeks later, God told her, "I want you to buy seed and return to Snake Mountain." So she bought the seed and fertilizer and returned. The day she arrived with the seed, the people knelt down. Bree said, "God told me to bring seed." They said, "God speaks to us too. He told us to start plowing our fields two weeks ago, and He would supply the seed. We finished plowing our field today! God brought the seed through you." They sowed seed in the field that same day, and then the rains came.[5] Not only does God provide seed for the sower, but He also just may use you to be the answer to someone's prayer.

I once heard an evangelist share about how God called him to do a great work in New York City. The outreach would cost millions of dollars. When the money didn't come in for the outreach, he said, "God, I thought you called me to do this. You always provide for what You order." God told him, "I spoke to people to give, and they disobeyed." God has chosen to partner with people. That is why our obedience is so important when it comes to generosity.

We have to understand this about kingdom finances. It's not just for us. It's for others. This is completely true for every bit of power God will ever give us. God's power isn't just to help us and meet our needs. God's power is given so we can help others. This must be the motive behind sowing and reaping. We don't sow just to reap for our own selfish wants. We sow so we can reap so we can more effectively help others. It's all in the motive! (See James 4:3.)

Throughout my years of growing up in church, I never heard a teaching that taught me the principle of sowing and reaping and that I could trust God for His provision in my life. I was always taught, "You never give to get." While that may sound good, it's not biblically accurate. If we give to get for selfish reasons, it won't work. If we give to get so we can give into spreading the work of God in people's lives, that's the right motivation.

Kingdom prosperity is not about self. It's about touching as many people's lives as possible with the resources God blesses us with. I love what John Wesley once shared: "Do all the good you can, by all the means you can, in all the ways you can, in all the places you can, at all the times you can, to all the people you can, as long as ever you can."[6]

Many people never properly learn the sowing and reaping principle. They are taught giving more in a legalistic sense, that if they don't tithe, their finances will be cursed. But the New Testament teaches that Jesus became the curse for us and that any curse in the Old Testament was placed on Jesus at the cross. We are no longer under a curse! Neither are our finances. When you sow your tithe to God, it must be done in faith, not fear. This is what produces results.

Without faith it is impossible to please God (Heb. 11:6). Many people give and give, motivated by fear, and it produces no results in their life. God wants us to sow and give in faith, trusting Him as our heavenly source and provider. Faith is what pleases God, and faith is what releases the supernatural into operation, even in our finances.

I know over the years the manipulation of man has crept into the teaching of sowing and reaping, but we can never lose the revelation of God's heart in this principle. The power of generosity found in understanding how to sow in faith, expecting a harvest, goes way beyond our finances. It touches every area of our lives. It goes to the core of God's very heart and nature.

God knows our hearts. Our motives have to be pure. The more selfless we are, the more blessing God pours out on us because He knows He can trust us with it. Financial blessing is not just so we can live nice and enjoy our lives. Sure, God wants us to enjoy the good things of the earth, but He admonishes wealthy people in 1 Timothy 6:17–19 "not to be proud and arrogant and contemptuous of others, nor to set their hopes on uncertain riches, but on God…to do good, to be rich in good works, to be liberal and generous of heart, ready to share [with others], in this way laying up for themselves [the riches that endure forever as] a good foundation for the future, so that they may grasp that which is life indeed."

It's all in the heart. Money and finances are merely tools to do His will in the earth.

Sowing Into Your Field of Inheritance

We don't always realize that what we do today sets the stage for our tomorrow. Another powerful principle I have learned that has empowered me to be a generous person is the need to sow into my field of inheritance. God really taught this to me as we were launching into media ministry. While I was in prayer, God spoke to my heart saying that He had called me to invade the media industry with the power of God. I knew it was His desire for our ministry to go onto television.

I was speaking at a conference in the United States, and while I was ministering, the Lord spoke to my heart to sow my honorarium as a speaker back into the host's ministry who had brought me in. I felt very distinctively to sow into his media ministry. He had a weekly television program. My first thought was, "Well, God, I think he has more money than I do, and I don't think he needs my money." God replied, "Do you want to have a media ministry?" I thought about it for a bit and said, "Yes. I believe it is Your will for me to go into television." God replied, "Then sow your honorarium into his media ministry. You are sowing into your own inheritance."

A joy erupted in my heart, and I cheerfully gave into my host's ministry. I had an excitement and anticipation for what was to come. The Lord then led me to the account in Genesis 26 of Isaac coming into the land of his inheritance. A principle would unfold before me that would change my life forever.

When Isaac entered his land of inheritance, it was a barren wasteland. Just like many of us, he probably said, "God, is this my inheritance? A barren desert? There has to be more." Then Isaac did something very strategic and very smart. Rather than getting discouraged with his land and just packing it in and moving on, he stayed where God had sent him, kept what God had given him, and began to sow seed into his land. Within the same year he reaped one hundredfold. (See Genesis 26:12–14.) The supernatural favor of God went before him, releasing a supernatural blessing over his life and inheritance. His entire inheritance was transformed as he sowed into it.

I have walked this truth out in my own life. After the Lord instructed me to sow into my ministry colleague's television ministry, just three months later the phone rang in my office. It was GOD TV, an international television network, calling to see if we had interest in launching a TV program on their network. God had spoken to me earlier, "You will not have to run after the TV networks. They will come to you." I had divine instructions from the Lord not to run after the networks. So I took it into private prayer. As I prayed and sowed into my land of inheritance by sowing finances into another person's TV ministry, God released His favor on my life, opening doors I could not have opened on my own. Never forget this: obedience brings favor! And you don't need favor with everyone! God will give you favor with key people that will open doors for you. He will put you in the right place at the right time with the right people to unfold His plan and purpose for your life. Ever since I prayed and sowed in obedience, our media ministry has been continually expanding worldwide.

When I sow seeds, I've learned to be specific. When I sowed into this other ministry, I was very specific in my heart. I wrapped faith around my seed. I sowed intentionally believing God for a specific harvest. I sowed into TV ministry believing God for my own TV ministry. I sowed into my land of inheritance. When you sow financially, always sow in faith believing God for a specific area of breakthrough. If you know God has called you to travel on a missions trip, sow into missions and trust God that He will provide for your missions ministry. If God has called you to revival, sow into revival ministries. If God has called you to media, sow into media ministries. Be specific in your faith, and identify your land of inheritance.

Sow a Seed of Gratitude

One thing I have learned about the power of generosity is the power of sowing a seed of gratitude and thankfulness. When someone does something nice for you, take the time to express thankfulness and gratitude. It will go a long way. And it's the right thing to do. Never take any blessing for granted. If God has someone show you favor, thank them. Pray for creative ways to be a blessing back to those who have blessed you. This means a lot to God and to other people.

I heard of a man and woman who gave a sizable contribution to the church to honor the memory of their son who lost his life in the war. When the announcement was made of the generous donation, a woman whispered to her husband, "Let's give the same amount for our boy!" Her husband said, "What are you talking about? Our son wasn't killed." "That's just the point," she said. "Let's give it as an expression of our gratitude to God for sparing his life!"[7]

When I look at my own brother's life, it amazes me. We came into relationship with God when I was fourteen and my brother was fifteen. About a year later, my brother backslid away from God. For twenty years my mom prayed for him. Then, when he was in one of my meetings, the Lord powerfully encountered him; he turned back to God and was ignited in his relationship with God. Right after he came into relationship with God, something supernatural happened in him. I brought my brother, Rick, to a ministry event so he could be further exposed to the anointing of the Holy Spirit. During the offering time I was amazed when he pulled out his checkbook and wrote out a thousand-dollar check! He instantly received a heart to give. The more he gave, the happier he became! He loved to give.

He shared with me privately what God was doing in him. "Matt, I am so thankful and appreciative to God for what He has done for me I just want to give back. I love Him so much." I realized my brother was giving solely out of a thankful heart of love and gratitude. What happened next shocked us all.

My brother owned his own heating and air conditioning business in New Hampshire. As things began to slow down with the economy, businesses were going down all around him. He called me to say, "Matt, I don't know where my next job is going to come from. I have no work." Yet he was sowing a thousand dollars into an offering! Many people would think that was crazy. If they see possible lack ahead of them, they hold on to what they have; they don't give it away. Not my brother! He gave and gave and gave. He had stumbled right into God's law of generosity.

As he gave even during a time of great need, suddenly he started to get phone calls for new jobs. While other businesses were collapsing, my brother's soared and prospered. The more he gave, the more jobs came to him. Since then he has sowed in the thousands, and thousands have come back to him. His harvest has come through divine opportunities set before him, favor with contractors, and favor with customers. He has favor with God and with man.

But his motive is very important. He learned to sow seeds of gratitude and thankfulness. He sows out of love for God, and he sows back into people who have been a blessing to him. This gratitude has opened even more doors and brought more kingdom wealth to him.

One of Rick's builders was producing a costly TV show to promote their business. Because my brother was thankful for the work this builder had provided for him, he felt a peace to sow $7,500 into his TV show. He sowed a seed of gratitude. That month not only did the $7,500 come back to him in work, but much, much more. As a result of my brother's act of appreciation, he gained even more favor from that builder. Now he does predominantly all this builder's work. This builder has given Rick 90 percent of his homes and more recommendations for business in the community, which has resulted in even more work. As I said earlier, you can't out-give God! Generosity, thankfulness, and appreciation attract blessings like a magnet. It's important that we cultivate the same heart that was in the one leper who came back to Jesus to thank Him for healing him. Ten were healed, but only one was thankful. (See Luke 17:17–18.)

Discerning Your Harvest

You can believe for and expect a harvest. I remember a popular minister once shared how Dr. Oral Roberts rebuked him for how he received his offerings. Dr. Roberts said to the evangelist, "You teach people to sow a seed, but you don't tell them about the harvest." He went on to explain that it is important for people to believe there is a harvest in order for them to access it by faith.

Scripture teaches in Luke 6:38, "Give, and [gifts] will be given to you; good measure, pressed down, shaken together, and running over, will they pour into [the pouch formed by] the bosom [of your robe and used as a bag]. For with the measure you deal out [with the measure you use when you confer benefits on others], it will be measured back to you."

It's important that we learn to discern our harvest. Many times when we sow finances, we think somehow money is going to fall out of the air into our laps. While God most definitely can provide you with miracle finances by having money appear in your bank account, it doesn't always happen that way. Many times our harvest can come in different forms of blessings and provision.

Deuteronomy 8:18 says that God gives us "power to get wealth." Sometimes our harvest can come in the form of a creative idea that will produce kingdom finances in our lives. It may also come in the form of an open door or by God giving you a relationship with someone who will end up being a super blessing in your life. Look for divine opportunities that God puts before you. God may open up a new job opportunity for you or give you such wisdom in your job that you end up getting a raise. One thing I have learned about favor: when you solve a problem for someone else, there is a favor released on you with that person that can come in the form of a raise, bonus, or promotion on the job. This is what happened to Joseph. He solved Pharaoh's problem by interpreting his dream. As a result, God's favor promoted him over the entire nation.

If you just want to maintain where you are and not excel or go beyond the status quo, you will probably not move forward or experience any extra blessings on your job. It's part of being a good steward. When we look for ways to go beyond the norm and even do things that are beyond what is required of us to do, God sees it all, and He is the rewarder. He can easily speak to the heart of your boss to give you an increase. But that probably won't happen if you are being lazy and just getting by. Here are some things to think about. Do you arrive to work early? Do you ever leave late? Do you ever do things that are not required of you just because you see that it needs to be done? Do you ever pray for God to give you creative ideas that will be a blessing to your work place and bring increase to those you may work for? These are all things we can do to sow into our land of inheritance. Reaping the harvest God has for you can take place in your everyday life Monday through Friday. As you sow seeds of excellence, character, integrity, hard work, diligence, honor, and a good attitude, you will surely reap a harvest of blessing. Sowing good seeds releases God's favor on your life.

Power in Partnership

Paul taught a powerful principle concerning partnership. Regarding those who sowed into Paul's ministry, he made this statement in Philippians 4:17–19: "Not that I seek or am eager for [your] gift, but I do seek and am eager for the fruit which increases to your credit [the harvest of blessing that is accumulating to your account]. But I have [your full payment] and more; I have everything I need and am amply supplied, now that I have received from Epaphroditus the gifts you sent me. [They are the] fragrant odor of an offering and sacrifice which God welcomes and in which He delights. And my God will liberally supply (fill to the full) your every need according to His riches in glory in Christ Jesus."

Paul taught that as people partnered with him in the work of the gospel by sowing into his ministry, they would have increased fruit and have every one of their needs met out of God's riches in glory in Christ Jesus. I firmly believe this for every person who partners with us in the work of the gospel. As we touch and transform lives together, we can confidently trust God that He will more than take care of us.

It's More Than Just Money

Sowing into your land of inheritance is not just sowing money. Everything you do is an act of sowing! When you show love to someone, say a kind word, encourage them, pray for their breakthrough, live with integrity, go beyond what's expected of you, pick up the lunch bill, support an orphan in India, or sow into an offering received at church—all of these things are sowing. Do for others what you want to see happen in your own life. If you want more open doors, help to open a door for someone else. If you need finances, give finances to someone else. If you want to have friends, be a friendly person. If you want to receive love from others, start giving love to others. Leo Buscaglia said, "Too often we underestimate the power of a touch, a smile, a kind word, a listening ear, an honest compliment, or the smallest act of caring, all of which have the potential to turn a life around."[8] Never underestimate the smallest seed you sow into another person's life. Many times the smallest seeds turn into the biggest trees.

Mother Teresa couldn't have said it better: "Every time you smile at someone, it is an action of love, a gift to that person, a beautiful thing. We shall never know all the good that a simple smile can do."[9]

Living a life filled with power will be reflected in the legacy our lives leave behind. The more giving of a person we are, the greater the impact our lives will have on others and the greater the legacy we will leave behind. Winston Churchill once said, "We make a living by what we get. We make a life by what we give."[10]

"There are three kinds of givers—the flint, the sponge and the honeycomb. To get anything out of a flint you must hammer it. And then you get only chips and sparks. To get water out of a sponge you must squeeze it, and the more you use pressure, the more you will get. But the honeycomb just overflows with its own sweetness. Which kind of giver are you?"[11] Let's be the kind of person whose life overflows with the sweetness of giving God's love, leaving a trail of transformed lives behind us all the way to eternity.

Activate and Release Your Generosity

Giving will create a legacy that will far outlive your time here on earth—this is the way of the hero.

Let's start a movement, change the world, and leave a legacy for generations to come through the power of generosity. Pay it forward. When you do an act of generosity for someone, ask them to "pay it forward" by doing something nice for three other people. Here's some ways how:

1. Buy a homeless person dinner.

2. Buy someone's groceries who is struggling financially.

3. Donate some of your good clothes to the poor.

4. Participate in a food outreach at a homeless shelter or ministry.

5. Give a charitable donation and financially partner with a ministry that is impacting lives.

Make this a daily commitment, and not only will you see transformation in someone else's life, but you will also see it in your own as well!

CHAPTER 14

The Power of Love

Let's Start a Revolution

IN EVERY MOVIE there is a protagonist and there is an antago-
nist, a good guy and a bad guy. The key elements that differentiate the good guy from the bad guy are issues of the heart. The
hero wants to save the world but must go through a process of self-
discovery. The villain is usually just after power from the start. Just
like Superman and Lex Luthor, Batman and the Joker, Spider-Man
and the Green Goblin, the villain's intention is to rule the world
without love. What makes a hero great is his desire to serve the
world through his sacrifice of love.

Faith without love is power without fruit. God wants His power
to flow through the fruit, not apart from it. Love is the most powerful force in the world. It has the power and ability to pull people
out of the darkest pit of pain and despair. To live a life filled with
power means living a life filled with love. Usually when we think
of living in the power of God, we automatically equate power with
faith. For sure, faith is an important ingredient in experiencing
God's power in your life. Jesus often said to people, "Trust Me; by
your faith you are healed." The release of God's power in people's

lives was often connected to faith. We have faith, hope, and love. But the greatest of these is love (1 Cor. 13:13)!

The Demonstration Power of Love

Many people refer to my mom as "Mama Sorger." She is truly a spiritual mother to many. Whenever my mom travels with me on the road as part of our team, I see faces light up wherever she goes. It's true. From airport attendees, to store clerks, to hotel workers, to those who attend our meetings—just one hug, kind word, or smile from my mom can heal and soften the hardest of hearts. She has a way of bringing the pure light of God with her wherever she goes. It's who she is. She doesn't have to act loving; she is loving. The love of God exudes from her wherever she is. When we are home and visit the local diner for dinner, all the waitresses run over to her to hug her when she walks through the door. It's amazing to see. People aren't drawn to her because of her charismatic personality or because of some natural thing. They are drawn by the love. I have seen women totally healed on the inside and out as my mom wraps her arms around them. I've seen women sob in her arms as God's love heals them of years of emotional hurt and pain.

I was in a service praying for the sick. Both my parents were with me that night. As I was praying for people at the altar, I noticed a woman who literally looked like a skeleton. She was so weak she couldn't even stand. She sat in the front row, patiently waiting for me to notice and pray for her. I asked my mom to come and agree with me for this woman's healing. We found out that she was suffering from bone cancer. She was just skin and bones. I grabbed her hands and prayed the prayer of faith. After I prayed for her, my mom proceeded to wrap her arms around this woman and just simply speak the Word of God over her. The love of God exuded from my mom right into this woman. As God's love surged into her, suddenly I heard a commotion in the room. I looked up to see this woman, who could not even stand on her own, jumping, leaping, and dancing around the altar. She was yelling out, "I'm healed! I'm healed! The pain is gone!" She exclaimed, "I have to go tell my family Jesus healed me!" She ran out of the service to her son who was waiting in the car for the meeting to be over. What a night of rejoicing that family had.

I saw it right there in front of me. Love had healed this woman. The more I saw God's love in operation, the more I realized its power to bring healing, restoration, and freedom in people's lives. Then God brought me to Galatians 5:6, which says, "For [if we are] in Christ Jesus, neither circumcision nor uncircumcision counts for anything, but only faith activated and energized and expressed and working through love."

It was there in Scripture the whole time. It's not just faith that releases power. It's faith working through love. The Amplified Bible explains that love causes faith to be activated, energized, and expressed. Love puts faith into motion and action. Faith is like the battery cylinder, and love is the power within the battery. Love will propel our faith into motion, releasing the unlimited power of God! Love removes all the limits!

Mother Teresa said, "Open your hearts to the love God instills. God loves you tenderly. What He gives you is not to be kept under lock and key but to be shared."[1] God's love releases His power to be shared with others.

A Father's Heart

> And he shall turn the heart of the fathers to the children, and the heart of the children to their fathers.
>
> —MALACHI 4:6, KJV

As a child I remember that my dad was always working. He made the choice to work six to seven days a week and sometimes sixty to seventy hours a week just to make ends meet. It was important to my parents that my mom have the ability to stay home and raise my brother and me. Because of my dad's sacrifice of love, I was able to grow up in a safe and loving environment where all my needs were met.

My father's love was shown very differently than my mother's. While she showed a lot of physical affection, his love was shown through acts of service. Due to old age, my grandparents on my mother's side both needed to come live with us for the last ten years of their lives. My dad made the choice to sacrifice and help my mom care for them twenty-four hours a day. I remember how he used to bathe my grandfather and give him haircuts. It would be a fight the whole way, but in the end my grandpa couldn't stop thanking my dad. It left a lasting impression on me.

One of my mom's brothers faced some serious mental health issues. He lived in a boarding house in extremely unsanitary conditions. My dad would take a bucket of hot water and soap and get down on his hands and knees and scrub the room from top to bottom until it sparkled. My dad made it the cleanest room in the building. Whenever my "Blue Bomb" or any other car my family had would have mechanical difficulties, my dad would lie under the car for hours fixing it. One time my car broke down at college, and my dad drove four hours in the rain to get to me so he could fix the engine in the pouring rain. That's love in action. Even though I didn't see my dad a lot as a kid due to his sacrificial work schedule, God has more than made up for it, as now he is my full-time travel partner in ministry around the world.

Love Looks Like Your Family

A lot of people want to have ministries of power or successful careers; meanwhile they have family members at home in pain. Ministry starts with your family. If you save the whole world, but lose your family, what are you left with in the end? Nothing. Love looks like your family. At one of our conferences we host in New York, a dear friend of ours, Heidi Baker, shared a moving testimony on how God dealt with her heart concerning her family. In sincere vulnerability and humility, Heidi opened up and shared that there had been a dysfunctional mind-set finding its way into the Baker household. "We put the lost before each other," she truthfully admitted.

Heidi then shared how the mercy of God shook her family, causing her and Rolland to truly understand the love of the Father. God "broke in" on them in a deeper way through a sudden breakdown that hit Heidi's husband, Rolland. He was diagnosed with dementia, cerebral malaria, and a series of mini-strokes that left him totally helpless with a few weeks to live. But God had a redeeming plan for the Baker family. He showed them what His love looked like through selflessly loving each other and the importance of putting your family first. Heidi continued to share "that God's plan is that we will have victory and flow with such radical love that the world will run to the church."[2]

Heidi was driven to a point where she was willing to give up everything for Rolland, and when she held and loved on her husband as she would her African children, God ultimately blessed the Bakers by saving fifty thousand souls in two years through their ministry and then totally and completely healing Rolland. We learn firsthand through these experiences and testimonies shared by Heidi Baker that God's love clearly looks like your family! As God commissions you to love the world, remember it starts in your own home. When you pass this test, it will position you to break a generation through.

The Forgotten Ones

I'll never forget the day I entered into my first leper colony in India. The stench was almost unbearable. The site of rotting flesh, swarming flies, and dilapidated shacks shocked my senses. As I walked along the dirt road toward the leper colony, a gentle rain began to descend from above. I looked to see the faces of my team who had come with me from America. Some were in shock. Others were bewildered. As we passed dilapidated shacks, some with no doors and with walls that were falling down, lepers began to come out of their places of hiding to greet us. This was home to a group of fifty or more lepers who lived on the outskirts of the city of Chennai, India. One man sat in a makeshift wheelchair. It was more like a wagon that needed to be pulled by others. He had no hands, no legs, and was suffering from open sores all over his body and face. He sat there looking up at us with eyes of pain and despair. His face was half sunken in. Flies swarmed in his open wounds.

I stood amazed as my team entered into this colony of forgotten people, God's children cut off from society. They were cut off from their families and long-forgotten friends, alone, rejected, despised, and cast out. Mother Teresa has said, "The biggest disease today is not leprosy or tuberculosis, but rather the feeling of being unwanted."[3] Imagine the deep pain of isolation and rejection these individuals have endured. This was their existence. Some would call it hell on earth.

An unusual warmth filled my heart as I saw my teammates running to these people, opening their arms wide, hugging them, and just pouring out the love of God. Some of our women sat in the dirt as the leper women lay in their laps. You could see desperate eyes being filled with hope and life. That day we wrapped our arms around each leper one at a time. We loved them. We prayed for them. We fed them. We held them—the rejected of the earth.

As I prayed for one woman, she began to wail and cry out with tears streaming down her face. The power of God was touching her. Something deep inside was being set free by the love and power of Jesus. Her face of desperation turned to a face of joy as she reached out her arms to hug me and thank me. It very well could have been the first human touch and contact she had in years, maybe the first in her entire life. Never underestimate the power of a touch! It can bring healing.

As I stood before each leper, I laid my hands on them, praying for their healing and freedom. Some may say, "Matt, don't you know leprosy is contagious? Should you be laying your hands on them with open sores and wounds?" Well, I would say, "God is more powerful than leprosy! Love is more powerful than disease. Love is more powerful than the deepest pain and scars people carry, on the inside and out." The ultimate answer for man's need is love. Love is the one thing that will never fail. It has a 100 percent success rate.

Shortly after returning home from my trip to India, my phone rang. It was a pastor from India who had accompanied us on our trip to the leper colony. He was weeping on the other end of the phone. "Matt, I have to tell you what has happened. We have brought other ministers out with us to the lepers. One was so afraid of catching leprosy that he sat in the car and prayed for the lepers through the car window with the window up. Another team we brought in left the food at the front of the colony and wouldn't go in. They didn't want to get too close to the lepers." He continued, "But you and your team, when you went, you sat with the lepers. You fed the lepers. You prayed for them." He began to tell me how he went back to the leper colony two weeks after we were there to follow up. When he visited, the lepers told him, "When that white man came and prayed for us, when he touched us and put his hand on us, something happened. The leprosy has stopped in our bodies!" The pastor wept as he testified of the healing power that had touched these lost and forgotten people. It was the power of unconditional love.

A Cripple Boy Walks

On another trip to India, one of our team members experienced the amazing power of God's love. I was praying on the platform, during one of our Healing Festivals, for those who needed healing. Our team was out in the field also praying for people. One of our team members, Rich, found a young boy lying in the dirt, unable to walk due to paralysis in his legs. Rich's heart became overwhelmed with

God's love for this young boy. He picked him up in his arms and held him as he prayed. Suddenly Rich could feel the young boy's legs beginning to kick. As he placed him down on the ground, strength came into his legs and he walked! He was healed by God! Oh, what healing power there is in God's love!

I think the most powerful love of all is the love that gives expecting nothing in return. So many times we give with strings attached. We think, "Well, if I do this for you, then what are you going to do for me?" That's not real love. Love gives expecting nothing in return. Love gives to those who have nothing for you. It's this kind of selfless love that truly moves the heart of God.

Living a Life of Unlimited Power

How would you like to live with unlimited power? Power to heal the sick. Power to see people set free. Power to live a life of wholeness and victory over your own pain and weaknesses. I think this is what we all desire, but many times we live beneath all God has for us because either we haven't fully received or we haven't fully given His love to others. Love will not only transform you, but it will also transform others through you.

Tremendous supernatural power flows through love. Jesus was a man who saw all the sick healed. He never turned one person away. He never said, "Sorry, I can't help you. Your problems are just too difficult. That's beyond Me." No. He had the power to help every person who ever reached out to Him. He was not motivated by selfish gain. He didn't give to others based on what He could get back from them. He gave simply because He loved. This was His main mission in life, to reveal the love of God to broken, messed-up people—people who seemed beyond repair. These are the ones He came for.

As I study the life of Jesus, I realize a truth that has transformed my own life and ministry: love was the secret source of Jesus's power. It's what enabled Him to heal every sick person who came to Him. It was what gave Him the ability to move in a power that broke through the natural laws and limitations of the earthly realm. Let me explain.

Jesus really established a model and example for us to follow and learn from. One moment that stands out to me the most is in Matthew 14 when Jesus receives the news that His cousin, John the Baptist, just had his head cut off for standing up for truth and righteousness. It was a deep loss.

We must never forget that although Jesus was God in the flesh, Jesus was also a man just like us. He had feelings and emotions and was even tempted in every way we have ever been tempted. He has experienced it all. That's why He can relate so well to us.

But as Jesus went to a solitary place to pray and work through what He was experiencing, the crowds found out where He was going to be. They followed Him. While Jesus was going through His own problems, He was confronted with the deep needs and pains of the people around Him. His response to this reveals why He had so much power present in His life to help others: "When He went ashore and saw a great throng of people, He had compassion (pity and deep sympathy) for them and cured their sick" (Matt. 14:14).

When Jesus saw the deep pain and needs of the people, He was moved with compassion. As compassion and love flowed in His heart, power flowed through His hands and body, healing the sick people around Him. Somehow love was connected to the power Jesus had. It was a selfless love that caused Jesus to put His own problems aside to help others in their moment of need.

If you really want God to use you to help others, you will quickly discover that ministry will not always be convenient. So many wait until everything is just right in their lives. They say, "When I have enough money…" "When this situation is dealt with…" "When this person acknowledges my call, then I will be used by God." If you wait for every situation in your life to be perfect before God uses you, you will be waiting a long time.

Sometimes the greatest power flows through you when you feel the least ready. It's not about everything being perfect. It's about having God's heart for people. You can be facing serious situations in your own life, and in the process God will still use you to help others, but you have to be willing to be inconvenienced.

Not only was Jesus willing, but He also showed us why such power could flow through Him. He was moved with compassion. This was the key! He actually cared about people. His heart was genuine and sincere. Something happened in Jesus that day. As love flowed in Him, God's healing power was released to minister healing and freedom to multitudes of others.

Compassion Draws God's Power to You

Not only will God's compassion in you release His power through you, but it will also draw His power to you! Delia Knox was crippled in a wheelchair for twenty-two years, paralyzed from the waist down. She couldn't even feel her legs. For the first ten years of her paralysis, she woke up each morning wondering if that day would be the day for her healing. With each passing day, month, and year her hope became deferred, and she wondered if she would just have to live this way forever. Now twenty-two years had come and gone, and she found herself in a healing meeting; truthfully she didn't want to be there. She was uncomfortable in such places because she didn't want to be let down again, but something miraculous happened that night.

A mother brought to the platform her baby, who needed healing from a kidney disease. As Delia saw this child's condition, her heart was moved with deep compassion. She began to pray, "Lord, You have to do something for that baby!" Then suddenly the evangelist and pastor came off the platform and began to pray for her. Her heart at that moment was filled with compassion for the baby, so much so that something deep inside of her softened. Suddenly she could feel hands on her legs! Sensation was coming back. As the pastor said, "Let faith arise in this woman," she heard the Holy Spirit say, "Get up!" And up she went! For the first time in twenty-two years she was standing. As those around her helped her begin to take her first steps, God's healing power surged through her.

Today she is 100 percent healed and is fully walking and praising God for her healing. She testifies that as God's compassion filled her heart for another person, it actually drew God's power back toward herself for her own healing. Delia's husband says, "When compassion goes out, virtue comes in. What happened was a boomerang effect." Faith came alive in Delia's heart for healing through the power of compassion.[4]

A Personal Meeting With Dr. Oral Roberts

One of America's great healing evangelists was Dr. Oral Roberts. Known for his large tent meetings across America in the 1950s, Dr. Roberts witnessed the tremendous healing power of God on a regular basis. A few months before he passed away on December 15, 2009, at the age of ninety-one, I had the privilege of sitting with him in his living room for several hours. We shared some wonderful conversation, and then he prayed over me. I asked him what the secret was to his healing ministry. I was amazed by his answer. He said, "Well, many think I would say faith. And true, faith is important, but I knew I had faith. The Bible teaches that all men who believe in Christ have a measure of faith. So all Christians have faith. Because the Bible tells me I have faith, I simply believe it. But I would find myself before a healing crusade meeting going into my hotel room and praying and seeking God for His love to fill my heart. I would pray for God to cause me to love the people and to care about their conditions. As I sought after the love of God, the miracles exploded in my meetings." In another meeting Dr. Roberts shared, "If you want to heal the sick, you must love the sick."

It was just as Paul taught in Galatians 5:6. Faith was activated by love, releasing the power of God to help people overcome the most impossible situations.

Releasing God's Love

I will never forget the night I was ministering in Wales. It had once been the home of an amazing move of God back in 1904. I felt led that night to call people forward for prayer for healing. As I was praying for people at the altar, my eye caught a woman sitting down in her seat about halfway back in the auditorium. I felt prompted by God to go and pray for her. But my mind said, "God, if she wanted prayer, she would be up at the altar." I couldn't shake the impression I was feeling.

So I made my way back to where the woman was sitting. I asked her, "May I pray for you?" She looked up at me and with a scowl on her face said, "No! I don't want you to pray for me!" She continued, "I didn't even want to be here tonight. My husband made me come!" I looked up at God and said, "I told You." Again I felt, "Pray for her." So I asked again, "May I pray for you?" She said, "I've had everyone pray for me, and I'm still sick! I've gone to the doctors and had operations and nothing has worked. God doesn't love me, and He doesn't want to heal me!" She was mad, angry, and depressed—not a good combination for the prayer of faith. She began to tell me all the sickness she had in her body. It was a long list! I never knew one person could have so much wrong with them.

I finally had to stop her and ask her one more time if I could pray for her. She now reluctantly agreed. As she stood to her feet, she just looked at me with an icy cold stare. I wasn't sure where I was going to muster up the faith to believe God for her healing. I was just acting in obedience to God.

It would have been very easy for me to react to her anger and animosity toward me. I could have easily walked away with my own flesh offended by her bad attitude. But I knew I had to obey God. As I closed my eyes and began to pray, suddenly something began to happen inside of me. I didn't care one bit how angry this woman was with me. My heart began to be overwhelmed with a supernatural love for her! As this love filled my heart, I lost sight of her earthly condition and saw what God could do.

As love infused my heart, power flowed out of my spirit into her body. She began weeping and laughing at the same time. All the pain left her body, and she was completely healed and set free. Not only was she physically healed of all her pain and infirmity, but also she could feel God's presence again. "I have felt spiritually dead for five years. I haven't felt God's presence at all! But it's like a new life has flowed into me. I am close to God again," she exclaimed.

Love has the power to pull people out of the deepest pits of despair, heal them, restore them, and give them a new life. God's love can even overcome people's depression, anger, and lack of faith.

I remember one trip our team took to India to minister in a healing crusade. God's power was present to heal the sick, set people free, and bring people to faith in Christ. While I was preaching, my dad, Rich, was standing off to the side of the platform. As he was looking over the crowd, he couldn't help but notice this one particular man who was near the front. The man kept staring at my dad with eyes that said, "If I get near enough to you, I am going to kill you." My dad felt prompted simply to pray the love of God over him. Throughout the entire crusade meeting my dad silently prayed for this one man.

At the end of the meeting, as we were leaving, this man came running after us and was intercepted by some of our security. As he made his way through, he just wanted to testify of a miracle he received. For years he had suffered from mental torment. He said, "As I was staring at that man [referring to my dad], my mind was healed." As my dad simply prayed God's love over him, God's power was released, completely setting his mind free.

The Spirit of Adoption

> Pure and undefiled religion before God and the Father is this:
> to visit orphans and widows in their trouble, and to keep one-
> self unspotted from the world.
>
> —JAMES 1:27, NKJV

Another way of releasing God's love to those who need it most is through the spirit of adoption. Christians are becoming a part of the solution to the world's brokenness by opening their hearts up to foster parenting and adopting orphans—children that for one reason or another were given up by their natural birth parents. One such family is the Ragsdales, who began foster care about fifteen years ago and have had over seventy-five children in their home. Some children have stayed a few months, some for up to five years.

They adopted one child when he was four years old. He is eleven now. One day they asked their newly adopted son, "How did we become your parents and you become our son?" He replied, "I prayed to God for a new mom and dad, and God gave me you. When I get older, I will obey you. Now go and write that down." They gave him a new name, Josiah, which means, "Yahweh heals." "The Lord continues to expand our hearts with His presence, so we are able to reach out and pour His love into His children," shared Denise Ragsdale.

Heidi Baker, a missionary in Mozambique, Africa, shared a heart-wrenching story with me about a young girl named Angelique. As a child she had been tied to a tree by her uncle and raped over and over again by the men in her village. When Heidi and her husband, Rolland, rescued this young girl, she had human bite marks all over her body. She had been brutalized by the depravity of man's sin. But the love of God is more powerful! When she first came home with them, she couldn't even raise her head up. She was so weak. But as Heidi, Rolland, and their team loved her, held her, and prayed over her, God's healing power began to bring restoration. Soon she was not only able to lift up her head, but she also began eating and then walking. Today she is a beautiful young lady, healed and made whole by the power of God's love. She was able to completely forgive her uncle and the men who abused her and live the life God destined for her, a life of joy, peace, blessing, and fulfillment. She not only was made whole by God's love, but she was then able to release it to those who were the least deserving.

Fruit-Driven Life

> But earnestly desire and zealously cultivate the greatest and best gifts and graces (the higher gifts and the choicest graces). And yet I will show you a still more excellent way [one that is better by far and the highest of them all—love].
>
> —1 Corinthians 12:31

It's very important to know that Jesus's life and ministry were not gift driven; they were fruit driven. Sure, Jesus was empowered by the Holy Spirit and operated in tremendous gifts from God. But His life was not driven by these gifts. His life was driven and motivated by fruit. Jesus was motivated by the very thing God is—love. Jesus didn't seek after the gifts of God alone. He sought after the love of God. God's love and compassion compelled Jesus to release supernatural power to those who needed it most.

The reason love is so powerful is because love is what marks us as believers in God. (See John 13:34–35.) Love is what makes us different and sets us apart. Too many times we mark each other by our gifts. God marks us by our love—not just our love for Him but also our love for one another.

His love in you will release an overflowing power that will be far beyond just the manifestation of a gift. Love will cause you to manifest Christ Himself removing all the limitations to what God can do through you. When your life is compelled forward by fruit, it stays pure and clean. Motives remain pure, ambitions remain holy, and God is truly glorified. Not only will people see God's power, they will experience His heart and see His face.

I remember one day as a child walking through the front door and breaking down in tears because of a problem I was having with a kid at school. That day God spoke to my mom's heart, "Just love him." It sounded so simple. Yet it was that very love that helped me through that moment of pain. We may not have the ability to completely fix someone's pain or change their circumstances, but we can love them. Love in itself is a healing agent. Mother Teresa has said, "I have found the paradox, that if you love until it hurts, there can be no more hurt, only more love."⁵ This means that when we really love others, we will also feel their pain. But as we keep on loving, eventually the pain is replaced by love.

The unconditional love and support of both my mom and dad strengthened me during difficult times. They are my everyday heroes. I know it was because of their love that God was able to bring me through and use what I walked through to become more effective in helping others.

God has brought me from a survivor to an overcomer! In high school I was very bold in sharing my faith with others. Years later I would find out from different ones how my stand for God deeply impacted them and was a part of them eventually coming to know God in their own lives. I now stand whole in God and am able to minister God's power to others. We have seen thousands saved, healed, set free, and touched by God's power in more than twenty-five nations of the earth. He does a work in you so He can do a work through you! I learned by experience that when you set your love upon God, He works everything for your good, even the bad things. It really is true; love never fails (1 Cor. 13:8)!

The Ultimate Expression of Love

This is My commandment: that you love one another [just] as I have loved you. No one has greater love [no one has shown stronger affection] than to lay down (give up) his own life for his friends. You are My friends if you keep on doing the things which I command you to do.

—JOHN 15:12–14

Jesus Christ is the ultimate expression of God's love. He laid down His life so that we can lay down our lives and release His love to the world. There is no greater love than to sacrifice your life for another. Love compelled Jesus all the way to the cross. Love resurrected Him from the grave. Love set you and me free so that we can be fruitful vessels of His power.

Jesus is the ultimate hero. When you accept Him into your life, Jesus becomes the hero in you. He is your source, your harness, and your release. If you don't know Christ, please take a moment and say this prayer with me now.

> *Heavenly Father, I come to You and confess my faith in Your Son, Jesus Christ. I believe that He is the Son of God and that He was crucified, died on the cross, and was raised to life on the third day. I ask You to forgive me of all my sin and cleanse my life with Your precious blood. I repent of and renounce everything that has grieved You, and I surrender my entire life to You. Come and fill me with the Holy Spirit, and empower me to walk with You all the days of my life. In Jesus's name, amen.*

God now has an assignment for you to do. Go and share His love with everyone you know.

> You have not chosen Me, but I have chosen you and I have appointed you [I have planted you], that you might go and bear fruit and keep on bearing, and that your fruit may be lasting [that it may remain, abide], so that whatever you ask the Father in My Name [as presenting all that I AM], He may give it to you. This is what I command you: that you love one another.
>
> —John 15:16–17

Activate and Release His Love

It's time to start a love revolution that releases the authentic power of God within you. Here are some ways how:

1. Lay hands on the sick in Jesus's name.

2. Set the captives free in Jesus's name.

3. Share the gospel with someone who needs to hear.

4. Hug someone who is lonely.

5. Visit an elderly person in your local nursing home.

The Hero Movement

There's a hero in all of us. That hero is Christ.

Join me in the hero movement as we release the power of God to the world through Christ's fruit within us. It's time to unleash the hero within. So let's do it!

Submit your hero testimonies to www.powerforlifebook.com.

Notes

INTRODUCTION

1. Julia Cameron, *The Artist's Way* (New York: Penguin Putnam, Inc., 2002), 144.

CHAPTER 2
THE POWER OF INTIMACY

1. As quoted in Phil Pringle, *Inspired to Pray: The Art of Seeking God* (Ventura, CA: Regal Books, 2009), 3.

2. Smith Wigglesworth, *Ever Increasing Faith* (Radford, VA: Wilder Publications, 2007), 120.

3. Albert Hibbert, *Smith Wigglesworth: The Secret to His Power* (Tulsa, OK: Harrison House, 2009), 32.

4. Brother Lawrence, *The Brother Lawrence Collection: The Practice of the Presence of God* (Radford, Virginia: Wilder Publications, 2008), 23, 95, 19, 29.

5. As quoted in Bill Hybels, *1 Peter: Stand Strong* (Grand Rapids, MI: Zondervan, 1999), 52.

CHAPTER 3
THE POWER OF GRACE

1. As quoted in Thomas C. Oden, *The Justification Reader* (Grand Rapids, MI: William B. Eerdmans Publishing Company, 2002), 34.

2. "Proclamation for National Day of Humiliation, Fasting, and Prayer—April 30, 1863," Intercessors for America, http://www .ifapray.org/archive/PrayerGuides/ProclamationforNational DayofHumiliationFastingandPrayer.htm (accessed April 27, 2011).

3. Dwight Lyman Moody, *D. L. Moody's Little Instruction Book* (Colorado Springs, CO: Honor Books, 1996).

CHAPTER 4
THE POWER OF TRUTH

1. Dictionary.com, s.v. "align," http://dictionary.reference.com/browse/align (accessed April 28, 2011).

CHAPTER 5
THE POWER OF IDENTITY

1. Ian Gilbert, *Essential Motivation in the Classroom* (London: Routledge Falmer, 2002), 175.

2. David W. Freeman, "Tyler Perry, Oprah Talk Sexual Abuse: Who Victimized Little Tyler?," CBSNews.com, October 22, 2010, http://www.cbsnews.com/8301-504763_162-20020438-10391704.html (accessed May 12, 2011).

3. AllSands.com, "Gene Kelly Biography," http://www.allsands.com/entertainment/people/genekellybiogr_yzn_gn.htm (accessed April 28, 2011).

4. Yahoo! Movies, "Sidney Poitier," http://movies.yahoo.com/movie/contributor/1800025653/bio (accessed April 28, 2011).

CHAPTER 6
THE POWER OF FAITH

1. Hibbert, *Smith Wigglesworth: The Secret to His Power*, 91, 95.

2. F. F. Bosworth, *Christ the Healer* (Grand Rapids, MI: Chosen Books, 2008), 92.

3. TheVoiceMagazine.com, "Dr. Lilian B. Yeomans: A Physician's Experience With the Gospel," http://www.thevoicemagazine.com/health-and-healing/health-healing-drugs/dr-lilian-yeomans

-experience-with-a-physicians-the-gospel.html (accessed April 28, 2011).

4. Charles Price, *The Real Faith for Healing* (Gainesville, FL: Bridge-Logos, 1997), 56–57.

5. Ibid., 15–16.

6. As quoted in Nuggets of Wisdom, http://www.savedhealed.com/nuggets.htm (accessed April 28, 2011).

7. Creative Bible Study, "The Charles Blondin Story: A Lesson on Faith," http://www.creativebiblestudy.com/Blondin-story.html (accessed May 12, 2011). Permission to quote requested.

CHAPTER 7
THE POWER OF INTEGRITY

1. Ron Flatter, "Secretariat Remains No. 1 Name in Racing," ESPN .com, http://espn.go.com/sportscentury/features/00016464.html (accessed April 28, 2011).

2. Gus D. Nichols, "Secretariat—All Heart," HubPages.com, http://hubpages.com/hub/Secretariat-All-Heart (accessed April 28, 2011).

3. Derek Prince, *Rules of Engagement* (Ada, MI: Chosen Books, 2006).

4. Nathalie K., "Breaking in a Horse," EzineArticles.com, http://ezinearticles.com/?Breaking-in-a-Horse&id=1303437 (accessed April 28, 2011).

5. Nancy Leigh DeMoss, *Brokenness: The Heart God Revives* (Chicago: Moody Publishers, 2005), 51.

6. Kathryn Kuhlman, *A Glimpse Into Glory* (Gainesville, FL: Bridge-Logos, 1979), 142.

7. Smith Wigglesworth, *The Teachings of Smith Wigglesworth* (Radford, VA: Wilder Publications, 2007), 107.

8. John MacArthur, *Matthew 1–7: The MacArthur New Testament Commentary* (Chicago: Moody Press, 1985), 66.

9. FamilyLife.com, "FamilyLife Today Series: Love Renewed—the Reconciliation of Clint and Penny Bragg," http://www.familylife.com/site/c.dnJHKLNnFoG/b.6468077/k.3984/Love_Renewed_Clint_and_Penny_Bragg.htm (accessed May 12, 2011).

10. As quoted in Paige Lanier Chargois, *Certain Women Called by Christ* (Birmingham, AL: New Hope Publishers, 2008), 86.

11. Derek Quizon, "Tempe Homeless Man Returns $3,300 in Cash to ASU Student," *The Arizona Republic*, November 17, 2010, http://www.azcentral.com/community/tempe/articles/2010/11/17/20101117tempe-homeless-man-returns-money1119.html (accessed April 28, 2011).

12. Herbert Lockyer, *All the Men of the Bible* (Grand Rapids, MI: Zondervan Publishing House, 1958), 56.

13. As quoted in James Montgomery Boice, *The Gospel of Matthew: The King and His Kingdom* (Ada, MI: Baker Books, 2001), 49.

14. R. Kent Hughes, *Disciplines of a Godly Man* (Wheaton, IL: Crossway Books, 2006), 154.

15. Diane, "Little Decisions Add Up to Big Benefits," *Fit to the Finish* (blog), October 27, 2010, http://www.fittothefinish.com/blog/2010/10/little-decisions-add-up-to-big-benefits/ (accessed April 28, 2011).

16. Ibid.

17. Stanley Howard Frodsham, *Smith Wigglesworth: Apostle of Faith* (Springfield, MO: Gospel Publishing House, 1948), 125.

18. Jim Kasparek, *It Is Appointed* (Summerville, SC: Holy Fire Publishing, 2007), 109.

19. Frank E. Grizzard, *George Washington: A Biographical Companion* (Santa Barbara, CA: ABC-CLIO, Inc., 2002), 363.

CHAPTER 8
THE POWER OF PERSPECTIVE

1. Rob Garofalo Jr., *A Winner by Any Standard* (n.p.: Teen Winners Publications, 2004), 48.

2. BaldEagleInfo.com, "Bald Eagle—Nesting and Young," American Bald Eagle Information, http://www.baldeagleinfo.com/eagle/eagle4.html (accessed April 29, 2011).

3. Personal testimony sent in to author. Also, see AbortedYetAlive, "From an Ultrasound to Planned Parenthood," http://christian -topics.info/Article/From-An-Ultrasound-To-Planned -Parenthood/10229 (accessed April 29, 2011).

CHAPTER 9
THE POWER OF PERSEVERANCE

1. The information for this was given in a sermon James Goll preached at one of the author's conferences after Michal Ann Goll died.

2. The Quote Garden, "Quotations: Hang In There!," http://www .quotegarden.com/hang-in.html (accessed April 29, 2011).

3. Jeanine Basinger, *The Star Machine* (New York: A. A. Knopf, 2007), 79.

CHAPTER 10
THE POWER OF VISION

1. As quoted in John H. Zenger and Joe Folkman, *The Extraordinary Leader* (Columbus, OH: McGraw-Hill Professional, 2002), 16.

2. As quoted in Jakki J. Mohr et al., *Marketing of High-Technology Products and Innovations* (Saddle River, NJ: Pearson Prentice Hall, 2009), 112.

3. As quoted in Steve Little, *Leading God's Way* (Bloomington, IN: CrossBooks, 2010), 25.

4. As quoted in Mark Herringshaw and Jennifer Schuchman, *Nine Ways God Always Speaks* (Carol Stream, IL: Tyndale, 2009), 169.

5. Ibid.

CHAPTER 11
THE POWER OF BLESSING

1. Dictionary.com, s.v. "blessing," http://dictionary.reference.com/browse/blessing (accessed April 29, 2011).

2. James Allen, *Above Life's Turmoil* (New York: Cosimo Books, 2007), 39.

3. Joanne Ford, "Interview With Eduardo Verastegui, Film Producer and Pro-Life Advocate," *L'Osservatore Romano*, weekly edition in English, September 23, 2009, 10.

4. Ibid.

5. Ibid.

6. Hialmer Day Gould and Edward Louis Hessenmueller, *Best Thoughts of Best Thinkers* (Cleveland, OH: Best Thoughts Publishing, 1904), 33.

CHAPTER 12
THE POWER OF JOY

1. James B. Smith, *Embracing the Love of God* (New York: Harper Collins, 2008), 23.

2. Gwen Costello, *Spiritual Gems From Mother Teresa* (New London, CT: Twenty-Third Publications, 2008), 19.

3. Liz Szabo, "Number of Americans Taking Antidepressants Doubles," USAToday.com, August 4, 2009, http://www.usatoday.com/news/health/2009-08-03-antidepressants_N.htm (accessed May 2, 2011).

4. Harriet Fraad "Why are Americans Passive as Millions Lose Their Homes, Families and the American Dream?", Alternet.org, February 2, 2010, http://www.alternet.org/media/145481/why_are_americans_passive_as_millions_lose_their_jobs_families_and_the_american_dream?page=5 (accessed May 2, 2011).

5. Szabo, "Number of Americans Taking Antidepressants Doubles."

6. Charles Barber, "Are We Really So Miserable?", Salon.com, August 26, 2009, http://www.salon.com/life/feature/2009/08/26/barber_age_of_anxiety (accessed May 2, 2011).

7. Augustine, *The Confessions of Saint Augustine*, ed. Temple Scott (New York: E. P. Dutton and Co., 1900), 255.

8. Sonja Lyubomirsky, "Buying Happiness," *Spirit Magazine*, n.d.

9. Ibid.

10. As quoted in Mary Kathryn Clark, *In the Morning...Joy* (Bloomington, IN: iUniverse, 2010), 356.

11. As quoted in Robb Dunn, *Will God Heal Me?* (Colorado Springs, CO: Cook Communications, 2007), 238.

12. James Botkin "Laughing to Live Longer," Navy.mil, June 10, 2002, http://www.navy.mil/search/display.asp?story_id=1896 (accessed May 2, 2011).

13. Meredith Melnick, "Lack of Sleep Linked With Depression, Weight Gain and Even Death," *Time*, September 2, 2010, http://healthland.time.com/2010/09/02/lack-of-sleep-can-cause-depression-weight-gain-and-even-death/ (accessed May 2, 2011).

CHAPTER 13
THE POWER OF GENEROSITY

1. Pay It Forward Foundation, "The Miracle of Innocence: A Bittersweet, Unforgettable Novel About a Twelve-Year-Old Child Who Changes the World," http://www.payitforwardfoundation.org/about_novel.html (accessed May 2, 2011).

2. Famous-Quotes.com, "Famous Quotes by Bob Hope," http://www.famous-quotes.com/author.php?aid=3553 (accessed May 2, 2011).

3. Lloyd Cory, *Quote, Unquote* (n.p.: Victor Books, 1977), 130.

4. Adam Mayers, *Acts of Kindness: Inspirational Stories* (Toronto: Durdorn Press, 2010), 5.

5. As told to author by a friend who attended an April 2010 house meeting where Dr. Bree Keyton spoke. More information on Dr. Bree can be found here: www.breekeytonministries.com.

6. As quoted in Mark Victor Hansen and Art Linkletter, *How to Make the Rest of Your Life the Best of Your Life* (Nashville: Thomas Nelson, 2006), 45.

7. James S. Hewitt, *Illustrations Unlimited* (Carol Stream, IL: Tyndale House Publishers, 1988), 262.

8. As quoted in Mary Beth Simmons, *Second Acts That Change Lives* (San Francisco: Red Wheel/Weiser LLC), 83.

9. Costello, *Spiritual Gems From Mother Teresa*, 2.

10. As quoted in Warren Wiersbe, *The Wiersbe Bible Commentary: The Complete New Testament* (Colorado Springs, CO: David C. Cook, 2007), 361.

11. St. Peter's Lutheran Church, *St. Peter's*, vols. 1–4 (New York: Interest of St. Peter Lutheran Church, 1913), 288.

CHAPTER 14
THE POWER OF LOVE

1. Mother Teresa and Jose Luis Gonzalez-Balado, *Mother Teresa, in My Own Words* (n.p.: Liguori Publications, 1996), 18.

2. Taken from a transcript of the sermon Heidi Baker preached at Matt Sorger Ministries Conference in New York.

3. ThinkExist.com, "Mother Teresa of Calcutta Quotes," http://thinkexist.com/quotation/the_biggest_disease_today_is_not_leprosy_or/193811.html (accessed May 5, 2011).

4. GOD.TV, "The Bay of the Holy Spirit Revival," November 5, http://www.god.tv/node/839 (accessed May 6, 2011).

5. Costello, *Spiritual Gems From Mother Teresa*, 9.

MATT SORGER MINISTRIES

Leading a cutting-edge ministry, Matt Sorger travels the globe empowering believers, churches and regions to move higher in the power and presence of the Holy Spirit. By connecting with God's true power source they are transformed, healed and released to bring hope, healing, love and joy to those Jesus died for. The primary ways in which the gospel is shared and broadcast through MSM are:

- **Power for Life** - National and international TV programing reaching over 200 nations
- **Conferences** - National and international teaching and impartation gatherings
- **Missions Outreach** - Healing crusades, pastors and leaders conferences, girls home in India, drilling water wells in Africa, building homes in devastated earthquake hit regions such as China
- **Equipping** - Empowering believers with teaching resources including books, CD's, DVD's, mp3's and more
- **Healing** - Bringing the healing power of God to the sick

Help someone else receive power for life by partnering with Matt Sorger Ministries. Power Partners receive a teaching message every month from Matt.

For more information about Matt Sorger Ministries, to sign up for Matt's weekly Power Email, and to become a monthly Power Partner please visit **Mattsorger.com.**

MSM CONTACT INFORMATION

MAILING ADDRESS:
Matt Sorger Ministries
PO Box 1648
Selden, NY 11784

PHONE AND FAX
Telephone: 631-696-4950
Fax: 631-696-4995

E-MAIL & WEBSITES
info@mattsorger.com
mattsorger.com
powerforlifebook.com
mattsorgeronline.com

 Connect with Matt on Facebook at
facebook.com/mattsorgerpage

 Follow Matt on Twitter at
twitter.com/mattsorger

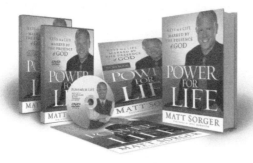

CD & MP3 Teaching Sets:

ADVANCING YOUR DESTINY
How to Pull Your Future into Your Now

Teachings Include:
- The Power of Vision and Destiny
- Advancing Your Destiny with Excellence
- Pulling Your Future into Your Now
- Unleashing Your Prophetic Promise

THE SECRET SOURCE OF POWER
Intimacy and the Anointing

Teachings Include:
- Digging Your Own Well
- The Prayer Life
- Birthing Revival Through Intimacy

OPERATING IN CREATIVE MIRACLES

Teachings Include:
- God's Will to Heal
- Faith for Creative Miracles
- Four Methods of Divine Healing
- Releasing the Healing Anointing

IS YOUR SHADOW DANGEROUS?
Moving in the Power Gifts

Teachings Include:
- Activating the Power Gifts: Gifts of Healing,
  Working of Miracles & the Gift of Faith
- Spiritual Protocol for the Miraculous
- Four Levels of Speaking in Tongues

THE PRESENCE DRIVEN LIFE

Teachings Include:
- Stress Free Living
- How to Overcome the Negatives of Life
- The Presence Driven Life
- Nine Keys to Living in Supernatural Joy

PROSTATE
CANCER
BREAKTHROUGHS

THE NEW OPTIONS YOU NEED TO KNOW ABOUT

JAY S. COHEN, MD

SQUAREONE
PUBLISHERS

COVER DESIGNER: Jeannie Tudor
IN-HOUSE EDITOR: Ally Cirruzzo
TYPESETTER: Gary A. Rosenberg

The information and advice contained in this book are based upon the research and experiences of the authors. They are not intended as a substitute for consulting with your physician or other healthcare provider. The publisher and authors are not responsible for any adverse effects or consequences resulting from the use of any of the information or suggestions presented in this book. All matters pertaining to your physical health should be supervised by a healthcare professional who can provide medical care that is tailored to meet individual needs.

Square One Publishers
115 Herricks Road
Garden City Park, NY 11040
(516) 535-2010 • (877) 900-BOOK
www.squareonepublishers.com

Library of Congress Cataloging-in-Publication Data

Names: Cohen, Jay S., author.
Title: Prostate cancer breakthroughs / Dr. Jay S. Cohen.
Description: Garden City Park, NY : Square One Publishers, [2018] | Includes bibliographical references and index.
Identifiers: LCCN 2017058964 | ISBN 9780757004704 (paperback) | ISBN 9780757054709 (ebook)
Subjects: LCSH: Prostate—Cancer—Popular works.
Classification: LCC RC280.P7 C62 2018 | DDC 616.99/463—dc23
LC record available at https://lccn.loc.gov/2017058964

Printed in the United States of America

10   9   8   7   6   5   4   3   2   1

Contents

PART 3

Weighing the Evidence and Making a Decision

To my mother, Dolores Cohen-Levy,
who always supported me through every undertaking.
When I was nineteen and questioning my choice of medicine
versus becoming a writer, she said,
"Why can't you do both?"

I didn't think it was possible,
but time proved her right.

Acknowledgments

I want to express my deep appreciation to the Informed Prostate Cancer Support Group. The willingness of its members to reach out and educate men like me who are newly diagnosed with prostate cancer is both generous and invaluable. Their new efforts changed the course of my medical care for the better. Groups like IPCSG are helpful not only for supporting men with this terrible and sometimes deadly cancer, but also in spreading the word about vital new tests and treatments, ideas that men with prostate cancer can take to their doctors, thereby facilitating much needed change in the medical approach to prostate cancer care today. For readers of this book, the IPCSG website (ipcsg.org) is an excellent source of information, particularly the monthly lectures and discussions, available on DVD, with top experts in all of the fields of medicine that are involved in the treatment of prostate cancer.

My sincere thanks also to the small group of fellows who met every week over Chinese food to discuss our individual challenges as well as new ideas and reports about prostate cancer.

I also want to thank my publication team of Beth and Ezra Barany of Barany Consulting, and my reliable proofreaders, Karen Lockwood and Barbara Isrow-Cohen. Thank you for your guidance, support, and encouragement in my new adventure as both writer and publisher. It has been an ongoing learning experience and a thrill.

Introduction

I learned I had prostate cancer six years ago. Dr. Summers, my highly experienced and knowledgeable urologist, recommended surgery or radiation therapy for my disease. As a writer, I am always open to new ideas for a book, but I decided against writing about my prostate cancer. I didn't want to think about it any more than necessary. I wanted to get treated and move on with my life.

And so, two weeks later I met with Dr. Frederick, the prostate surgeon. As he described the details of prostate removal surgery, or prostatectomy, in which he would remove the entire prostate gland, he asked me: "Do you want me to take out one or both neurovascular bundles?"

The neurovascular bundles contain the nerve and artery trunks to the prostate gland. Cutting them could render me impotent or incontinent, possibly both, perhaps for the rest of my life. I was too dumbfounded to answer.

The doctor continued, "Your cancer is on the left side, so we should definitely take that bundle out. If we don't, there's a 30 percent greater chance of your cancer returning. Still, to give you the best chance of getting all of it, we should take the right bundle, too." He paused for a second, then asked, "What do you want to do?"

Dr. Frederick was intelligent, experienced, calm, and personable. He had performed more than five hundred robotic prostatectomies, the treatment most often recommended for prostate cancer. Based on his demeanor and attention to detail, I figured he was a good surgeon.

What did I want to do? My left brain struggled to find an answer, while my right brain recoiled and cringed. I had been diagnosed with prostate cancer two weeks earlier, and everything I'd heard since then sounded worse and worse.

1

Dr. Frederick assured me that over time, most men get some return of normal sexual and urinary functioning, but what did "over time" and "some return" mean? Although I was a doctor, I wasn't a urologist or an oncologist, and I was as overwhelmed as any of the other 240,000 American men who face this situation each year.

Listening to the doctor speak so calmly about mutilating my body seemed unreal. This was serious, permanent, no turning back stuff. I imagined being single at sixty-six, impotent and incontinent. I couldn't fathom it. On the other hand, I imagined dying slowly, agonizingly, of prostate cancer. Tough choices.

I weighed the odds Dr. Frederick had given me. Part of me wanted to halt the debate in my head and simply say, "Okay, let's get it over with!" I figured I probably wouldn't become both impotent and incontinent. I'll be okay, I told myself. Empty words. I was in deep denial. I could not perceive myself as anything other than what I had always been. I'd had surgeries before and came out fine.

Suddenly I heard myself saying, "Let's do it."

Surely I had PTSD, post-traumatic stress disorder. It doesn't take a war to cause PTSD. Mine began with the C-word—cancer—and now with Dr. Frederick's graphic descriptions of severing nerves and removing prostates, my PTSD was peaking. I am not the only one to react this way. Heart attacks and suicide rates double after men receive a diagnosis of prostate cancer. You can see why.

Fate rescued me from my urge to rush ahead. The hospital's prostate surgery schedule was backed up by three months. They would call me. I told them to move me up if there was a cancellation. I wanted to get it over with. Until then, I would just worry about how much cancer I had, whether it had already spread, whether I had made the right choice, whether I would be impotent or incontinent or both for the rest of my life, whether the surgery would save my life or ruin it ... and so on, around and around in my mind.

The next day, when I could think again, my mind was beset with questions. The main one: How could I make an informed decision about surgery and whether to sever the neurovascular bundles with so little information? Was there any other area of medicine that demanded such dire decisions with so little data? Here's one example: surgery was not recommended for men whose cancer had already spread beyond the gland. With my cancer score low (more on this in Chapter 3), spread wasn't likely, but we didn't know for sure. If I underwent surgery and metastases were found, then the surgery would be for naught, and I might be left impotent and incontinent anyway.

The whole process seemed so backward, so twentieth century. With good reason, I realized, because it is the same method we've used since 1990. Before then, prostate cancer assessment was even more primitive.

At this point I knew the following: the amount of prostate-specific antigen, or PSA, in my blood was high, at 15 nanograms per milliliter (ng/ml). A second test indicated a PSA level of 13.4 ng/ml. A normal level is 4 ng/ml or less. The elevated amounts of PSA in my blood meant surgery or radiation was necessary. My biopsy showed a low-grade cancer on the left side of my prostate gland. However, because biopsies frequently miss areas of cancer, the cancer could also be on the right side, and it may have already spread, too. We didn't really know.

On digital rectal exam, my prostate was smooth without any tumors palpable along the posterior side of the gland. This was good, yet the cancer could have spread in a different direction beyond the reach of the doctor's finger. The cancer could be huge on the forward, anterior side of the gland, and we would not know it.

Multiple prostate surgeons told me that these questions do not matter, because if the biopsy detects one area of cancer, other cancers likely exist elsewhere in the gland. Pathology examinations of men's prostate glands after surgical removal proved this. Therefore, the only reliable treatment was the complete removal of the prostate gland by prostatectomy.

This is what many urological surgeons say to their patients. In other words, the way the system works is that the doctors doing the biopsy and delivering the diagnosis are almost always urologists, many of whom are prostate surgeons. Hence, most men receive the recommendation one would expect from a prostate surgeon: prostatectomy. Yet more and more today, experts disagree with this approach. Not every diagnosis of prostate cancer requires aggressive treatment. As *Prostate Cancer Breakthroughs* will explain, other and often safer options do exist for the great majority of men diagnosed with prostate cancer.

If you have been recently diagnosed with prostate cancer, you might be thinking like I did—go ahead, cut out the damn cancer and be done with it. Yet even if you agree to surgery or radiation therapy, these are not always cures. The cure rate for these methods is around 75 percent. The cancer returns about 25 percent of the time. The other disturbing fact is that in doctors' efforts to eradicate all degrees of prostate cancer, prostate surgery or radiation is frequently recommended and performed on men who don't need these aggressive treatments. It is estimated that *of the nearly 100,000 American men who undergo radical treatment for prostate cancer each year, 85,000 do not actually need it.*

Where did I stand in this continuum? At this point, I didn't know. My work in medicine has included general medicine, pain research, psychiatry, psychopharmacology, and research into how to prevent the medication side effects that kill 150,000 and hospitalize one million Americans a year. What did I know about prostate cancer? Very little.

I asked Dr. Summers, "Can we do other tests to better clarify the picture? Perhaps an MRI?" This standard test is performed in the diagnostic workups of people who undergo surgery on their knees, lungs, hearts, brains, and just about everywhere else in the body. Why not the prostate?

"Unfortunately, MRIs are not helpful for prostate cancer," Dr. Summers explained. "The prostate is situated so deep in the pelvis, an MRI would not be able to give us a clear picture of the cancer."

Three weeks later, I was having lunch with a group of men, none of them doctors, but instead prostate cancer survivors. I learned from them that advanced diagnostic tests do indeed exist, and the fellows encouraged me to get them. These men had been where I was now, with a cancer diagnosis and a frightening lack of details.

I got the tests, and the results changed everything for me. Six weeks from the day I received my diagnosis of cancer, I finally knew what I had, where it was, and whether it had spread. I also learned that with my low grade cancer, I had time to deliberate about the best way to proceed. In fact, most men diagnosed with prostate cancer have time to obtain other tests and other opinions and to consider multiple treatment options. In the great majority of men, prostate cancer is slow-growing and slow to spread. There is usually time to obtain a thorough medical assessment, which most men with prostate cancer do not receive today. And there is time to consider other, less invasive treatments that can remove a localized cancer with far less damage, which most men today never hear about.

Unfortunately, when most men receive the diagnosis "cancer," their instinct is to decide quickly and try to get rid of it as soon as possible. Family members tend to think the same way. This is why so many men choose aggressive therapies such as prostatectomy or radiation treatment, each of which can cause serious, often lifelong damage to a man's sexual functioning or bladder control.

The problem with this approach is that it provides inadequate information and leads to the overtreatment of 85,000 men annually. This is how it usually goes: Elevated PSA levels and/or abnormal digital rectal exam will lead to a "blind" biopsy. If the biopsy is positive, you have cancer. If negative, another biopsy may be recommended. A cancer diagnosis will then lead to a recommendation for prostatectomy or radiation therapy.

Sometimes, men are given a third option: watchful waiting. "Watchful waiting" means waiting passively, which is unacceptable to most men. Men diagnosed with cancer want to do something. That's how I felt and why I placed myself on the surgery schedule. I did not want to spend the rest of my life watching and waiting and worrying about the cancer within me.

The root of the problem is that PSA levels and biopsy specimens are just not sufficient for making an accurate diagnosis of a man's prostate cancer. Yet these are the only tools that doctors have had for the last twenty-four years and that they continue to rely on today for recommending treatment options to 240,000 men a year. When you understand the inadequacy of PSA levels and biopsy results for making accurate diagnoses, coupled with doctors' determination to not let any man die from prostate cancer, it becomes clear why so much overtreatment occurs with this disease.

WHAT'S IN THIS BOOK

The day of "all or nothing"—radical treatment or no treatment—is ending. A better approach exists, and it is already being used in many of the most highly respected medical centers in the United States. The first few chapters of *Prostate Cancer Breakthroughs,* 1 through 6, will take you step by step through the new diagnostic process I recommend, with the tests you need to obtain and where you can get them. Chapter 7 describes genetically-based tests that are now available for improving the accuracy of prostate cancer biopsy interpretations, for determining the aggressiveness of a man's prostate cancer, and for identifying the most effective drugs for high-risk prostate cancer. The introduction of genetic tests represents another breakthrough, a quantum leap in diagnosing and treating prostate cancer, and many more genetic tests will be coming soon. Chapter 8 describes the C-11 PET/CT scan, a huge advancement in the early and accurate detection of metastatic prostate cancer.

If you follow the steps I outline, you will acquire a full picture of your disease: where it is, how large it is, and whether it has spread. These are essential questions that must be answered, yet most prostate cancer evaluations today do not answer them or even try to. This may be because many urologists are not aware of, or not convinced about, the new tests I describe, so your doctor may not mention them to you. Many of you will have to learn about these new methods on your own, from a support group, from other doctors, from web surfing, or from this book.

Most doctors are sincere, yet many are conservative and cautious about change. In researching my books and medical articles on medication side effects and how to prevent them, I learned long ago that new ideas take far too long to be accepted and implemented in the healthcare world. It can take ten to twenty years for a new idea or method to be verified by studies, accepted by medical leaders, approved by their governing associations, and reimbursed by insurance companies. If you rely on what your doctor tells you, you may not learn about and obtain the new tests you need to fully know what you have. Like me, you will be asked to make an all or nothing decision about treatment with insufficient information.

Once you know the nature and extent of your prostate cancer, making a decision about treatment becomes much easier. Part 2 discusses the broad range of twelve treatment options now available for men with prostate cancer. Chapter 9 covers the more aggressive therapies, including prostatectomy and four types of radiation therapies. Non-invasive therapies, such as medication treatment and active surveillance, are explained in Chapter 10. The chapter also discusses Xofigo, a treatment for men with metastatic bone disease, as well as finasteride (Proscar), a drug that obtained recent attention as a preventative for prostate cancer—but as you will see, there is a big downside. Finally, Chapter 11 will introduce you to focal therapies, a set of newly developed, minimally invasive techniques that aim to destroy the cancer while preserving as much of the prostate and surrounding areas as possible. The focal therapies I will discuss include cryotherapy, focal laser ablation, and high intensity focused ultrasound, or HIFU.

Section 3 contains two chapters. Chapter 12, "What Does Your Data Say?" explains how to organize your test results and make a decision about treatment. Chapter 13 offers thirty questions you can ask your doctor. The questions are listed in categories, some appropriate at your first visit, others for when you are making choices about diagnostic tests, and the remainder about treatment options. You may not need to ask every one of them, and there may be other questions you want to ask about the specifics of your individual case.

Prostate cancer is the most common cancer, other than skin cancer, in men. It can be a deadly disease, killing 30,000 men in the United States and 280,000 men worldwide each year. Because of this, every case of prostate cancer today is treated as deadly. Yet, approximately 85 percent of men with prostate cancer will not die of it, so treating every case as deadly has lead to massive overtreatment and much unnecessary, often permanent pain. In the past, we have treated every case as deadly because we have lacked a way of separating the dangerous cancers from the non-threatening ones. This is why performing surgery or radiation on so many men with prostate cancer has been the accepted course of treatment, until now.

With the new tests available today, this one-size-fits-all method is no longer necessary. As prostate cancer oncologist, Dr. Mark Scholz says:

Only about one out of seven men with the disease—perhaps 15 percent—are truly at risk. New research shows that there is an indolent variety of the disease that is not life-threatening, a type that can be safely monitored without immediate treatment. The tragedy is that most men don't know this.

How can you find out if you are in this 85 percent group that does not require depressive intervention? This is what *Prostate Cancer Breakthroughs* will explain.

The problem with the current medical method is that it hasn't caught up with the new advancements. To make the right decisions, you need to have the right information. For men with prostate cancer, no easy treatment options exist. All have risks. This is why it is so important for you to obtain all of the tests necessary for defining your cancer, and as many second opinions as you need to know all of your choices.

Medically and legally, you have a right to complete knowledge of your situation. This right is called *informed consent*, a right written into the medical code. I have written about this issue many times. The fact is that patients rarely obtain adequate informed consent, and this is certainly the case today for most men with prostate cancer. This is why I finally decided to write *Prostate Cancer Breakthroughs*, to pass along what I learned and to tell you about the new tests and treatments you can get today.

With the emergence of these new diagnostic tests and treatments, a renaissance in prostate cancer is quietly underway. It is a large wave, building slowly now, that will hit the shore in full force later in this decade. Just as the last decade saw great progress in the medical approach to breast cancer, major breakthroughs are now on the verge of irrevocably changing our approach to prostate cancer.

The problem for you, as it was for me, is that if you have been diagnosed with prostate cancer, you can't wait for the renaissance in prostate cancer to fully unfold. You can't wait for your doctor to get up to speed in a year or two or five. You have prostate cancer *now*, and must make decisions now.

I encourage you to take the time to now learn about these breakthrough options in prostate cancer diagnosis and treatment. The information can expand your choices and change the course of your care for the better, as it did mine.

TO THE WOMEN WHO ARE READING THIS BOOK

Thank you. You must care very much about your husband, boyfriend, father, son, brother, or other men in your life. This is so important, because one of every six men you know or have ever known will develop prostate cancer.

Women read health books more often than men. Some men with prostate cancer are avid readers, but many men just want to "deal with it," meaning action, meaning surgery or radiation. Some men need these aggressive therapies, but many more do not. Women reading this book can help steer their men to doctors who are informed about the new tests and treatments.

I greatly admire the work women have done during the past twenty years in raising awareness about breast cancer. Pink ribbons and breast cancer walks and fundraisers have done much to advance our knowledge about screening, testing, and treatment. Men have taken a lesson and prostate cancer support groups are growing, but we are far behind the ladies. I tip my hat.

In the great majority of cases of prostate cancer, there is time to obtain all of the useful diagnostic tests. With these, treatment decisions become easier, and for many men, safer. If some women have to push their men to follow the approach I have spelled out in *Prostate Cancer Breakthroughs*, you have provided your men a great service.

PART 1

A Better Diagnostic Approach

1

An Annual PSA Test

Nearly 30,000 men die each year from prostate cancer. This number will climb to roughly 55,000 over the next few years. Why? Because in recent years, government panels and medical associations have decided to no longer encourage PSA testing, a blood test that screens for prostate cancer and other complications, for any man, not even men with a higher risk for developing the disease. Hard to believe, isn't it?

How did this happen? First, the United States Preventative Services Task Force (USPSTF) recommended that doctors should abandon routine PSA testing in healthy men. Their reasoning: elevated prostate-specific antigen (PSA) levels in the blood lead to too much unnecessary treatment that causes serious, permanent harm. The task force was referring to the tens of thousands of unnecessary prostate biopsies, surgeries, and radiation therapies that doctors rush men toward based on high PSA levels. The USPSTF was correct about the rampant overtreatment of men with prostate cancer, but rejecting PSA testing was like ordering doctors to put their heads in the sand, as if the disease would simply disappear.

Then other prestigious organizations jumped on the anti-PSA bandwagon. This included the American Urological Association (AUA), which released an in-depth report instructing doctors to discontinue routine PSA testing for all men forty and older. For men at higher risk of prostate cancer, including those with a family history of it, as well as African-American men, the association meekly suggested that they discuss the benefits and risk of PSA testing with their doctors. Of course, having already been told by the AUA to dispense with routine PSA testing, this is probably what most doctors would tell these higher-risk men.

To me, the AUA's approach is not a solution. It is a retreat to the past, to the 1980s and earlier, before PSA testing began. It is true that thousands of men are rushed each year to radical, often damaging treatment when found to have elevated PSA levels. This is why I wrote this book: to inform men about the newer, better options that can allow them to obtain proper treatment when necessary while avoiding overtreatment.

A timely study was recently published in the *Journal of the American Medical Association* on this issue. The study demonstrated that the overtreatment of those diagnosed with prostate cancer is a serious problem affecting tens of thousands of men—and it is getting worse. Yet, the problem isn't the PSA test itself. The problem is a system that is tragically outdated in its approach to diagnosing and treating prostate cancer.

THE VITAL ROLE OF PSA TESTING

Abandoning PSA testing is shortsighted for another reason: it is irreplaceable today. No other test is as simple, convenient, inexpensive, and proven for the early detection of prostate cancer.

In the 1980s, before PSA testing commenced, the main method of diagnosis was from a digital rectal examination, an internal procedure in which the doctor checks the prostate gland for abnormalities, such as tumors or enlargement. By the time the cancer could be felt, it was often well advanced and frequently untreatable—and 50,000 men died annually from prostate cancer. After PSA testing began in the early 1990s, only 30,000 died annually. The test produced a breakthrough in the early detection of prostate cancer, saving thousands of men each year from slow, painful deaths. And yet, doctors are being told to stop performing PSA tests.

This is why many experts have spoken out against the new guidelines and in favor of continuing annual PSA testing. These experts warn that if routine PSA testing is abandoned, deaths from prostate cancer with rise significantly back to pre-PSA levels, which amounts to an additional 25,000 men's deaths a year from prostate cancer. I share this concern.

PSA Testing Saves Lives

PSA is shorthand for prostate-specific antigen, a protein released by prostate cells into the bloodstream. It's normal to have a small amount of PSA in your blood, up to 4 nanograms per millimeter (ng/ml). Abnormal PSA levels can be, but are not always, an early indication of prostate cancer.

A study published in the *New England Journal of Medicine* demonstrated unequivocally that PSA testing saves lives. This large study showed that the death rate from prostate cancer was reduced 29 percent in a group that received annual PSA testing in comparison to another group that did not. This study confirmed another study published a year earlier with similar results. These studies proved another astounding statistic: for every 1,000 men who receive PSA testing, one prostate cancer death is prevented. Somehow, the anti-PSA faction interprets this as a reason to stop annual PSA testing. Again, hard to believe.

The PSA test is inexpensive. One thousand men getting a PSA test costs about $22,000. I wish we could prevent a death from breast or lung or colon cancer so inexpensively. The cost of treating a man with terminal prostate cancer is many times more expensive. And first and foremost, beyond the numbers, what is the value of saving a man's life? Of saving 25,000 men's lives annually—the ones that could be prevented but won't be if we discontinue PSA testing.

As we see so often with large bureaucracies, the debate has boiled down to a numbers game. This is not a good way to make decisions that will affect the lives of tens of thousands of men. If the PSA test can save thousands of lives each year, how can we stop using it? Especially since the problem isn't the PSA test, but doctors who misinterpreted an elevated PSA result.

I once appeared on a National Public Radio show, during which a man called in to explain that his doctor had recommended radiation treatment for him. "Why did your doctor recommend radiation?" I asked. The man explained that his PSA level had increased from 1.7 to 2.5 ng/ml. Understand, these levels are normal, not even close to being abnormal. Although there was no medical basis to do so, the doctor performed a biopsy to look for cancer. The biopsy was normal. And although a more recent test indicated that his PSA level had dropped down to 1.9, the doctor nevertheless advised radiation treatment. I strongly advised the man to get a second opinion.

This case is an extreme example of doctors recommending biopsies and aggressive treatments with no sound medical basis. The regrettable thing is that it happens many times every day. Although urologists are seen as the expert on prostate issues, they treat many other conditions and are trained surgeons. Many are not experts on interpreting PSA results, and many recommend prostate biopsies when they aren't needed.

The PSA test wasn't the problem for the radio caller. His doctor was the problem. Discontinuing PSA testing doesn't solve it. Besides, it isn't always the doctors' fault. The PSA test is useful as a general indicator of a prostate concern, but it is often not accurate enough for making treatment decisions.

Being Proactive About PSA Levels

It is said that generals always prepare for the last war, not the next one. And so it seems with the doctors and medical organizations mulling over PSA testing today. The problem is, they have based their decision to dump the PSA test on statistics and treatment models from yesterday. These models we have been using for twenty-four years are the reasons why so many men are sent unnecessarily for aggressive, injurious treatments they don't need. With the new methods I describe throughout this book, the decision to halt routine PSA testing becomes short-sighted.

FINDING ALTERNATIVES TO THE PSA TEST

Everyone involved in treating prostate cancer knows that we need a test superior to the PSA, but until it arrives, the PSA is better than nothing. Meanwhile, research centers across the land are working on a PSA successor.

For example, the University of Michigan Health System offers a urine test called the *Mi-Prostate Score* (MiPS). Already validated on 2,000 samples, the PSA test and MiPS together were significantly more accurate than PSA alone for predicting prostate cancer. In addition, MiPS also predicted the level of aggressiveness of cancer. The test measures not only PSA, but also two genes that are specific for prostate cancer: TMPRSS2:ERG and PCA-3. MiPS is not 100 percent accurate, but may be a significant step forward from PSA alone.

University of California, Los Angeles is also developing an improved PSA test called *A-PSA*. In addition to PSA itself, which indicates prostate cancer cell activity, the test measures six antibodies the body created to fight prostate cancer. The A-PSA test is still undergoing study and not yet available clinically.

I am not recommending MiPS or any other advanced test now undergoing study to replace the PSA test. These new tests require the test of time, are expensive, and may not be covered by insurance. However, MiPS is available to the public, so you might want to check it out.

In coming years, men with repeatedly elevated PSA levels will be sent first for advanced diagnostic testing, not biopsies. For the first time, we will have—indeed, we already have!—tests that can sort out the men who need biopsies from those who don't. And the ones who need aggressive treatment from those who don't. These advances will greatly improve our accuracy when interpreting PSA results. This is why I encourage men to obtain PSA testing, because it can save your life!

John's doctor had stopped ordering annual PSA tests at regular check-ups. But as part of his pre-operative evaluation prior to a colonoscopy, John's proctologist tested his PSA levels. The result was 9 ng/ml, triple John's previous test three years earlier. The result showed prostate cancer that needed immediate treatment. The treatment should extend his years and maybe cure him. Without the PSA test, John would have been like the men before 1990, before PSA testing, whose cancer was often untreatable by the time it was discovered.

So if you are over fifty years old, or over forty if you are African-American, or have a family history of prostate cancer, my advice is to request a PSA test among your blood tests for your annual physical exam. Most doctors will do so if you ask. If you don't get an annual exam, ask your doctor to order a yearly PSA test. Obtaining PSA testing is important not only as a check for prostate cancer, but also to serve as a baseline for comparison with future PSA tests. And keep your own log of PSA test results.

IT'S NOT ALWAYS CANCER

Because prostate cancer cells produce more PSA than healthy cells, doctors get worried when a man has a PSA result above 4 ng/ml. Yet an elevated PSA level does not automatically mean prostate cancer. There are other factors that may cause your PSA to rise. And just because your PSA level is higher than 4 does not automatically mean you must rush to a prostate biopsy.

George, a member of my support group Chapter 4, always tells men to think of an elevated PSA level as similar to an engine light signal on your car's dashboard. When it lights up, it indicates a problem, but not specifically. Likewise, when your PSA level is elevated, it signals a problem, but not necessarily cancer.

Impact of Prostate Size on PSA Levels

As soon as Dr. Summers finished taking the biopsy samples, he inserted a small ultrasound device and measured my prostate size. The proper name for this procedure is a *Trans-Rectal Ultrasound*, or TRUS. My prostate measured at 75 cc, almost twice the average size for men my age. The ultrasound test was needed, but it should have been done two weeks earlier when Dr. Summers performed the digital rectal exam. When trying to interpret my high PSA levels, it would have been helpful to know that I had a 75 cc prostate gland. Even now, Dr. Summers did not explain how the size of my prostate affected the interpretation of my PSA numbers. It was my new support group friends who explained this and a lot more to me, changing the course of my care.

One common reason for an elevated PSA is the benign prostate hypertrophy (BPH), which means prostate enlargement, that commonly occurs as men age. The average prostate size of a man age forty-five is around 40 cc (cubic centimeters). A general rule of thumb is that the PSA level should not exceed 10 percent of the prostate size, or 4 ng/ml or less in a man with a 40 cc prostate gland. As the prostate size increases in some men as they age, their PSA levels may rise, too.

Some doctors do not know this and will recommend a biopsy if your PSA level is higher than 4 ng/ml. However, they need to gather more information first. Prostate biopsies can have serious complications (bleeding, infection), another reason one should be performed only if needed. A friend of mine was hospitalized because of a dangerous blood infection from a prostate biopsy. He almost died.

Using my own case as an example, in 1996, when I was fifty-one years old, my PSA level was 7.1. Most urologists would have immediately recommended a biopsy, but my cautious urologist understood that the high PSA could simply reflect my large prostate. He also knew I had had previous prostate infections, which can also elevate PSA levels. The next year, my PSA level was 3.7, within the normal range.

My urologist then ordered another test, the PCA-3, which measures a type of RNA (ribonucleic acid) that is released from prostate cancer cells, but not normal cells. This test can sometimes be helpful in determining whether an elevated PSA represents cancer. Often, however, the results are equivocal and therefore the PCA-3 is not widely used. My PCA-3 result was unhelpful. I watched my PSA levels gyrate up and down for many more years after.

Another factor that can elevate PSA levels is orgasm within 48 hours prior to a PSA test. So can riding a bicycle or exercise bike, a prostate exam or massage, or other activities that place pressure on the prostate gland, forcing more PSA material into the bloodstream.

If your prostate examination suggests you may have a prostate infection, it should be treated with antibiotics first, and a few weeks after treatment, you should have another PSA level drawn. If the antibiotics eradicated the infection, the PSA level may drop back into the normal range. One man's PSA level jumped from normal amounts one year to 37 ng/ml the next. His doctor thought he had an infection, prescribed antibiotics for three weeks, and the level returned to normal. The lesson is: don't panic if your PSA level is suddenly high.

It is important to understand that a single PSA test is not absolutely reliable. Levels of the prostate-specific antigen measured by the test can fluctuate. You can obtain a PSA test and then repeat it two weeks later, and the results may differ. The PSA test's accuracy as an indicator of prostate cancer is considered to be around 75 percent, not 100 percent. For this reason, interpreting PSA levels is not always cut and dried. Nevertheless, you should consider any rise in your PSA level significant until proven otherwise, and you should discuss with your doctor whether any of the other causes of an elevated PSA may apply to you.

Seven Common Causes of an Elevated PSA Level

- Enlarged prostate (benign prostate hypertrophy)

- Prostate infection

- Orgasm within 48 hours prior to testing

- Pressure on the prostate gland (such as bicycle riding, exercise biking, prostate massage)

- Laboratory error

- Prostate cancer

A major part of the problem of overtreatment is the current method of reliance on PSA levels and biopsy results to make treatment decisions. Until now, doctors haven't had much choice. But PSA and biopsy results are not accurate enough and do not provide enough specific information for doctors to make accurate treatment decisions. We know this now, but the old system continues to prevail: of the 50,000 prostatectomies performed each year for prostate cancer, over 40,000 are unnecessary. The numbers are similar for radiation therapy.

Abnormal PSA Tests

Some men are biopsied based on a single, slightly elevated PSA test. If the biopsy does not reveal cancer, the urologist may do further biopsies just to be sure cancer hasn't been missed. One expert tells of a man who was biopsied five times on a single elevated PSA test. The biopsies never found cancer. Turns out, his prostate was huge, at 164 cc, compared to the average prostate size of 40 cc. The man's large prostate explained his markedly elevated PSA. A repeat test in this man may have shown a lower PSA level.

At its highest, my PSA level was 8.4 ng/ml. Yet it had been bouncing up and down between 1.6 and 7.2 for fifteen years. Was this just another upward bounce or a sign of something more serious? I was worried. My urologist and I agreed to delay a biopsy until we repeated the PSA test. The next result was 4.6, low for me compared to my other PSA results over recent years. We decided to postpone a biopsy.

Time slipped away, and I did not check the PSA until two years later—poor judgment on my part! My PSA was 15.3, nearly double my previous high. I knew this was serious. Not even my large prostate could explain a result this high. I had another PSA test, and it came back high, too: 13.4. My prostate size was 75 cc, which inflated the results somewhat, but even when I corrected for this, my PSA levels were still too high. This was a red flag I could not ignore. A doubling of PSA numbers within two years is a worrisome sign. That's when my urologist used the B-word: biopsy.

THE IMPORTANCE OF A DIGITAL RECTAL EXAM

By the time you are reading this book, you probably have had a digital rectal exam (DRE). If not, and your PSA level is high, a DRE should be done. The doctor will insert a gloved finger into your rectum and feel your prostate. Before he does so, make sure he spreads plenty of lubricant on your anus. Then tell him to give you a few seconds' warning, take some deep breaths and exhale slowly, thereby relaxing your muscles as the doctor inserts his finger. Keep taking slow, deep breaths to keep your muscles relaxed until the DRE is over. It only takes about 20 seconds.

Why is the DRE important? First, the doctor can feel the surface of the posterior aspect of your prostate gland, feeling for any irregularities, bumps, or elevations. Eighty-five percent of prostate cancers occur in the posterior area. A prostate with a smooth posterior wall is a good sign. Irregularities are important because they may indicate cancer.

With a DRE, your doctor can get a sense of the overall size of your prostate. If your prostate is elevated, it is important to get more precise information. Before starting the DRE, ask your doctor to also perform an ultrasound test (known as a TRUS, for transrectal ultrasound) that will accurately measure the size of your prostate. Most urologists have this device.

It is estimated that 50 percent of prostate biopsies in the United States are performed because of elevated PSA levels in men with benign prostatic hypertrophy (enlargement). This is why it is important to know your actual prostate size. If it is large enough to explain your elevated PSA level, you may not need a biopsy.

A year after my initial prostate cancer diagnosis, my DRE was normal, but my PSA numbers had been consistently high. Even if I factored in the other possible causes of my elevated amounts of PSA, they were not enough to explain the levels of 13 and 15 ng/ml. There was no escaping the fact that I needed a biopsy.

2

Blind Biopsy, Targeted Biopsy, or No Biopsy?

Why is a prostate biopsy necessary? A biopsy is the only way to directly examine prostate tissue and to determine whether cancer is present. Thus, a prostate biopsy is essential for men whose PSA levels or digital rectal examination suggest the possibility of prostate cancer.

If cancer is found, the pathologist will study the tissue, identify the type of prostate cancer, and grade the level of aggressiveness. No other tests can provide this information. This is why the biopsy is such an important procedure in the diagnosis of prostate cancer.

THE BLIND BIOPSY

In my case, I went ahead with the biopsy because it was clear from my PSA numbers that one was needed. In retrospect, I should have waited for further testing, but at the time I did not know there were other tests that could guide the biopsy needle to the most suspicious areas of my prostate. Equally important, I was anxious to learn if I had cancer. You may feel the same way. Most men do.

Dr. Summers did a good job. A prostate biopsy is unpleasant, but mine was not as painful as I expected. He numbed the area and took fourteen samples from various areas of my prostate, following a deliberate pattern. The one problem with my biopsy was that it was "blind"— there was no way to know for certain whether cancer was present on my prostate or not.

"Amazingly, prostate cancer is being diagnosed today almost exactly the way it was twenty-five years ago. Prostate biopsies are performed in a systematic but blind manner," says Daniel Margolis M.D., Department of Radiology, UCLA.

By "systematic," Dr. Margolis means that today's standard biopsy is performed following a grid pattern that was developed a couple of decades ago. This is the best most doctors can do because they have no tests indicating where the cancer might actually be. When Dr. Summers performed my biopsy, he was shooting in the dark. This is why blind biopsies miss about 20 percent of prostate cancers. Many of these men will undergo a second or third blind biopsy, because their doctors want to be as sure as possible that they have not missed prostate cancer. Some doctors are so concerned about missing cancer, they perform a procedure known as a *saturation biopsy*, in which they take twenty to thirty prostate samples while the man is under anesthesia.

The Downside of a Prostate Biopsy

For urologists, a prostate biopsy is standard procedure, part of their daily practice. It is no big deal. Dr. Summers did warn me about the possibility of excess bleeding or infection, but I was not warned that these adverse effects could be severe enough to require hospitalization, mostly for blood infection, in 2 to 4 percent of men after biopsy. One in a thousand men die.

Another significant risk of prostate biopsies is currently under-appreciated. With 1.2 million prostate biopsies done annually in the United States, tens of thousands of low-risk cancers are discovered. In fact, by age fifty, 30 percent of men have cancer cells in their prostate. By age eighty, 50 percent have prostate cancer cells. These cancers are usually low-risk and will not harm the great majority of the men. Yet many of these men receive aggressive treatment anyway. In the United States, a diagnosis of prostate cancer leads to aggressive treatment 80 percent of the time, even in men who are diagnosed with low-risk cancer, the type that experts agree can be followed without invasive treatment. This method of observation is known as *active surveillance* (Chapter 10).

All of this confusion and overtreatment are the result of one problem: our inability to reliably differentiate dangerous prostate cancers from non-threatening ones. Until now, if your blind biopsy revealed cancer, your doctors had to assume you had a life-threatening cancer unless proven otherwise. This is why so many men are treated aggressively (often over-aggressively) with prostatectomy or radiation therapy. The great fear of urologists is to assume a cancer was non-threatening, only to have it spread and kill a man. PSA levels and biopsy results are simply not adequate for making accurate treatment recommendations for thousands of men. With few tools to tell the doctor otherwise, all cancers had to be considered high-risk. If I were a urologist, I might feel the same.

If you have any question about whether a biopsy is necessary, do not hesitate to get a second opinion, preferably from a urologist in an unaffiliated office or health system or a prostate oncologist.

THE TARGETED BIOPSY

The traditional method of performing prostate biopsies is already beginning to change. Now in selected medical centers, for the first time, we have tests that allow us to see inside the prostate gland. *Targeted biopsies* are being performed at many hospitals and cancer centers using new technologies such as the DCE-MRI (Chapter 5) and the color Doppler ultrasound (Chapter 6). The targeted biopsy is a safer and more accurate method than today's standard blind biopsy. These new tests can locate areas of possible prostate cancer within the gland itself. If done before your biopsy, the tests can inform your doctor where to direct the biopsy needles. The advantages of this new type of guided biopsy is that fewer needles are needed, trauma to the prostate gland is reduced, and accuracy of results is improved. As doctors begin to learn about this method, the targeted biopsy will become the standard of care. This will make today's blind biopsies and saturation biopsies under anesthesia things of the past.

MRI-guided biopsies are being implemented at several top medical centers in the United States (for a list of these medical centers, see the *Resources* section at the back of this book). Samir Taneja, M.D., of the NYU Langone Medical Center, states, "The prostate remains the only organ in the body that doctors will biopsy without good imaging. In every other organ, biopsies are directed by imaging to a specific location." The doctor added that at his medical center, "We now routinely do MRI imaging on every newly diagnosed prostate cancer patient to help us in both assessing risk and directing treatment."

Biopsy or No Biopsy?

Robert, a sixty-seven-year-old former surgical assistant at a major hospital and now an artist, told me he had been following his PSA levels for many years.

"It used to be 1.75 ng/ml, but gradually rose up to 3.5. Last March, it jumped to 8.4. The doctor said I needed a biopsy. I was shook up. From my former work, I had learned that one should not rush into surgical interventions," Robert explained. "Then I found your book. It really enlightened me. I have had two severe prostate infections in previous years and suspect I still have some inflammation down there. I took some anti-inflammatory supplements and told my doctor I wanted to repeat the PSA test before we made any decisions. A month later, the PSA was 3.4."

"With your previous prostate infection," I said, "you should be cautious about letting a doctor biopsy your prostate unless there are no other alternatives. You are high-risk for a prostate infection after biopsy. Taking antibiotics before and after the biopsy may protect you, but may not. Four percent of men develop infections severe enough to require hospitalization after prostate biopsies, and nearly one in 1,000 die."

I recommended Robert take the advanced diagnostic tests I discuss in Part 1. These would determine whether a biopsy was necessary. "If your PSA jumps up again, do the tests first, before anyone sticks a biopsy needle in you," I told him. "The tests can tell whether there is anything worth biopsying."

One of my patients in my psychiatry and psychopharmacology practice asked me about his father, age seventy-six, who had undergone repeated annual biopsies of his prostate gland: "They diagnosed him with prostate cancer several years ago, but told him it is low-grade and will probably never harm him. As part of the surveillance, his doctors required a prostate biopsy once a year. My father dreads them. He says they are very painful. He would do almost anything to avoid a biopsy."

Most experts now agree that prostate biopsies are performed far too often. Does this mean that they should never be done? Biopsies are essential for accurately identifying and grading prostate cancer. My criticism of our current method of biopsying men suspected of having prostate cancer is not about the biopsy itself, but that approximately half of the 1.2 million prostate biopsies performed annually in the United States are unnecessary. For men like my patient's father who require an annual biopsy to monitor prostate cancer, the new tests may reduce the necessity for many of these biopsies. After all, if the DCE-MRI does not show any change in the man's cancer or any new areas of suspicion, and if the PSA tests have remained level, a repeat biopsy may not be needed.

You May Need a Prostate Biopsy if:

- An abnormality is felt on digital rectal examination.

- Your PSA level is repeatedly high.

- Your PSA level is 4.0 or less, but the level has doubled in one year or less.

- Your abnormal PSA levels cannot be adequately explained by an enlarged prostate, prostate infection, or other factors.

- Tests such as the DCE-MRI or color Doppler ultrasound identify areas in your prostate suggestive of cancer.

I have come to believe that whenever a doctor recommends a prostate biopsy for a man, other tests, especially the new DCE-MRI, should be performed first, if possible. These tests can tell the doctor and the man whether there are any suspicious areas in the prostate worthy of a biopsy. If the tests reveal suspicious areas in the prostate gland, then the biopsy can be targeted towards these areas instead of being done blindly. A targeted biopsy is much more likely to retrieve adequate amounts of suspicious tissue and to answer key questions about diagnosis. Fewer biopsy cores may be required overall, thereby reducing the pain of the procedure, the trauma to the prostate gland, and the risk of post-biopsy bleeding, infection, or other adverse effects. And if the advanced prostate DCE-MRI shows no suspicious areas, then the biopsy may be withheld altogether.

If you need a prostate biopsy because of high PSA levels or other reasons, and you cannot get a guided biopsy, then get the blind one that is more commonly available today. One man spent a year trying to learn about the targeted biopsy. Meanwhile, his PSA level went from 6 to 9 to 11 ng/ml. Even when I encouraged him to obtain a biopsy as soon as possible, he wanted to put it off a few more months so he could take a long vacation. Apparently he did not realize the worrisome significance of his rising PSA levels. Maybe he was in denial. The moral is: if you need a biopsy, get it. A targeted biopsy is preferable if you can obtain it, but if not, get a blind one.

3

Assessing Your Findings

You have now finished the standard diagnostic tests for prostate cancer: PSA levels, digital rectal exam, and biopsy. If you are following the standard model, you will be asked to make a decision about treatment. In the standard model, your choices are all or nothing: prostatectomy or radiation therapy, which destroy the entire prostate gland, or watchful waiting, which amounts to doing practically nothing. If you have advanced prostate cancer, your choices may differ, such as radiation therapy plus hormone suppression therapy or chemotherapy. As you can see, there are no happy choices in the old model.

Yet whatever your situation, you may have more diagnostic and treatment options than you have been told. The first step involves assessing the diagnostic information you already have. The first question is: based on the Gleason score, *what grade of cancer do I have?* If, like me, your Gleason score is 6, you may fit into the low or intermediate-risk group.

Then the key question is, *which risk category?* The survival statistics between the two groups differ significantly, and so do the treatment options. For example, if you are in the low-risk category, active surveillance may be a safe choice and also allows you to avoid surgery or radiation. If you are in the intermediate risk group, surgery or radiation or other invasive treatments become more likely options.

PSA FINDINGS

If your PSA results are between 4 and 10 ng/ml, you may fit into the low-risk group. My case was atypical in that my two PSA results were 15.3 and 13.4 ng/ml. These numbers were significantly elevated, well over the 10 ng/ml ceiling for the low-risk category. I was in the intermediate risk category, defined as PSA levels between 10 to 20. Even if I factored in my large prostate, I was still in the intermediate-risk group, just slightly above the low-risk ceiling. If your PSA levels are above 20, you may be in the high-risk group.

NUMBER OF BIOPSY CORES POSITIVE FOR CANCER

Another important factor in risk assessment is how many cancerous cores are obtained from biopsy. Usually twelve cores are taken, and inclusion in the low-risk group requires zero to two cores (zero to 17 percent) positive for cancer. Sometimes fewer or more than twelve cores are taken. My urologist took fourteen cores, and four were positives (29 percent). Yet one core contained just one percent cancer, hardly worth counting, I decided. Three cores out of fourteen (21 percent)—did this equal two cores out of twelve? Not quite. Again, I was in the intermediate-risk category, which requires three to six cores out of twelve to have cancer, but at the low end of the category. If more than 50 percent of your cores have cancer, this would place you in the high-risk category.

DIGITAL RECTAL EXAM FINDINGS

A normal digital rectal exam is required for inclusion in the low-risk group. Inclusion in the intermediate-risk group requires a normal DRE or a single, palpable small nodule. Multiple nodules or one large nodule would place you in the high-risk group.

GRADING YOUR PROSTATE CANCER

Of the fourteen biopsy specimens that Dr. Summers took from my prostate, four showed cancer, all on the right side of the gland. The pathology report summarized my cancer state as "T1c." The "T1" meant that the cancer was found within the prostate via surgical intervention. The T1 grade also implies that the doctor was not able to feel the cancer on the digital rectal exam (DRE).

Prostate Cancer Grades

- The subtypes of the **T1** grade are:

    - **T1a**—The cancer was found unexpectedly during a pathology examination of tissue removed from surgery for an enlarged prostate.

- **T1b**—Found unexpectedly as above, the cancer involves more than 5 percent of the removed tissue.

- **T1c**—Cancer found on biopsy.

■ The next higher grade, **T2**, means that the cancer was found during a DRE:

- **T2a**—Cancer involves less than 50 percent of one lobe of the prostate.

- **T2b**—Cancer exists in more than 50 percent of one lobe of the prostate.

- **T2c**—Cancer exists in both lobes of the prostate.

■ When the DRE indicated that the cancer has spread outside of the prostate gland, the stage is **T3**:

- **T3a**—Cancer has spread outside of the prostate on one side.

- **T3b**—Cancer has spread outside of the prostate on both sides.

- **T3c**—Cancer has spread into one or both seminal vesicles, two pouches that hold semen located just above the prostate gland.

■ The **T4** stage means that on DRE, the cancer was found to have invaded other nearby structures:

- **T4a**—Cancer was found in the bladder, urinary sphincter, or rectum.

- **T4b**—Cancer has spread to other structures such as lymph nodes, pelvic wall, or muscles.

THE GLEASON SCORE

The *Gleason Scoring System* is used to describe the appearance of the prostate cancer cells when viewed under a microscope. The Gleason score is determined by examining prostate tissue retrieved from biopsy. The pathologist evaluates the size, shape, and appearance of the normal prostate cells and cancer cells, and then classifies the type of cancer and its level of abnormality. The score rates the degree of abnormality and apparent aggressiveness of the cancer cells. Low-risk cancers look similar in many ways to normal prostate cells, whereas high-risk cancer cells have lost the normal organization of prostate cells and appear aggressive.

The total Gleason score represents the sum of two grades. The first is the grade given to the most prominent pattern of cancer cells in your biopsy specimens. The second grade is given to the second most common pattern of cancer cells. Sometimes the pathologist sees only one cancer pattern, but sometimes more than one pattern is present. Prostate cancer cells with a mild degree of abnormality are given a Gleason score of 3. Cancer cells with a high degree of abnormality receive a score of 5.

A Gleason score of 6 or less is required for inclusion in the low-risk group, a Gleason 7 for the intermediate-risk category, and a Gleason 8 or above for high-risk. Most men whose biopsies show prostate cancer receive Gleason scores of 6 to 10, representing less aggressive to more aggressive degrees of cancer, respectively. A Gleason score of 6 indicates a consistent pattern of low-grade cancer, scoring a grade of 3 on both Gleason assessments. Gleason 6 is the most common score for newly discovered cases of prostate cancer.

Another common Gleason score is 7. This score is a bit more complicated in that it sometimes indicates a 4 for the most common pattern of cancer cells and a 3 for the next most common pattern. However, a Gleason 7 can also indicate a 3+4 pattern. The distinction is important. A 3+4 means the most common cancer pattern is 3, the lowest grade, whereas a 4+3 means the most common pattern is 4, an intermediate grade cancer. These distinctions can be significant when making treatment decisions with your doctor.

My Gleason score of 6 indicated that my cancer had a low level of risk. Still, cancer was clearly identified. A Gleason 6 score is less worrisome than higher scores, yet it is still cancer and can kill. Dr. Summers, my urologist, urged me to consider surgery or radiation as soon as possible. Thinking these were my only alternatives, a week later I met with Dr. Frederick, the prostate surgeon.

The Meaning of Gleason Scores

Gleason grades can range from 1 to 5 for each side of the prostate gland; then the top two scores are added together for the final Gleason score (2 to 10).

What Is Your Gleason Score?

- **Gleason 1:** Cancer cells look almost normal.

- **Gleason 2:** Cancer cells appear almost normal but early cancerous changes are apparent.

- **Gleason 3:** Some cells are clearly cancerous to a mild degree and have some degree of irregularity.

- **Gleason 4:** Many cells display cancerous abnormalities and are crowding out normal cells.

- **Gleason 5:** No normal prostate cells remain, and cancer cells are highly abnormal.

Because the Gleason scoring of the cancer in your biopsy cores is so crucial, some experts recommend always getting a second opinion. Gleason scoring is a subjective process that depends entirely on the eye and experience of the pathologist. Studies have shown that variations can occur in Gleason scoring from one pathologist to another, even when they evaluate the same specimens.

WHAT IS THE RISK LEVEL OF YOUR PROSTATE CANCER?

The severity of your prostate cancer depends on a combination of the factors discussed in this chapter. These include:

Low Risk

- PSA less than 10 ng/ml
- Less than three biopsy cores (out of twelve) with cancer
- Zero cores with more than 50 percent cancer
- Clinical stage of T1 or T2a
- Gleason score 6 or less
- Digital rectal exam normal

Intermediate Risk

- PSA 10 to 20 ng/ml
- Three to six (out of twelve) biopsy cores with cancer
- Clinical state T2b or Gleason score 7
- DRE normal or small nodule

High Risk

- PSA above 20 ng/ml

- More than 50 percent of biopsy cores with cancer

- Clinical state T2c or Gleason score above 7

- DRE reveals large or multiple nodules

HEADING FOR TREATMENT?

Hopefully, your findings place you into one of the well-defined groups, so that you can determine your next step. Even then, it is not always that simple. Or perhaps you have findings that fit different risk groups. My PSA and biopsy cores said intermediate risk, but my Gleason score and normal DRE said low risk. This raised questions for me, but not for Dr. Frederick, the surgeon.

"Two high PSA levels, four cores—this places you squarely in the intermediate risk category," he said. "You are not low risk or a candidate for active surveillance. You need surgery."

I heard him. After all, Dr. Frederick had done more than 500 prostatectomies. He had vast experience in removing prostate glands and then, after the gland was dissected by pathologists, seeing how much cancer they had actually contained. In many cases, far more cancer is discovered in prostate glands when dissected following a prostatectomy than initially indicated by the biopsy. This is why urologists lean towards aggressiveness in recommending surgery. They want to be sure to get all of the cancer right away.

I understood Dr. Frederick's point of view. The only findings that argued otherwise were my normal DRE, which didn't mean much once the biopsy found cancer, and the Gleason 6 score. The Gleason 6 was the most important single finding of all, because it indicated that my cancer was early and slow growing. This alone, however, could not guarantee my safety.

Trying to clarify my picture further, Dr. Summers ordered bone and CT scans. These tests can be helpful in high risk cases, for they can determine whether the prostate cancer has spread to bone, lymph nodes, or other tissues near the prostate. They are used most often with men who have PSA levels above 20 or Gleason scores indicating aggressive cancers.

(These scans are now being superseded by a new, more accurate test, the Carbon-11 PET/CT scan—see Chapter 8).

My scans were negative, fortunately, but this did not change my risk status. I was at intermediate risk, although in my opinion, not by much. At this point, I had pretty much decided on treatment. The only question was: prostatectomy or some form of radiation therapy?

Just then, new, hopeful ideas emerged from an unexpected source. No matter whether you are low, intermediate, or high risk, you must check out this source before making any final decisions.

4

The Support Group

As mentioned earlier, in their haste to rid themselves of prostate cancer, many men rush right into treatment. You may be tempted to do so, but consider this: Neither surgery nor radiation is a guarantee of cure, and with either treatment you run the risk of serious, permanent side effects. Besides, because prostate cancer is very slow growing in most cases, you have time to do some research on your own.

Many men do not realize that they don't have a full picture of their disease. Many accept at face value what their urologist tells them and never consider obtaining a second opinion. Many urologists are good doctors, but they are surgeons and are trained to look at things from a surgical perspective. With this disease, second opinions can be helpful and sometimes quite enlightening.

Unfortunately, most men do not bother going to a support group. Why? Most men do not think they need it. For some men, the idea of seeking support implies emotional weakness. This is what I thought after being diagnosed. Yet I went anyway and learned that a good support group can offer far more than a place to share your concerns and exchange consolations. It can also provide important information you will not get anywhere else.

MY UNOFFICIAL SUPPORT GROUP

Two weeks after meeting with the surgeon, I sat down for lunch with seven prostate cancer veterans. Over several meetings, this small support group played a pivotal role in increasing my knowledge of my disease, which in turn decisively altered my decision about treatment. Without this group, I would have had a prostatectomy. From the questions they raised and the tests they told me about, I realized there was far more diagnostic work to be done and far more treatment options to consider.

Fortune played a role in my meeting this group. Dr. Summers sent me to a nurse specialist who did a good job of providing information about the standard treatment options, answering my questions, and then suggesting the hospital's prostate cancer support group. Because it was December and the group was not meeting that month, she also told me of a nearby independent support group, the Informed Prostate Cancer Support Group (IPCSG). I had pretty much decided on a prostatectomy, and I had spoken to two men who had done well with the surgery, so I thought I had enough information. Why should I bother finding out what other men had to say?

Still, knowing that the more information I had about prostate cancer, the better, I called IPCSG and left a message. The next day, I received a call from a leader of the organization. IPCSG was not meeting in December, either. However, there was a small group of men who met informally for lunch once a week. Although all of the men were members of IPCSG, their small group was not formally affiliated with the organization. I had lunch with them the following week.

Many prostate cancer support groups serve as a meeting place where men can share information and tips about how to handle the long-term impacts from surgery or radiation therapy. These groups serve a useful purpose. However, my little group functions differently. Most of the three to ten men who show up for lunch each week, as well as others who drop in occasionally, are past the recovery stage. Some have had prostatectomies, others radiation. One has had both. Some men continue to struggle with problems of impotence or incontinence, others with recurrence of their cancer, and still others are coping with the side effects from their testosterone-suppressing or anti-cancer drugs.

The meetings consist of the men updating each other on their status, latest test results, or treatments they are considering or already receiving. They also spend time discussing new information in news reports, online, or in the medical literature. These are educated and assertive men, who, before retiring, held important and demanding jobs. For their work, they had to know their stuff, and they now know their stuff about prostate cancer. They spend considerable time reading current studies, contacting institutions and experts around the country, and obtaining details about new therapies that go beyond what we find in typical public relations press releases.

The fellows in the group were the first to explain how my large prostate and my earlier prostate infections could contribute to my high PSA levels, information my urologist never explained. They were the ones who pointed out that the huge jump in my PSA level of 13.4 to 22 ng/ml a month later, which worried me greatly, was probably due to my biopsy, another fact my urologist neglected to explain. And they answered my questions about what more could be done to better define the size and location of my prostate cancer, and determine if it had already spread.

These men told me about the latest diagnostic methods such as the advanced prostate DCE-MRI and color Doppler ultrasound, tests that can identify and define prostate cancer within the gland itself. My doctor never mentioned these essential tests, because most urologists do not know about them, or there are no nearby facilities that offer them.

Most of all, Gene and my other support group buddies helped me put things in perspective. They reminded me again and again that I had time to check things out. I was Gleason 6, wasn't I? Most prostate cancer grows slowly, especially G6, so there was time for me to learn more about my disease and the various treatment options. There was time for me to be thorough, so when I made my treatment decision, there would be no "If only I had …"

PASSING IT FORWARD

Every month or so, newly diagnosed men appear at our lunch meetings. Like me, these men are worried and confused about how to make vital decisions regarding their prostate cancer. We answer their questions and impart information as best we can. None of us are experts, so our goal is not to direct their cases or make decisions for them, but to merely let them know their options for diagnosis and treatment, something they rarely obtain in full elsewhere.

Every man's case is different. You may not be interested in joining an ongoing support group, but I think it is helpful to take the opportunity at least once to speak with men who have previously walked the path you are now walking. Most men get a lot of support from family and friends, and useful information from their doctors, but there is nothing like speaking with men who have been through it.

Different support groups offer different formats. You may find that you prefer a formal, moderated group that provides speakers, allowing you to do more listening than interacting. Or you may feel more at ease with a group of men in a casual environment. No matter the kind you choose, a support group can offer practical advice and tips, resources to help you better manage your situation, and feedback about the doctors the men have seen.

Some men join us for lunch one time and do not return. That's okay, because there are no expectations or obligations. We keep meeting because we enjoy it, we like helping newly diagnosed men and each other, we're always coming across new science to discuss, and we all share a chronic condition that can change and evolve over time—and all that aside, we like and respect each other. The fields of prostate cancer diagnosis, testing, and treatment are evolving so fast now that our group never suffers from a lack of issues to talk about. And with so many men keeping an eye on developments, we can keep up with things as well as, or sometimes better than, many of the doctors.

That said, I hope you decide to try a prostate cancer support group. Whether you go once or several times, learn as much as you can from the men. Add their input to the information you have received from your doctors, your reading, and other sources. When it is time for you to make a treatment decision, your thoroughness will serve you well.

The Informed Prostate Cancer Support Group's website, ipcsg.org, is a great resource where you can learn more about the group's purpose, articles and links to research on the disease, and much more. For more information, see the *Resources* section at the back of this book.

5

The Dynamic, Contrast-Enhanced MRI

You are probably familiar with the test known as the MRI (magnetic resonance imaging). MRI technology employs strong magnetic fields and radio frequency impulses translated by computers into highly detailed pictures of internal body structures. The MRI was one of the great advances in medicine in the late twentieth century, and the technology keeps evolving and improving today. Some experts, including me, believe MRI technology has advanced to the point of use for prostate cancer.

Although MRIs have long been used as vital diagnostic tests for orthopedic, gastrointestinal, pulmonary, brain, and other conditions, MRI technology has not been useful for identifying cancer in the prostate gland in the past. Because the gland sits so deeply in the pelvis, and because with PSA testing prostate cancers are initially very small, MRIs have been unable to obtain a clear enough picture to differentiate prostate cancer from normal prostate tissue—until now. A new type of MRI known as the Dynamic Contrast-Enhanced MRI, or DCE-MRI, is changing the way we diagnose and treat many kinds of cancer, including prostate cancer.

"I think imaging is really the future in cancer care in every organ," says Samir Taneja, M.D. "Up until recently, imaging did not allow us to see prostate cancer. These cancers are microscopic, so seeing them on an X-ray or film of any sort is almost impossible. One of the reasons the surgeons remove the whole prostate gland is because we haven't known where the cancer really is. If we can now treat patients through image guidance, then our treatments could be far less radical in some patients than they are now."

A BREAKTHROUGH TECHNOLOGY

The DCE-MRI machines are newer, wider, and not as deep as the old, coffin-like versions. A contrast material, gadolinium, is injected intravenously before the exam begins. The blood vessels of cancerous prostate tissue absorb gadolinium more readily than normal prostate cells, thereby making the cancerous tissue visible.

In some centers, a sensor is placed inside the rectum to provide further clarity to the picture. This type of MRI is known as an *endorectal* MRI. Another type is the *multiparametric* MRI, which provides more data than the others. In my experience, the differences between these tests are slight, and any of them can be very helpful in identifying cancer in the prostate gland. For the remainder of this book, I will refer to the test as the DCE-MRI, although the specific test used by different centers may vary.

You will have to be specific about the DCE-MRI with your doctor, because many health systems use the standard MRIs to rule out metastases near the prostate gland, but this older MRI cannot see into the gland itself. Many doctors are not aware of the new DCE-MRIs and will not think you mean the latter. A friend of mine went to an Ivy League medical center. He had a high PSA and asked the doctor for a DCE-MRI. The doctor did not know the difference, and sent him for a standard MRI.

The rating of my DCE-MRI machine was 1.5 Tesla. *Tesla* is the measurement of the magnificent quality of a MRI machine's magnetic field. Until recently, 1.5 Tesla was the highest strength available. New 3.0 Tesla MRI machines, with their greater magnification of microscopic structures, are now being used at many medical centers. However, the resolution of the MRI machine is not the only key factor in identifying prostate cancer. One of my group members received a 3.0 Tesla MRI at the university, but it could not identify his prostate cancer because it lacked the sophisticated software needed to do so. Several centers now possess advanced prostate MRI 3.0 Tesla machines, and you should choose this if possible. If not available, a 1.5 Tesla MRI will usually do.

I received the results from the test the next day. The radiologist wrote:

> The test identified a right-sided and posterior peripheral zone tumor, small but more than one cc in size. No extracapsular [beyond the prostate] extension into the seminal vesicles or pelvic metastases.

I sighed with relief. These were the kind of details about my cancer that I had been seeking: size, location, and signs of spread. The cancer was not tiny, but small nonetheless, about the size of the tip of my pinkie. It was in the right lobe of the gland. The left lobe was clean. This matched the biopsy findings, which found cancer in the right but not the left. There was no sign of spread to the edge of the prostate gland, seminal vesicles, lymph nodes, bone, or elsewhere.

Finally, I had a complete picture of my cancer. This made a huge difference for me, and it can do so for you and most men with newly diagnosed prostate cancer.

How Reliable is the DCE-MRI?

Just as PSA levels and biopsy findings are not entirely reliable, the findings with a DCE-MRI are not 100 percent reliable, either. Experts rate the accuracy at 85 to 90 percent. This is very good, but the DCE-MRI can miss some cancers, especially small ones, those below five millimeters in diameter. These cancers could cause trouble eventually, but with close follow-up and repeated tests, these small cancers should be identifiable before becoming a problem.

More and more, I see proof building in support of the prostate MRI. One study concluded: "DCE-MRI can accurately identify intraprostatic [within the prostate] cancer foci. Possible applications are guidance for biopsies, selection of patients for watchful waiting, and focal treatment planning."

Dr. Peter Scardino, chief of urology at Memorial Sloan-Kettering Hospital, which specializes in treating cancer, is known for his great skill in performing prostatectomies in the treatment of prostate cancer. About the DCE-MRI, he writes in his book, "It has been proven to be the best means we have today for seeing a cancer in the prostate."

When asked how he uses the DCE-MRI results, Dr. Scardino replied, "If I don't see anything on an MRI, it helps reassure me you probably don't have a large, life-threatening cancer." Then he added an important statement: "I don't rely just on the digital rectal exam, the PSA, the biopsy results, or the MRI. But if we put all that information together, we can get a pretty good idea of what's going on."

Exactly! As it is in many areas of medical endeavor, the basic method is to obtain all tests that can help define the problem. For you and other men with prostate cancer, this means PSA levels, DRE, biopsy, and a DCE-MRI. For me, this MRI confirmed I was low-risk, not intermediate, and suddenly I could consider newer, less aggressive treatment possibilities.

A DCE-MRI Could Save Your Life

In a broad article about prostate cancer, the *Wall Street Journal* included a story about Richard, a fifty-four-year-old man whose PSA had doubled within two years, then jumped even higher. This was a large red flag. Richard's prostate biopsy was normal, and the plan was to wait and repeat the PSA test some months later. At the same time, however, Richard enrolled in a study using the DCE-MRI. His test identified areas suspicious for prostate cancer. These findings led his doctor to perform a second targeted biopsy. Two of the twenty-one core samples contained cancer. Because the Gleason score was 6, indicating a less aggressive cancer, and the number of positive cores was low, Richard's doctors recommended watchful waiting.

A few months later, Richard obtained a second DCE-MRI. The test showed more cancer, this time larger than on the original MRI, and the cancer was now present on both sides of the prostate. With a complete picture of his prostate cancer condition, Richard decided to undergo a prostatectomy. Based on his findings, I believe he made the right decision. Just think, without the DCE-MRIs, Richard's cancer would have continued growing until later, when it was finally identified by biopsy.

I read Richard's story six months later after I had gone through my own prostate cancer odyssey. Like Richard, I received differing medical opinions, test results that did not jive, and a DCE-MRI that finally shed much needed light on my situation. For me and for Richard, the DCE-MRI was a game changer. It could also be a game changer for you.

SLOW TO ACCEPT NEW TECHNOLOGY

Dr. Summers had no faith in the DCE-MRI and was unwilling to write a prescription for me to get one, even if I went outside my health care system and paid for it myself. The majority of urologists today probably agree with Dr. Summers. Gerald Chodak, M.D., author of *Winning the Battle Against Prostate Cancer,* has excellent credentials and is very knowledgeable. In his book, he states, "At present, there is not enough proof that the MRI should be done routinely [for prostate cancer], but research is ongoing to find out."

Dr. Chodak may be right about one element. It is true that we lack published studies convincing enough to persuade today's doctors to order DCE-MRIs for prostate cancer patients. But after I was diagnosed with prostate cancer, I could not wait for some medical authority or insurance panel to grant approval five or ten years down the road. For decades, I have been writing and lecturing about the difficulty people have in obtaining individualized care in our huge medical-pharmaceutical complex. My emphasis has been on prescription drugs. For example, when Prozac was introduced in 1988 at a one-size-fits-all 20 mg starting dosage, it greatly helped some of my patients, yet provoked serious side effects in others. My research uncovered evidence that 5 mg was all that many patients needed. Because the only available dosage at the time was a 20 mg capsule, I had patients dump out half or three-quarters of the pills' contents. Many of them did great on these lower dosages. It took the manufacturer a decade to finally market lower dose pills. In the medical world, sometimes you cannot wait for the systems to catch up with what is known and needed now.

The usual complaint from doctors is that they practice evidence-based medicine, and if they do not see enough evidence to convince them, or if their medical association has not yet approved a new test, they will not recommend it. However, in my experience, most doctors do not know what the term "evidence-based medicine" actually means. In my research and writings about why medications cause thousands of deaths and one million hospitalizations in the United States each year, I point out that "proof" differs in meaning to doctors and to patients. Many doctors think evidence-based medicine means proof from large, placebo-controlled clinical studies, like the ones done by drug companies. Doctors readily dismiss any other type of information as "inadequate" or "anecdotal," a word they often use with derision.

Yet evidence-based medicine encompasses all types of information, including large studies, small studies, individual case reports, and personal experience. Doctors often scoff at case reports or personal accounts, yet these are what the FDA uses to identify toxic drugs and ban them. If such reports are good enough for the FDA, they are good enough for me. And if eight intelligent, well-informed prostate cancer survivors in my group tell me about a new MRI that can accurately identify prostate cancer in the gland, I am going to check it out. I might discover they were wrong, or maybe they were right. Either way, it could not hurt to be thorough. At that time I was hovering between a diagnosis of low-risk versus intermediate-risk prostate cancer. Right then, prostatectomy or radiation therapy seemed the likely choices for me, but I would rather avoid both, providing it would not jeopardize my survival. If another test could shed more light on my case, I welcomed it. So should you.

If you think about the factors I discussed in the last chapters—PSA levels, biopsy cores with cancer, Gleason score—none of these provide information on the location, size, or extent of a man's prostate cancer. Perhaps an advanced prostate DCE-MRI might help clarify whether a man has low-risk or intermediate-risk cancer—as the test did for me. My thinking going in was, even if the MRI showed cancer throughout my prostate gland, then I would know specifically what I had and undergo surgery or radiation with an accepting mind. Consult the *Resources* section to learn how to find institutions offering the DCE-MRI in your area.

6

The Color Doppler Ultrasound

f you now have your PSA levels, prostate size, biopsy, and prostate MRI results, you are ready to talk about treatment options. Then again, you might consider one more diagnostic test that can confirm or clarify the findings you already have. In fact, if the color Doppler ultrasound test were easier to obtain, I would recommend it earlier in your diagnostic process, because it is the easiest way, right there in your doctor's office, to make your biopsy targeted rather than blind.

In my case, I didn't hear about this breakthrough technology until after my DCE-MRI. I didn't think I really needed a color Doppler ultrasound test, but I was still perplexed by the disparity of my high PSA levels and limited DCE-MRI findings. An elevated PSA of 8 or so would have been consistent with my biopsy trouble. This fact was brought home by another test you can use and that many doctors rely on.

If you go to prostatecalculator.org, you will find the Prostate Calculator, a method that determines the risk of your prostate cancer having already spread beyond the gland. All you have to do is input your age, T stage (e.g., T1c), your two Gleason scores (e.g., 3, 3) and PSA level. I inputted my data using my first PSA result, 15.3 ng/ml. The calculator result: a 49.6 percent risk that my prostate cancer had already spread into the seminal vesicles, lymph nodes, or bone!

I adjusted my PSA numbers downward by subtracting the impact of my large prostate. Using a PSA result of 10, I ran the number through the calculator again: 42.2 percent risk of cancer spread outside the prostate! This sounded bad. I thought I was in the clear after receiving the MRI results. The Prostate Calculator said I was wrong.

I sent an e-mail to a highly knowledgeable member of IPCSG, the local support group I discussed in Chapter 4. He replied that I should ignore the PSA results. The test is only 75 percent reliable, he said, pointing out that my PSA results were inconsistent with all of my other test results.

I also contacted my internist, who personally called one of the top prostate surgeons in the area. Because of my fifteen-year history of gyrating PSA levels, the surgeon felt strongly that the calculator was probably exaggerating my risk of spread. Nevertheless, risk still existed, she said, and urged me to have a prostatectomy as soon as possible.

I wasn't really seeking more confusion, but there it was. I hope your case is less complicated than mine, but dealing with prostate cancer is not always simple. This is when I decided to go to Los Angeles to see a doctor with expertise in color Doppler ultrasound. I needed confirmation of what I had and what it meant.

COLOR DOPPLER ULTRASONOGRAPHY

Ultrasound is used in many areas of medicine to produce images of internal organs or tissues by bouncing sound waves off of them. In urology, the standard ultrasound apparatus is inserted into the rectum to measure prostate size. This device is called a trans-rectal ultrasound (TRUS).

It is important to differentiate the TRUS machine from the color Doppler ultrasound. The latter is an adaptation of the standard ultrasound device. By using advanced computer analysis of the sound waves it generates, the color Doppler device has much greater resolution than standard ultrasound. The color Doppler device is able to measure blood flow within prostate tissue and to translate these findings into color images on a computer screen. Because prostate cancer areas have greater blood flow than normal prostate areas, the cancerous areas produce intensely colored "hot spots" on the screen.

Color Doppler ultrasound is controversial among urologists, partly because they are not trained in its use. And although the technology has been available for many years, the best practices guidelines for urologists do not advocate for the use of color Doppler ultrasound in the evaluation of men with prostate cancer. My personal experience is that it can be quite helpful. If I had learned about color Doppler ultrasound earlier, I would have gone to a doctor who uses it for targeting a biopsy. The doctor can look at the computer screen and aim the biopsy needles at the targets the computer indicates. With a targeted biopsy, fewer cores are often needed. Fewer cores mean less trauma to the prostate gland and less likelihood of bleeding or blood infection. This capability alone should motivate urologists to consider using the device. The accuracy of biopsies would be increased, adverse effects would be reduced, and the necessity for repeat biopsies would be diminished. In some cases, the color Doppler ultrasound does not identify any sign of cancer, and a biopsy may be postponed.

Dr. Duke Bahn, who has lead the way in bringing the color Doppler ultrasound to the United States, explains:

> The role of the color Doppler ultrasound is in examining the prostate by blood flow pattern (color) in addition to black and white images. In a color-Doppler study, we pick up about 15 to 20 percent more cancers. The color Doppler ultrasound also helps us identify the exact tumor size. The tumor size seen on color Doppler is usually larger than it is in black and white. So the black and white image underestimates the cancer size. In addition, if we see a suspected lesion in black and white and that suspicious lesion shows increased blood flow, it is most likely cancer. The more flow in the lesion, the higher the Gleason grade in general. Then we perform a targeted biopsy rather than a blind, systemic, random biopsy.
>
> A targeted biopsy has a higher yield with fewer tissue cores taken. By getting tissue from the middle of the action, we can get a more accurate Gleason grading. Also, based on the cancer location, we can anticipate where the cancer would have spread out, if at all. We can take a tissue sample from the most probable area of cancer escape. By doing so, we can determine the exact stage of the cancer. Since color Doppler ultrasound can identify the cancer clearly by location, size, and blood flow pattern, it can be objectively monitored over the years, especially if someone is undergoing active surveillance.

The color Doppler ultrasound does have some limits in its ability to identify prostate cancer. Like the prostate MRI, color Doppler ultrasound can miss small prostate cancers less than five millimeters in size. On the other hand, color Doppler technology has been studied intensively in Japan for more than a decade. Studies show that color Doppler ultrasound can identify 77 to 95 percent of prostate cancers. In one study, the accuracy was determined to be 88 percent.

A Clearer Look at Prostate Cancer

Color Doppler testing can also serve to provide clarity to a complicated case. This is what I sought in Los Angeles, which was the nearest place with doctors experienced in performing the color Doppler test.

I left San Diego at 5 A.M., hoping to beat the Los Angeles traffic for my 8:15 appointment. Dr. Mark Scholz met with me at the appointed time. Highly regarded in my prostate cancer community, Dr. Scholz is neither a surgeon nor a radiologist. He is an oncologist, an expert in the treatment of cancer with medications. Most oncologists treat many different types of cancer, but Scholz works only with prostate cancer, so he has vast experience in evaluating and treating the disease.

We talked for quite a while. Dr. Scholz was not fazed by my PSA levels. "Many men do not fit the typical criteria," he assured me. "Believe me, I see many men with much higher PSA levels than yours. The PSA test may be helpful, but it is not always reliable. A high PSA level itself should not dictate your final treatment decision."

Dr. Scholz noted the DCE-MRI results. It is a test he ordered frequently, and he explained how useful it is to obtain in the DCE-MRI and the color Doppler test. If the tests are consistent, they are highly reliable.

We proceeded with the color Doppler test. Lying on my side on the examination table, Dr. Scholz placed the ultrasound sensor in my rectum. It was uncomfortable but not painful. He placed the computer screen where both of us could see the color images. He showed me the prostate area and pointed to a spot within it. I could see the cancer in exactly the same spot in my prostate gland as the MRI had depicted. The size and shape of the color Doppler image were also consistent with the MRI findings. More important, like the MRI, the color Doppler analysis did not indicate cancer anywhere else. "No cancer in the left lobe, no cancer in the seminal vesicles," Scholz commented.

After the test, Scholz said: "Despite your high PSAs, you are a candidate for active surveillance. This cancer of yours is located in a rather safe area of the prostate gland. It is not near any major structures and shows no sign of spreading beyond the prostate capsule. It is highly likely that this cancer will never bother you."

Music to my ears.

And yet, as I was driving back to San Diego, I remembered an old saying in medicine: the more doctors you see, the more likely you will find one who will say exactly what you want to hear. I believed Dr. Scholz. He was knowledgeable and current in his thinking, and he seemed better informed than the other doctors I consulted about this newly accredited approach, active surveillance.

Still, I had to consider: did I like him because he said what I wanted to hear? Yes, he certainly did that. But his reasoning made sense. I would strongly consider his recommendations.

A REDUCED NEED FOR INVASIVE TESTS

In a letter to the *Wall Street Journal,* a man named Frank related his experience with the color Doppler ultrasound. Frank was seventy-four years old and had benign prostate hypertrophy since age fifty-six. His PSA test indicated a level of 5.5 ng/ml. Because the result was above the normal range of zero to 4, his prostate gland was biopsied. No cancer was found. Several years later, Frank's PSA jumped to 9.5. Another biopsy was done. It was negative, too. Hoping to avoid further biopsies, he obtained color Doppler testing from Dr. Duke Bahn in Ventura, California, an hour north of Los Angeles. Dr. Bahn has published multiple papers on color Doppler ultrasound testing in men with prostate cancer and is considered a pioneer of the technique.

Frank's color Doppler test was normal. In his letter, Frank mentioned that he was unable to find a urologist in the Denver area who performed the color Doppler test. "Every urologist I talked to starts with a biopsy with a high PSA." However, Frank wrote, if the color Doppler test is normal, there should be no need for a biopsy. From his perspective, the current approach did not make much sense. "It seems the medical profession is still in the dark ages regarding examination techniques for benign prostatic hypertrophy and cancer detection," Frank continued. "I get the impression that urologists cry 'biopsy!' too quickly and loudly for any PSA above 4.0, no matter what the age."

Dr. Scholz says that more than half the prostate biopsies performed each year are unnecessary. If a color Doppler ultrasound were performed before each prostate biopsy, sometimes it would show no suspicious areas, and the biopsy could be postponed. These men would be followed closely and their PSA levels and other tests would be repeated frequently. Dr. Scholz told me that sometimes the first sign of a developing cancer appears on the color Doppler ultrasound, even while the PSA levels remains stable. As one of my group friends says, prostate cancer is an elusive disease. Nothing about it is absolute.

Meanwhile, as the medical establishment awaits studies to confirm the reliability of the prostate MRI and ignores the value of the color Doppler ultrasound, my color Doppler test confirmed the findings of my MRI. That was exactly what I had hoped it would do. While driving home, I thought about how lucky I was to have learned about these tests before rushing into surgery. I now felt fully prepared to consider the many treatment options available to me. And, thanks to the input of my support group, I had more options to consider than I'd known—and you have them, too.

Just to clarify, the DCE-MRI is a more important test than the color Doppler ultrasound. The major medical centers that are already employing the newer methods rely on the DCE-MRI or the most advanced multiparametric MRI. Yet, if you can obtain it, the color Doppler ultrasound can also be helpful for diagnostic purposes as well as for obtaining a targeted biopsy in the doctor's office. Check the *Resources* section to find out if the color Doppler ultrasound is available in your area.

7

Genetic Diagnostic Tests

Although we have long known that there is a genetic link to prostate cancer—sons of fathers with prostate cancer have a higher risk of contracting the disease—the clinical use of genetic testing for prostate cancer is just beginning. Yet we already have a handful of genetic tests that may vastly improve our methods of diagnosis and treatment. These tests are just the tip of a new wave of genetically-based breakthroughs that will change our methods for decades to come.

Within a decade, no prostate biopsies will be done without genetic tests that can identify the presence of prostate cancer, even when the visual pathology examination identifies none. No prostatectomy will be done without genetic tests to calculate the tumor's aggressiveness and whether immediate further treatment is warranted. No metastatic prostate cancer will be treated without genetic testing to match the sensitivity of the cancer with scores of potential drug therapies.

This chapter describes a number of newly emerged tests that have proved to be effective in accurately detecting prostate cancer. Many, many more tests are on the way. Clinical trials have demonstrated the usefulness of these new tests, yet their accuracy and reliability will ultimately be proven in the clinical cauldron, that is, via their use with tens of thousands of men with prostate cancer.

"It's a little tricky to find out which one applies to you and whether it will be paid for by insurance," says Jan Manarite, who runs the telephone help line for the Prostate Cancer Research Institute, a patient education organization.

The tests are already making a difference. Even though they may not yet be perfect, they can add valuable information when making difficult decisions. A *New York Times* article described the case of Angel Vasquez, who wasn't comfortable with his urologist's recommendation of active surveillance. "I said, 'No, my philosophy is if there is something in my body that is not supposed to be there, I want it to come out.'" His doctor ordered a test that showed the cancer was more aggressive than thought. After his prostatectomy, the pathology examination confirmed the accuracy of the test. "Had I left it alone, it would have really progressed," Vasquez said.

Although the shaking out period will take awhile, I find all of these advances incredibly exciting. They are providing us a keyhole's glimpse of an amazing future to come in the medical treatment of prostate cancer and all disease. For a comprehensive list of the websites for each of the treatments mentioned in this chapter, see the *Resources* section.

IMPROVED ACCURACY OF BIOPSY INTERPRETATION

Approximately 1.2 million prostate biopsies are performed each year in the United States. Of these, 700,000 are determined on pathology examination to be negative (not containing cancer), and 25 percent of these determinations are wrong—cancer is found on a second biopsy or via other methods. It is easy to understand why this happens. Each core of prostate tissue taken during a biopsy represents just a tiny fraction of the entire prostate volume. The typical random biopsy takes twelve or fourteen cores of prostate tissue, less than one percent of the full gland. This is why today's standard blind biopsy misses prostate cancer so often.

A negative biopsy can cause a lot of uncertainty. Is the biopsy result accurate? Is there really no cancer in the prostate gland? Or did the biopsy simply miss a cancer that actually exists? Can the result be relied on for making life-and-death treatment decisions? If you have a rising PSA level, a negative biopsy can cause more concern than relief.

In today's medical approach, a negative biopsy often leads to another biopsy. Hundreds of thousands of men each year would be relieved to avoid these additional prostate biopsies, because they all too often prove unnecessary. So is there a better way to tell whether a second biopsy is truly needed? This is the purpose of the following three genetic tests. These tests are most helpful for men with high PSA levels whose prostate biopsies are negative.

Prostate Core Mitomic Test

The Mitomic Test is performed on the tissue obtained from your biopsy. Even if your biopsy result has been reported as negative, the test can identify prostate cancer by finding aberrations and deletions in cells' mitochondrial DNA that are consistent with prostate cancer. In other words, although the cells do not appear cancerous upon visual inspection, the Mitomic test can find molecular markers of cancer.

When the Mitomic test is negative, it is accurate 91 percent of the time. If the biopsy and Mitomic test are both negative, a second biopsy might be necessary. Thus, hundreds of thousands repeat biopsies each year might be avoided. When the Mitomic test is positive for prostate cancer, the finding is accurate 85 to 90 percent of the time. This would suggest a second biopsy, preferably targeted, in order to obtain a cancer specimen for grading and Gleason scoring by a pathologist.

The parent company of the Mitomic test, Mitomic Technology, is developing similar tests for breast cancer, endometriosis, melanoma, and bladder, cervical, thyroid, ovarian, and pancreatic cancers.

The ConfirmMDx Test

ConfirmMDx uses patented technology to identify signs of prostate cancer in prostate tissue obtained on biopsy. Even when the visual examination of the biopsy tissue indicates no cancer, this test can find genetic markers in these normal cells, suggesting they were near cancer cells in the prostate gland. The test is 90 percent reliable in determining that a negative biopsy is truly negative, thereby possibly obviating the need for an additional biopsy. If the ConfirmMDx test is positive for prostate cancer markers, a targeted biopsy may be needed to obtain cancer for grading and Gleason scoring. ConfirmMDx has been tested in studies involving over 4,000 prostate cancer subjects.

The parent company of the ConfirmMDx test, MdxHealth, is also developing genetic-based tests for lung and colon cancer. In addition, it is developing tests that can distinguish between aggressive and non-aggressive cancers, and also tests to predict the medications and treatments that are most effective for an individual's cancer.

The QuadVysion Test

The QuadVysion test identifies a protein present in prostate cancer cells, but not in normal cells. The test can be used to confirm that when biopsy material is read as negative, it is truly negative, or to determine if tiny areas of prostate cancer actually exist in some of the biopsy specimens. The parent company of the QuadVysion test, Bostwick Laboratories, also makes another prostate test, the ProstaVysion test, which I discuss in the next section.

No matter whether any of these biopsy specimen tests are positive or negative for prostate cancer, a DCE-MRI should be done before a second biopsy is considered. The MRI can identify a prostate cancer tumor of 0.5 cm or greater and could facilitate a targeted biopsy with its greater likelihood of obtaining cancer tissue or pathology inspection. If the biopsy, the Mitomic, ConfirmMDx or QuadVysion test, and the DCE-MRI are all negative, a second biopsy might not be necessary.

You may ask, if the DCE-MRI is done, are these genetic tests necessary? This is a good question. Because the tests are performed directly on prostate tissue obtained from the biopsy, they can tell us about the state of the prostate tissue on a molecular level. For example, if the pathology examination of biopsy tissue is negative and so is the MRI, yet one of these tests identifies prostate cancer markers, what then? One interpretation might be that prostate cancer exists or is beginning to develop in the prostate gland, but it is too early to be detected on MRI. An active surveillance approach might then be adopted.

ASSESSING AGGRESSIVENESS AND ASSISTING TREATMENT DECISIONS

As mentioned earlier, the degree of a prostate cancer's aggressiveness is a key factor in determining a man's treatment. Currently, the Gleason score indicates a cancer's aggressiveness. This score is determined via visual and microscopic inspection of prostate tissue obtained by biopsy. The new genetic tests can allow the Gleason determination to be confirmed on a molecular basis.

The Prolaris Test

A prognostic test for measuring the aggressiveness of a man's prostate cancer, the Prolaris test measures the frequency of tumor cell division in the prostate cancer tissue obtained from biopsy or prostate surgery. The test measures RNA expression levels of genes related to cellular proliferation. The faster the rate of cell division and proliferation, the more aggressive the prostate cancer, and the higher the Prolaris score.

The Prolaris test does not measure whether you have prostate cancer, but how fast your cancer cells are dividing. The Prolaris website states: "Two patients with the same PSA and Gleason scores may have a different estimate of mortality risk when their Prolaris score is included in their evaluation."

The Prolaris test is intended to help men with low-risk prostate cancer and their doctors decide whether they are a good candidate for active surveillance or should consider an intervention. The test is also used for men who have had a prostatectomy. In the latter case, the Prolaris score can help determine if further treatment, such as radiation therapy, is needed after the surgery. If you have low-risk prostate cancer, a low Prolaris score may support your choice of active surveillance. If the Prolais score is high, you may want to choose a more active approach.

The Prolaris test has been examined in four clinical studies involving hundreds of patients each. In each study, the Prolaris test was shown to be a statistically significant predictor of clinical outcomes in men using active surveillance and in men who had received prostatectomies. Over ten years, the test has demonstrated 97 percent accuracy.

The OncotypeDX Test

OncotypeDX analyzes the RNA from genes in prostate cancer tissue obtained from biopsy and prostatectomy. This approach reveals a gene signature that can help predict your cancer's level of aggressiveness.

In a study of 395 men with prostate cancer, the OncotypeDX test led to the reclassification of thirty-five men originally deemed low-risk to an even lower risk category, thereby allowing the men to choose active surveillance with greater certainty. Conversely, in the same study 10 percent of men defined as low-risk were reclassified into a higher risk category, allowing the men to consider other treatment options. The OncotypeDX test can also be helpful in determining whether further treatment is necessary after a man has undergone a prostatectomy. If the test indicates a cancer that is more aggressive than indicated by the pathology examination, post-operative radiation or androgen blocking therapy might be considered.

The ProstaVysion Test

For determining the aggressiveness of prostate cancer from tissue obtained on biopsy, the test's methodology involves the identification of two major mechanisms of prostate carcinogenesis: gene fusion/translocation and loss of a key tumor suppressor gene. The approach includes a projection of your long-term outcome based on analyses published in the medical literature.

The Decipher Test

For men who have had a prostatectomy, the Decipher test determines the activity of a score of prostate cancer genes to assess the likelihood of the cancer returning and spreading. The results can help high-risk men and their doctors know whether radiation and/or androgen deprivation therapy should be initiated soon after the prostate surgery.

In studies, the Decipher test allowed for the reclassification of 60 percent of high-risk men into a lower risk category. Based on the test, their risk of metastases was low, so they could wait before deciding on further treatment. In contrast, in another subgroup the risk of developing metastases was markedly elevated, and additional treatment was recommended. In this way, the Decipher test could prove very helpful for men and their doctors in making accurate treatment decisions following prostatectomy.

Caris Molecular Intelligence Profile and Profile Plus Tests

Performed on tumor tissue from any source, the Caris Molecular Intelligence (MI) Profile test identifies thirty cancer biomarkers and determines the likely response to treatment with each of forty-six FDA-approved cancer drugs. This method is particularly helpful for difficult-to-treat prostate cancers, such as the uncommon, hard-to-treat small cell prostate cancer, or for the more typical adenocarcinoma cancer that is unusually resistant to standard chemotherapy. The "Plus" test performs an advanced sequencing panel for testing an additional forty-four biomarkers for matching more drugs. Moreover, the manufacturer, Caris Life Sciences, will attempt to match patients with ongoing clinical studies.

LOOKING TOWARD THE FUTURE

In broad perspective, the recent development of genetic tests to improve three major areas of prostate cancer diagnosis—biopsy interpretation, cancer aggressiveness grading, and the matching of drug therapies for each man's prostate cancer—is amazing. The big question remains: How accurate are these tests today? There is no doubt that in time we will have accurate tests for each of these categories and more. Will some of today's tests prove highly reliable? Or will they all be replaced by better tests that are being developed right now?

Bottom line, no matter the stage and Gleason category of your prostate cancer, it is certainly worth investigating these tests. Ask your doctor. Go to the websites I have listed above. Do a search on the Internet. Be sure to access the Mayo Clinic website about its new genetic endeavor: the Prostate Cancer Medically Optimized Genome-Enhanced Therapy (PROMOTE) study. Its purpose is to analyze the genetic characteristics of each man's prostate tumor and predict the most effective treatments. The Mayo Clinic effort seems similar to the purpose of the Caris Molecular Intelligence Profile test. Will it be better than the Caris test? Time will tell.

The University of California, San Diego has recently established a Center for Personalized Cancer Therapy at its Moores Cancer Center. The UCSD website states, "Our goal is to transform cancer therapy by using advanced technological tools to predict who will respond to a specific treatment, and to match each patient with the best drug for a particular tumor." The center will treat patients with many other types of cancer, including prostate cancer.

Soon, centers like these will be popping up everywhere. This is very encouraging. The momentum is building and appears unstoppable. My gosh, we are learning to use a cancer's own genetics against it! Soon we will be designing specific, genetically designed molecular missiles against the cancer instead of crude, side-effect prone drugs.

Suddenly, the decades-old unfulfilled promise, *a cure for cancer*, does not seem so beyond comprehension. Of course, cancer is a cagey enemy. Still, the next decades will be remarkable in transforming the treatment of prostate and other cancers toward the molecular and atomic levels. Ideas like this used to be considered science fiction, but now it is only a matter of time until they become real.

8

The Carbon-11 PET/CT Scan

Five years ago, the FDA approved the use of a new Carbon-11 PET/CT scan. This advanced form of scanning is a major breakthrough in our ability to better identify prostate cancer metastases in men with aggressive cancer (Gleason 8 to 10). The new scan can allow doctors to determine whether men with aggressive cancer already have metastases before making decisions about initial treatment with surgery or radiation. In men whose prostate cancer has already spread beyond the gland, prostatectomy is *contraindicated*, or inadvisable, because removing the prostate will not remove all of the cancer. Treatment will therefore involve radiation to the prostate gland as well as areas of metastases; medication therapy, such as Xofigo (Chapter 10); or a combination of therapies.

The key advantage of the new Carbon-11 PET/CT scan is that it can identify prostate cancer metastases earlier and with better accuracy than current techniques. The scan is specific for prostate cancer cells, which it can distinguish in bone, lymph nodes, and seminal vesicles.

With the new scan, much smaller metastases can be recognized, thereby making diagnosis sooner and treatment more capable of cure. Unlike other scans, the Carbon-11 scan identifies heightened fat metabolism, a sign that reflects the heightened metabolic activity of prostate cancer cells in comparison to normal prostate cells. Current methods for identifying metastatic prostate cancer include ultrasound, biopsy, CT scan, standard MRI, and bone scans, but none of these is as able to identify prostate cancer recurrences as the Carbon-11 PET/CT scan. The other tests show changes in bone that may represent metastatic prostate cancer, but may also be from other causes.

CARBON-11 PET/CT SCAN FOR PRIMARY PROSTATE CANCER

Research on this scan has mainly been directed toward men with signs of cancer recurrence after surgery or radiation treatment. The Carbon-11 Choline PET/CT scan that the FDA approved is being used at the Mayo Clinic in Minnesota for this purpose. However, the use of a similar method, the Carbon-11 Acetate PET/CT scan, is also being studied for initial diagnosis of aggressive cancers by Dr. Fabio Almeida at the Arizona Molecular Imaging Center in Phoenix. I wrote to Dr. Almeida asking about this application for primary evaluation. He replied:

> In addition to running the protocol with C11-Acetate for detecting recurrence, we have been running a protocol to answer the question you have asked. We are using C11-Acetate in those who are about to undergo surgery who have higher risk features on their biopsy: Gleason grade of 7 to 10, a PSA greater than 10, or a large amount of prostate cancer in the gland. The goal is to determine if C11-Acetate PET can help detect prostate cancer metastases in lymph nodes or bone that would alter the treatment plan. We are seeing good results, but the study is in its early stages.

Dr. Almeida enclosed an article published in the Journal of Nuclear Medicine. The study concluded, "In patients planning for or completing prostatectomy, carbon-acetate PET/CT detects lymph node metastases not identified by conventional imaging and independently predicts treatment-failure free survival."

A LONG-AWAITED ADVANCEMENT

After a man receives treatment for prostate cancer, his PSA level should drop considerably because all of the prostate cancer cells have been removed by surgery or killed in radiation. For example, after prostatectomy, the PSA should drop below 0.2 ng/ml and remain at that level. After radiation therapy, the PSA should drop below 2 ng/ml. After these procedures as well as after HIFU, cryosurgery, laser therapy, or other treatments, a rising PSA may indicate a recurrence of cancer.

Recurrence of prostate cancer after treatment is not rare. Recurrence rates after prostatectomy are about 25 percent after ten years. Rates are slightly higher following radiation therapy.

When the PSA rises repeatedly, it is imperative to identify the location of the recurrent prostate cancer. Did some of the cancer cells survive in the gland when it was bombarded by radiation? Or in the remaining prostate bed after prostatectomy? Or the recurrence from prostate cancer cells that have spread to local lymph nodes, to the seminal vesicles, or bones or other distant areas?

CASE REPORTS ON THE CARBON-11 PET/CT SCAN

Dr. Almeida provided these case reports in a newsletter sent out by the Patient Advocates for Advanced Cancer Treatments Organization, an excellent resource for men with prostate cancer.

When a man's PSA level began to rise nine years after prostatectomy, his doctors directed radiation to the area of the prostate bed. Nevertheless, his PSA kept rising. A Carbon-11 Acetate PET/CT scan identified a lymph node with cancer in the left pelvis. No other cancerous lesions were seen. This time, radiation aimed at the PSA indicated that the Carbon-11 scan had accurately identified the metastatic cancer. The radiation treatment was successful.

After radiation, a man's PSA level dropped to 0.43 ng/ml, but four years later, his PSA climbed again to 3.9. A Carbon-11 Acetate scan identified a suspicious area on the right side of his prostate gland. With this information, a targeted biopsy revealed the cancer, and brachytherapy (pellet radiation) was performed. The man's PSA level decreased to 0.6.

Twelve years after brachytherapy and external beam radiation (forerunner of IMRT), a man's PSA level had risen from 0.26 to 2.17 ng/ml. Carbon-11 Acetate scan identified a single, suspicious lymph node in his upper pelvic area. Surgical intervention removed thirteen lymph nodes. The node identified by the scan was found to have metastatic cancer, while the other nodes did not. In other words, the identification of this node by the scan was accurate. After removal, the man's PSA level dropped to 0.19.

Nine years after prostatectomy, a man's PSA rose to 4.8. Carbon-11 Acetate scan identified a single metastasis in a bone in the cervical (neck) spinal area. No other measures were identified in bone, lymph node, or prostate bed areas. Radiation was directed at the lesion, and the PSA dropped to 0.2 ng/ml. No other testing or scanning method today could have identified these lesions this early and accurately.

The availability of the Carbon-11 PT/CT scan is limited, but check the *Resources* section for a short list of the medical centers where it is currently being offered.

PART 2

When the Diagnosis is Prostate Cancer, What's Next?

9

Aggressive Therapies

The following procedures have been the standard for prostate cancer treatment for decades. These *aggressive* therapies treat the entire prostate in an effort to slow the growth of the cancer or eradicate it entirely. In the past, men have opted for these approaches—in particular, prostatectomy—regardless of the intensity or risk level of their prostate cancer. They would rather do anything they can to rid themselves of the cancer at the risk of severe, sometimes life-altering side effects, including urinary incontinence and impotence.

PROSTATECTOMY

Today, prostatectomies take the leading role in the treatment of men diagnosed with prostate cancer. More than fifty thousand prostate surgeries are performed in the United States each year. Most of these are *radical* prostatectomies, surgeries that remove not only the prostate gland but also the seminal vesicles and, when necessary, adjacent nerve bundles. Most prostatectomies today are done with robotic technology.

There is far more data on the long-term survival of men receiving prostatectomies for prostate cancer than for any other treatment method. Studies show that in men having radical prostatectomy for prostate cancer, approximately 70 percent show no sign of a return of the cancer after ten years. This is a very good result. This is why each of the four prostate surgeons I consulted strongly encouraged me to have a prostatectomy. Their intentions were good. They wanted me to have the greatest chance of cure.

Other prostate surgeons give the same advice to men newly diagnosed with prostate cancer. This explains why over 80 percent of men who fit the criteria for active surveillance (Chapter 9), men who could safely watch, instead opt for prostatectomy. Many doctors strongly believe that even in men with low-risk prostate cancer, the survival rate beyond ten years favors prostatectomy. In their zeal to prevent any man from dying of prostate cancer, they recommend the surgery to virtually all their patients diagnosed with the disease. This in turn adds to the massive degree of overtreatment that we see.

I leaned toward surgery at first because I had so many unanswered questions and so little specific information about my prostate cancer. I had to make a decision seemingly in the dark, and in that state I wanted the treatment most likely to cure me despite its serious risk effects to my quality of life.

Many men choose prostatectomy because they are uncomfortable with the idea of living with a potentially lethal cancer in their body while having only crude tools—PSA levels and biopsies—to monitor it. They are not comfortable with the limited information they receive about their cancer. They are uneasy about their lack of knowledge about the size, extent, and possible spread of their cancer. Thus, although more than 50 percent of men diagnosed with prostate cancer have low-risk, localized disease, the majority of these men opt for some form of treatment, most often surgery. Is this because the doctors who diagnose them are usually surgeons?

Now, with the growing use of the DCE-MRI and to a lesser extent, color Doppler ultrasound, the statistics are slowly changing. If men know their prostate cancer is localized, and that the cancer can be followed using these new tools, along with PSA levels and biopsy, far more men may choose active surveillance or a type of focal treatment such as cryotherapy, focal laser ablation, or the high-intensity focused ultrasound (see Chapter 11).

Does One Cancer Indicate Many Cancers?

Urologists often recommend prostatectomy because removing the prostate and having it examined by a pathologist has, before today's DCE-MRI, been the only way to determine exactly how much cancer the prostate actually contains. Many prostate surgeons view prostate cancer as a *multifocal* disease, with cancer developing simultaneously in multiple areas even if only one is located by biopsy. I spoke to four prostate surgeons and each one told me the same thing: "If you have prostate cancer in one area, you likely have it in many other areas, too."

Or maybe not. A study conducted at the Cleveland Clinic examined this issue. Over the course of four years, 431 men were diagnosed with unilateral prostate cancer based on their biopsy findings. 179 chose prostatectomy for treatment. Examination of the removed prostate glands of these 179 men revealed:

> In fifty of the 179 men (28 percent), prostate cancer was present only on one side of the gland. In 129 men (72 percent), cancer was found on both sides. In seventy-seven of these 129 men, the cancer on the other side was small and insignificant, and did not need treatment.

In only fifty-two of these 129 men, the cancer on both sides of the prostate was serious and required treatment. In summary, of the 179 men in this study with unilateral prostate cancer who underwent prostatectomy, only 29 percent actually needed surgery. 127 men (71 percent), who had no cancer or only insignificant cancer on the other side of the prostate gland, did not need surgery. They got the surgery anyway—and all of the adverse effects that often come with it.

Overtreatment or Undertreatment?

Experts continue to debate this ongoing issue regarding prostate cancer: Which is worse, overtreatment or undertreatment? Most surgeons believe undertreatment is worse, which is why they lean toward overtreatment. Undertreating prostate cancer can lead to a slow and painful death. No doctor wants that on his or her conscience. Nevertheless, many experts are no longer supportive of treatment for every prostate cancer patient without giving thought to the serious impact on a man's quality of life.

Words have never quelled the debate. Today's new technologies will. Yes, the DCE-MRI has limitations. It will not identify tiny cancers, but it will identify small and large cancers, along with unilateral (affecting one organ) and bilateral (affecting a pair of organs) ones. It will identify whether the cancer has spread to the edge of the prostate or into other tissues. If your DCE-MRI shows a large or bilateral cancer, or that the cancer is pushing against the capsule or beyond, your decision becomes simple: surgery or radiation.

But if your prostate cancer is shown by DCE-MRI to be limited to one lobe, and this is confirmed by biopsy and by color Doppler, you have other choices. If the DCE-MRI, color Doppler, and biopsy miss a cancer, then it is very small. If you follow up with ongoing surveillance including repeated PSA levels, DCE-MRI, biopsy, and perhaps color Doppler ultrasound, these other potential cancers can be identified as they reveal themselves. If they are caught when they are small, focal therapy may be all that is needed.

ROBOTIC RADICAL PROSTATECTOMY

There are several techniques for removing the prostate gland surgically, but increasingly popular today is the minimally invasive, robot-assisted radical prostatectomy. This procedure has advantages in that it does not require a large incision across the lower abdomen, thereby causing less blood loss and scarring. It also allows better visualization of the prostate gland during the surgery and enables the surgeon to identify and spare some of the nerves around the prostate.

If you have a higher-grade cancer and no sign of spread beyond the prostate gland, your main treatment choices come down to surgery or radiation. In terms of long-term cure, statistics seem to slightly favor surgery. And as urologists point out, if your prostate cancer returns after surgery, you can still have the radiation. But if the cancer returns after radiation, surgery is difficult because the irradiated tissue does not heal well. Today, however, focal therapies such as cryotherapy or HIFU can be used for some cases of local cancer recurrence.

The Downside of Prostate Surgery

Most men would strongly consider surgery if it did not come with a sobering array of side effects. The surgery itself is associated with:

- Blood loss requiring transfusion in 2 percent of patients

- Infection in 2 percent of patients

- Blood clots in the legs of 3 percent of patients

- Injury to bladder or rectum in 1 percent of patients

- Heart attack or heart failure in 2 percent of patients

- Death in one to two per thousand surgeries

These statistics are not so bad considering how deep in the lower abdomen the prostate sits and that the surgery is performed mostly on men over age fifty. The adverse effects following prostatectomy that worry most men are those involving bladder and sexual functioning. Even with modern robotic methods, removing the prostate always causes some damage because many delicate nerves and blood vessels run through or very close to the gland. There is no way to completely avoid these structures.

Urinary leakage may persist in 5 to 25 percent of men undergoing prostatectomy. Some men need an occasional pad, others always need them, and a few require corrective surgery. To many men, incontinence reduces quality of life immensely, even more than sexual dysfunction.

Normal sensations in genital areas and the ability to orgasm remain, but ejaculations are dry, and the quality of ejaculation and/or orgasm may change. Some men ejaculate urine. Over many months, sexual functioning can improve. Many men require erectile dysfunction drugs like Viagra, or penile injections or vacuum pumps to obtain a better erection. Shortening of the penis by .25 to one inch can occur and may not improve even with therapy.

The ability to spare the neurovascular bundles is an important factor in sexual functioning after prostatectomy. If both bundles are removed, as recommended to me by Dr. Frederick, impairments are often severe and permanent.

Not all men encounter these problems after prostatectomy. I have spoken to men who bounced back with a nearly full return of urinary and sexual function after a few months' recovery from the surgery. Factors indicating your likelihood of normal or near normal sexual functioning after prostatectomy include your age and your sexual functioning prior to surgery. The skill and experience of the surgeon are also key. Many urologists perform only a handful of robotic radical prostatectomies a year, but it is better to have a surgeon who has done hundreds or thousands of these complex procedures. You can find surgeons with this level of experience at major medical centers or in practices that specialize in treating prostate cancer. Do not be shy about asking surgeons how many prostatectomies they have performed. Also ask about the rates of short and long-term adverse effects, and whether there is a support team to help you with post-operative problems and long-term rehabilitation of bladder or sexual functioning.

The potential adverse effects of prostatectomy are enough to cause many men to pause. However, here is the upside: This intervention has been studied more than any other current treatment method and many experts still believe it offers the best chance for cure. A study published in the *Journal of Urology* reported on the results of 18,209 men who underwent prostatectomy at Johns Hopkins University between 1975 and 2009. The survival rate at ten years was 92.6 percent; at twenty years, 69.2 percent, which might sound low, except that the average age was fifty-nine at the time of the surgery. In fact, the overall death rate from prostate cancer in the group following prostatectomy was lower than the death rate in the general male population of the same age.

A study of robotic-assisted prostatectomy provided follow-up information on 1,384 men for up to seven years after surgery. After three years, 91 percent showed no sign of cancer recurrence (consistently low PSA levels); at five years, 86.6 percent; at seven years, 81 percent. This study demonstrated excellent, up-to-date results on survival following robotic radical prostatectomy.

As you can see, survival rates can vary from study to study. Many factors may contribute to this variability including the age of the men, the number of men in each risk category, cancer stages, and Gleason scores, the general health of the men, and so on. Nevertheless, the numbers of these studies, 70 to 80 percent cure at seven to ten years, are very good.

Attaining The Trifecta

Perhaps the number that may interest you the most is known as the *trifecta:* cure from prostate cancer, continued sexual potency, and continued urinary control. According to one study, about 62 percent of men obtained a trifecta in the hands of highly respected prostate surgeons at a top-notch hospital. This number doesn't sound too bad. It at least gives you a decent chance at having a normal life post-surgery.

At the same time, the 62 percent of men who regained sexual potency did not necessarily regain the same degree of functioning they had prior to surgery. In this study, sexual potency was defined as recovering enough hardness to penetrate successfully. It also counted men who required Viagra or erectile dysfunction medications to regain potency, and it included men for whom it took up to three years to regain adequate potency.

Most important in making your decision to have prostate surgery is to find a urologic surgeon you trust. In addition to having extensive experience with the technique being used, this surgeon should be willing to patiently and fully answer all your questions.

RADIATION THERAPIES

The great advantage of radiation therapy is that it can treat your prostate cancer without requiring an operation. The downside is that in some cases, cancer cells survive and the cancer returns. When this happens, surgery may not be possible because the injury to the area from the radiation might impede healing. However, a repeat course of radiation or a focal therapy such as cryotherapy or HIFU (Chapter 11) could suffice.

Another disadvantage is that as the radiation passes through surrounding tissues, it may cause damage that has an adverse impact on urinary or sexual function. Because the effects of the radiation are slow to develop, these problems may not appear for a year or more.

Intensity-Modulated Radiation Therapy

Intensity-modulated radiation therapy (IMRT) is the main type of radiation therapy for prostate cancer today. It emits charged particles, primarily photons, which easily pass through the skin and intervening tissues and into the prostate gland. The beam kills the cancer cells or renders them unable to divide by damaging their DNA.

Radiation therapy technology has been steadily improving for decades. Today, radiation therapy is no longer applied with one broad beam from a single angle, but instead with narrow beams applied from many angles. Although the radiation is directed at the prostate gland, the beam also has an impact on the tissues it passes through, in front, and behind the prostate. This is an important consideration. However, by changing the angles by which the radiation is administered, these other tissues are minimally affected. As an example, a new machine known as Rapid Arc emits its beam from a cylinder that rotates 360 degrees around the patient, thereby minimizing the impact on other tissues.

Using CAT or MRI imaging to define exactly where the prostate is represents another recent improvement. Studies have shown that the prostate gland moves a bit when the bladder expands with urine or the rectum fills with stool. Targeting the prostate as accurately as possible is key to obtaining the best results with the fewest problems.

As the accuracy of the equipment has improved, radiotherapists have been able to increase the intensity of the radiation beam, bringing higher cure rates. This has been one of the most important advances in the evolution of radiation therapy.

Still, IMRT can produce impairments in sexual or urinary function. These are usually less frequent, less severe, and slower developing than with prostatectomy. In addition, as the beam passes through the wall of the rectum, burn injuries can occur. This used to be a frequent and highly vexing problem with earlier versions of radiation beam therapy. Today, the adverse effect occurs in 2 to 4 percent of patients. With IMRT, there is also a slight increase in cases of secondary bladder or rectal cancer occurring five to ten years after radiation treatment. The increased risk is believed to be approximately two men per thousand per year receiving radiation.

Most forms of IMRT today require forty forty-five minute sessions spread over eight weeks. Higher intensity machines such as Rapid Arc require the same number of sessions, but each session requires about fifteen minutes.

Brachytherapy

This form of radiation therapy involves implanting small radioactive seeds into the prostate gland. The seeds are the size of tiny grains of rice, a few millimeters in diameter. They are placed via a needle inserted through the perineum (the area between the scrotum and the anus) into the prostate gland. The advantage of brachytherapy is that a high dose of radiation can be delivered directly into the prostate gland, thereby causing less injury to surrounding structures than occurs using IMRT. Another advantage of brachytherapy is that the procedure is accomplished in one outpatient surgery, rather than a lengthy series of visits. Some experts believe that overall, brachytherapy is the most effective form of radiation for prostate cancer.

Brachytherapy can affect the bladder, sexual, or bowel functioning. Approximately 10 percent of men develop urinary symptoms, including a constant urge to urinate, or slow or painful urination. These adverse effects can last for months.

Stereotactic Body Radiation Therapy

Stereotactic body radiation therapy (SBRT) is used for many types of cancers, including brain, lung, pancreas, kidney, and metastatic tumors. SBRT employs a specially designed coordination system to provide precise localization of targeted tumors. The precision of this method allows the delivery of highly potent, concentrated doses of radiation, higher than IMRT, with sub-millimeter accuracy and minimal exposure of normal tissue.

Because of the intensity of the SBRT beam, treating prostate cancer requires only five sessions, usually performed Monday through Friday. Sometimes the five sessions are staggered across two weeks, which may reduce side effects. IMRT or proton therapies usually involve smaller doses of radiation delivered over thirty-six to forty weeks.

SBRT therapy begins with diagnostic scans that pinpoint the exact location of the prostate gland and cancer within it. Their movements, which shift slightly due to breathing and the subtle movements of internal organs, are plotted over time. To more accurately define these subtle changes during treatment, tiny gold seeds called *fiducials* are implanted into the prostate days before treatment begins. This is done so that imaging before and during treatment can more accurately guide the SBRT. The placement of fiducials is similar to having a biopsy and also performed with imaging guidance.

The moment-to-moment precision of SBRT also allows the radiation therapist to avoid normal structures with the high-dose radiation. The SBRT beam is delivered from many angles, thereby further concentrating the radiation to the tumor. Each SBRT session takes thirty to sixty minutes.

SBRT is used for single localized tumors or a few distinct tumors for many types of cancer, but with prostate cancer it is usually delivered for the entire prostate gland. SBRT can also be used for men with recurrent prostate cancer after other treatment such as prostatectomy or other forms of radiation. The benefits of SBRT versus standard IMRT or brachytherapy have been hotly debated.

An article on long-term effects of SBRT showed that after five years, 97 percent of men undergoing SBRT for low-risk prostate cancer had no indication of cancer recurrence based on PSA monitoring. Moreover, 91 percent of men with intermediate-risk cancer and 74 percent of men with high-risk prostate cancer had no indication of cancer recurrence. These are pretty good numbers and comparable to other forms of radiation therapy. Adverse events with SBRT involving bladder or rectum were similar to those with IMRT. Impotence occurred in only 25 percent. The most commonly reported side effect with SBRT is mild fatigue for a week following treatment. Some men have reported intense, immediate adverse effects with SBRT, probably due to the high intensity of the beam used.

Proton Beam Radiation Therapy

Unlike IMRT, which irradiates with photon particles, proton beam radiation employs protons to kill prostate cancer cells. Theoretically, the advantage of proton beam therapy is that it only releases its energy when it reaches its target. Other tissues through which the proton beam passes are not affected, thereby greatly reducing adverse effects. The big question is whether proton therapy has perfected the ability to release its energy in the prostate and not elsewhere. Recent articles appearing in medical journals state that proton beam therapy is effective for prostate cancer, but it has not been shown to be superior to IMRT or brachytherapy.

The newest version of proton beam therapy, also known as intensity modulated proton therapy, utilizes a narrow "pencil beam," which allows greater control over radiation doses and shorter treatment times. This approach has less impact on surrounding tissues, thereby reducing the incidence of side effects. A study of men under age sixty-one found a low degree of impact on sexual functioning following treatment for prostate cancer with proton beam therapy. Proponents of proton beam therapy also claim that the therapy has little impact on bladder control. However, another large review of Medicare patients with prostate cancer who underwent proton beam therapy showed a slightly higher rate of rectal bleeding than others who received standard IMRT.

A bigger problem is that Blue Shield of California has announced it will no longer cover claims for proton therapy. Why? Because proton therapy costs tens of thousands of dollars more than other types of radiation therapy but, as the Los Angeles Times article puts it, " a slew of studies have found that proton therapy doesn't yield better results than older, cheaper alternatives."

"Proton beam is really the perfect example of all that is wrong with our healthcare system," said Cary Gross, a researcher at the Yale School of Medicine who recently compared outcomes for 30,000 Medicare patients who received proton beam or standard radiation. "The rush to adopt proton beam is far outpacing the amount of evidence to support its use." The study also found that one year after treatment, the side effects were not less than with other radiation therapies.

Another insurer, Cigna, has said it considers proton beam to be equal but not superior to standard radiation. As a result, Cigna does not consider proton therapy as medically necessary in many cases. Aetna also lists proton therapy as not medically necessary and not proven more effective than other radiation therapies. On the bright side, Medicare continues to pay for proton therapy for prostate cancer and, I believe, so do secondary insurers for people who have Medicare. Always check with your insurer as part of your planning for proton radiation therapy.

Notice, no one is claiming that proton therapy is less effective than other radiation approaches, and some men who have had it speak very highly of it. Tens of thousands of men have been treated for prostate cancer with proton beam radiation, and you can find hundreds of glowing testimonials on the Internet about its effectiveness. Consult the *Resources* section for a list of medical centers offering proton therapy.

Radiation for Prostate Cancer: How Effective Is It?

In terms of long-term survival from prostate cancer, many doctors believe that recent advances in radiation therapy have brought this approach to a level of equality with prostatectomy. Moreover, adverse effects from today's radiation therapies are less frequent and less severe than those with prostatectomy. The men in my group reflect a spectrum of treatment interventions, but the greatest number received IMRT. Several years post-treatment, they remain in remission and have had fewer adverse effects so far than those who chose prostatectomy. These men remain bullish on radiation treatment for aggressive prostate cancer. Then again, many of the most serious adverse effects from radiation therapy can appear years after treatment ended, so the final chapter for these men who chose radiation remains unfinished.

In an article published in August 2012, the survival rate after ten years among 2,658 men with prostate cancer was 89 percent following prostatectomy, 87 percent following external beam radiation therapy (an early version of IMRT), and 83 percent of brachytherapy. The study also focused on how many men developed a secondary malignancy such as bladder, rectal, or other pelvic cancer. At ten years, 3 percent of men who had a prostatectomy had developed a secondary malignancy, 2 percent following radiation, and 4 percent following brachytherapy. This study suggests that concerns about increased incidences of secondary pelvic cancer after IMRT are unwarranted. On a broader note, the ten year survival with these therapies are similar, with prostatectomy and IMRT being virtually equal and holding a slight edge over brachytherapy.

Other studies have indicated somewhat lower success rates with IRMT. A 2007 article revealed a five year cancer-free rate of 74 to 86 percent following IMRT. This study used a lower radiation intensity than employed today.

A 2011 study in the journal *Cancer* reported the outcomes of men with prostate cancer treated with IMRT. Ten years after treatment, 100 percent of men with low-risk cancer showed no indication of metastases, and in 81 percent of these men PSA levels remained low. The ten-year numbers for men with intermediate-risk cancer were 94 percent without metastases, and 78 percent had low PSA levels. For men with high-risk cancer, the numbers were 90 percent without metastases and 62 percent with low PSA levels.

Overall, these results suggest that if you require treatment for your prostate cancer, you should include radiation therapy among your considerations. This is not to say that radiation therapy always goes smoothly. During the months of uncertainty about my case, I decided to pursue radiation therapy treatment. I interviewed four radiation doctors, all of whom seemed first-rate. I was diligent about letting them know about my history of neuropathies, severe nerve injuries I have in my legs. These neuropathies had developed for no apparent reason in 1995 and were so painful and untreatable, they rendered me bedridden for five years and disabled me for another five. I finally developed a treatment regimen that worked, and I am doing fine now. However, when I talk to new doctors, I make sure to inform them about the condition.

The first radiation session went well, but after the second session, my severe neuropathies flared badly, causing pain and difficulty walking. I had told this radiologist about my neuropathies, but apparently he forgot during his treatment planning. For my part, I neglected to do adequate research. The medical literature has a half dozen reports about radiation causing neuropathies. My radiation oncologist could have designed the radiation beam to avoid the nerves as they exited the spinal cord and descended down my legs, but he didn't. Even good doctors make mistakes. We both erred in failing to recognize that the very intense beam of Rapid Arc would be risky in a person with highly sensitive neuropathies, and that a more gentle approach such as IMRT might be a better fit. After the incident, I spoke to another radiologist who suggested shaping the beam properly and eliminating the risk, but I was not going to chance it. As it was, it took weeks for me to get the neuropathies back under control.

I hope you will not have to deal with such complications, but if you do, you are not alone. In medicine, many cases have divergent results, unexpected reasons, or other idiosyncrasies. At times, only a minority of cases match the examples in the textbooks. If you have any medical conditions or sensitivities, be sure to inform your doctors and gather your own information from books, articles, or on the Internet.

I should not have assumed my radiation doctor had broad knowledge in this area. Perhaps he had never before run into this problem with a patient receiving radiation therapy. I should have been more circumspect and reviewed the medical literature myself. So, I repeat: Do not assume your doctors know how to deal with your individual conditions and circumstances.

10

Non-Invasive Therapies

The following treatments for prostate cancer are *non-invasive*, meaning they do not involve a surgical procedure, like a prostatectomy, or harsh radiation therapy. That is not to say that these therapies are not as intense as the others we've discussed, or will produce less severe side effects. With the exception of active surveillance, the treatments listed in this chapter are medications prescribed by your doctor.

ACTIVE SURVEILLANCE

Active surveillance is the treatment method chosen by many men with low, or sometimes intermediate-risk prostate cancer. During active surveillance, prostate cancer is closely monitored with frequent testing, including digital rectal exams and PSA tests, but treatment is deferred until there is evidence that the cancer is becoming too aggressive.

An older, similar approach called *watchful waiting* is sometimes used with some men with low-risk disease. Many men do well on this program, including Eddie Carrillo, a Los Angeles contractor who was diagnosed with prostate cancer at age fifty-two. According to an article in the *New York Times,* Mr. Carrillo's primary care doctor and urologist both recommended prostatectomy. Mr. Carrillo happened to hear about watchful waiting and decided to monitor his cancer. Now, fifteen years later, Carrillo remains healthy at age sixty-seven. "I wasn't ready to do the operation right away," Mr. Carrillo said. "I have two uncles with prostate cancer, and I have quite a few friends who have had their prostates taken out. The discomfort level and what they went through afterward, I didn't think that was the way I wanted to go."

Watchful waiting actually began in the 1970s. The idea was that prostate cancer was a slow-growing disease and people didn't die from it. This proved dead wrong in too many cases. So, with the advent of PSA testing in 1989, an opposite approach took hold. If your PSA level was high, a biopsy was done. If the biopsy showed cancer, aggressive treatment—prostatectomy or radiation—was recommended. The view was that if a biopsy showed cancer, the likelihood was that there was more cancer in the prostate, and radical treatment was needed to prevent death. The problem with this approach was that prostatectomy and radiation caused injury to surrounding tissues, often permanently impaired men's sexual or bladder functioning, and in about 25 percent, didn't cure the cancer anyway.

The only other alternative was watchful waiting. The problem with this approach was that it really did what it said—watched and waited—sometimes waiting too long for initiating treatment.

A Modern Perspective

Through the 1990s and into the 2000s, it has become increasingly clear that many men, as they age beyond fifty, develop small areas of prostate cancer. The percentage of men having these small prostate cancers generally reflects their age group. For example, around 70 percent of men at age seventy have these small cancers in the prostate. Yet, because men's prostate glands often enlarge as they age, their PSA levels also climb. With the findings of an elevated PSA and a biopsy positive for cancer, these are the men who have been sent for prostatectomy or radiation—often unnecessarily.

A key shift has begun in the recognition that these non-threatening cancers are usually Gleason 6, low-grade and non-threatening. Dr. Laurence Klotz explains:

> Active surveillance was an attempt to grapple with this by saying, okay, we know that guys who have bad prostate cancer need treatment, and benefit from it. And that's been clearly shown in randomized trials. But the patients dying of prostate cancer tend to have higher grade (Gleason) cancer. So maybe we can take the ones who have low-grade cancer, just manage them conservatively, and keep a close eye on them, because some may develop something worse . . . Patients flocked to this approach, because word was getting out that there were problems with the outcome of surgery and radiation in terms of quality of life.

Now, after more than fifteen years of study, it has been demonstrated that hardly any of these men with small, Gleason 6 prostate cancers die. Less than 2 percent die over ten years. Dr. Klotz adds:

> The vast majority of men who are found to have these little bits of low-grade cancer have absolutely no threat to their lives, and can be managed with conservative treatment.

Many other experts agree. Leonard Marks, M.D., Professor of Urology, UCLA states, "Prostate cancer is so prevalent, many men during their lifetime will be diagnosed with prostate cancer. Unlike a lot of cancers, breast, lung, colon, there are some prostate cancers that just sit there. They don't kill you. So even though these are, technically, cancers, they're not lethal cancers."

Active surveillance involves keeping a close eye on a man's cancer with repeated PSA tests and an occasional biopsy. To my mind, these tools are not enough to assure men that if their cancer grows larger or shows signs of spreading, intervention will be mobilized quickly enough. This is why I initially decided to have surgery. But if you add the new diagnostic methods—DCE-MRI and color Doppler ultrasound—active surveillance can be highly effective. When I obtained these tests, I decided to forego surgery and take the active surveillance route.

Who is a Candidate for Active Surveillance?

Ten years ago, the first national conference was held on active surveillance for prostate cancer. A consensus protocol was developed to define the men appropriate for active surveillance:

- Normal DRE (digital rectal exam)

- Gleason score of 6 or less

- 2 positive biopsy cores or fewer

- No biopsy cores comprised of 50 percent cancer cells or more

- PSA levels less than 10

Men who select active surveillance must be committed to working closely with their doctor. PSA levels should be drawn every three months for a year, then every six months. Digital rectal exams need to be done every six months at first. Biopsies have also been part of the protocol, but these may be less necessary today for men who are getting DCE-MRI or color Doppler ultrasound testing. None of these tests are 100 percent accurate, yet taken together they can provide an early warning of worrisome changes in your prostate cancer.

You may have noticed that my findings did not fit all of the criteria for active surveillance. I fit only three of the five factors: Gleason level 6; DRE normal; no biopsy cores greater than 50 percent cancer. However, my PSA levels were 15 and 13 ng/ml, well above the ceiling of 10 to be categorized as low-risk. Yet, with my large prostate and history of prostate infections, the PSA levels might not have been as bad as they seemed. PSA levels are accurate only about 75 percent of the time. In men like me, who have complicating factors, PSA levels are less reliable. Also, my biopsy revealed four (of fourteen) cores with prostate cancer, which are more than the one or two positive biopsy cores allowed under the usual definition of low-risk prostate cancer.

As you can see, decision making may be simple or complicated, depending on your findings. I discuss this further in the next chapter, *Weighing the Evidence and Making a Decision.*

When to Consider Treatment

If any of the tests above suggest worsening of your prostate cancer, consideration must be given to the possibility of active treatment.

Changes for the worse include:

- Increasing PSA levels

- Abnormal digital rectal exam

- Increase in cancer size or spread on DCE-MRI or color Doppler ultrasound

- Biopsy cores with a Gleason score of 7 or more

- Three or more biopsy cores with cancer

Foregoing Active Surveillance

Approximately 160,000 men in the United States are diagnosed with prostate cancer each year. About half have early stage disease that will probably never harm them. These men fit criteria for active surveillance, yet 90 percent of them will elect prostatectomy or radiation therapy. Why is this?

"Men have a strong belief that if they are diagnosed with cancer, they will die if it's left untreated. They believe that treatment will cure them," says Dr. Timothy Wilt.

The diagnosis of cancer produces so much anxiety, many men want to get rid of the cancer *right now*, no matter the risks of their quality of life afterward. The rate of heart attacks and suicide doubles in men who are told they have prostate cancer. Other men do their homework, weigh the benefits and risks, do not act rashly, yet still decide they will sleep better knowing the cancer has been removed. Others are pressured by family members, who are scared by the term "cancer." Other men listen to only one voice: their urologist, or a surgeon. Others are not told about the new diagnostic methods and multiple, focal treatment options. They have followed the traditional path: PSA, biopsy, surgery, or radiation.

A recent study showed that when men with newly diagnosed prostate cancer discussed treatment with only their urologist, only 10 percent choose active surveillance. This is just one fifth of the men who actually match the criteria for active surveillance. In contrast, when men with newly diagnosed prostate cancer met with a team of experts including a surgeon, radiologist, and MRI specialist, about 40 percent of the men eligible for active surveillance choose it. More information gave the men more choices.

Is Active Surveillance Safe?

An important study on the use of active surveillance for prostate cancer was published in the *New England Journal of Medicine*. The study consisted of 731 men with prostate cancer who, between 1994 and 2002, were treated with either prostatectomy or watchful waiting. 364 men received prostatectomy, and of these 21 (6 percent) ultimately died of prostate cancer. 367 men received watchful waiting, with 31 (9 percent) ultimately dying from their cancer. Overall, surgery for prostate cancer produced 3 percent fewer deaths than watchful waiting. In terms of preventing death from prostate cancer, prostatectomy was slightly superior.

But at what cost? During the thirty days after prostate surgery, complications caused one death, two cases of blood clots in the legs, two more in the lungs, one case of renal failure, one stroke, blood transfusions in six men, six others requiring urinary catheters more than thirty days, and

A Controversial Approach
to Preventing Prostate Cancer

A recent study titled "Drug Cuts Prostate Cancer Risk," announced that the drug finasteride (Proscar) significantly reduces the risk of getting prostate cancer. Finasteride is no use for men who have already been diagnosed with prostate cancer, but might be a preventative measure for those who are concerned about getting prostate cancer—in particular, men with a higher risk of developing the disease, such as African-Americans. But before you sign on, be sure to read the fine print.

Having analyzed thousands of medical studies, this one, "Long-Term Survival of Participants in the Prostate Cancer Prevention Trial," published in the *New England Journal of Medicine,* wins a prize as one of the most misleading and alarming studies I've seen. The study was big, including 18,000 men over eighteen years, costing $73 million. Back in 2003, when the first phase of the study was published, I saw many flaws in the approach it suggested. I wasn't alone. Dr. Peter Scardino, one of the most prominent urologists in the United States and chairman of the department of urology at Memorial Sloan-Kettering Cancer Center in New York City, wrote in an accompanying editorial. "Should finasteride now be recommended to men in order to lower their risk of prostate cancer? Several disturbing findings in the report argue that it should not."

Think of it this way. If we gave 10 million men finasteride, it would reduce their risk of prostate cancer by 38 percent. Sounds good, but at what cost? Finasteride blocks the conversion of testosterone into its more action derivative, dihydrotestosterone, which is ten times more powerful than testosterone itself. Thus, common side effects include reduced libido (10 percent), abnormal ejaculation (7.2 percent), impotence (18.5 percent), breast swelling, which is sometimes painful (2.2 percent), and abnormal sexual functioning (2.5 percent). These numbers are from the manufacturer of finasteride and the FDA, so they are credible, but be aware that manufacturer's numbers often underestimate the true frequency of side effects.

Worse, these symptoms do not always recede after the drug is discontinued. They can last for months or years. It is not believed to be a common problem, but nor does it seem to be rare. The condition has a name: Post-Finasteride Syndrome (PFS). It is believed to occur infrequently, but who really knows? Is "infrequent" one in ten men, in 100, in 1,000? From my research on the drug industry, it appears that drug companies do not really want to find answers to these types of questions, nor do they want the attention such answers would attract. Many doctors who treat sexual disorders are aware of PFS. So is the FDA.

The same problems have also been reported with Avodart (dutasteride), which is in the same family as, and often used instead of, finasteride. A study in the 2011 Journal of Sexual Medicine confirms it. Most men who take these drugs experience some of these side effects, but according to Abdulmaged Traish, M.D., lead author of the study, "some experience it more drastically than others." Dr. Traish added that in a small percentage of cases, "It is a life sentence. No sex. No desire. Potential depression."

So, of the 10 million men to whom we gave finasteride, the incidence of prostate cancer would probably drop from 16 percent to 11 percent. That's good. But *all* of the 10 million men would be subject to getting the side effects from blocking testosterone. Plus, 8.4 million of these men would never have gotten prostate cancer in the first place. Still interested, fellas?

The second reason finasteride for preventing prostate cancer is a terrible idea is that it only lowers your risk of the low-grade forms of prostate cancer. These are the types that rarely harm. So reducing the incidence of low-risk prostate cancer from 16 percent to 11 percent, as discussed above, may be good but it isn't really as big a deal as it sounds. Unless, of course, with today's backward methods, your doctor rushes you to biopsy, then surgery or radiation. If you have read this far, you know how to avoid overtreatment.

The study also found that finasteride was associated with a small increase in the incidence of high-risk cancer. If this is true, it is another good reason to trash this idea. Further analysis suggests that this finding might be a statistical artifact due to the design of the study. Nevertheless, the chief researcher of the study, Dr. Ian Thompson, felt the need to address it during his press conference. "Even if there is a higher risk of high-grade cancer, it doesn't appear to have an impact on how long a man lives, and that's reassuring." No, it isn't reassuring. If the drug truly increases the occurrence of high-risk prostate cancer, however slightly, it means more prostatectomies or radiation therapy. These in turn mean more sexual and bladder dysfunctions and reduced quality of life.

I doubt many men will opt to take finasteride every day for the rest of their lives to prevent prostate cancer of which they have only a 16 percent of getting, especially since the drug can markedly reduce their sex drive, performance, and pleasure. In addition, the drug only protects men from low-grade cancer, the kind that can be handled today with focal therapy or active surveillance.

Is it difficult to understand why this study was ever funded. Or why it made the national news. It just goes to show that in today's rush-rush world, members of the media often draw their reports from the press releases they are given. Few take the time or have the training to read a scientific article and sort the true breakthroughs from the busts.

ten cases requiring further corrective surgery. Problems with bladder control from dribbling to complete loss of urinary control occurred in forty-nine men with surgery, versus eighteen men with watchful waiting. 81 percent of men who had surgery developed erectile dysfunction, compared with 44 percent in the watchful waiting group.

Overall, prostatectomy slightly reduced the risk of death or metastases from prostate cancer in the high and medium risk groups, but at the cost of many serious adverse effects that clearly impaired men's quality of life. These adverse effects were experienced by men after surgery no matter whether they were high, intermediate or low-risk. Yet, in the low-risk group, the study found no benefit whatsoever from surgery in reducing the risk of death or metastases in comparison to watchful waiting.

This study was the first to clearly define the advantages of watchful waiting versus prostatectomy in men with low-risk prostate cancer. "I think this is game changing," said Dr. Leonard Marks, a urology professor at UCLA. "What this study does is call attention to the fact that there are a lot of prostate cancers that are diagnosed today that are not dangerous."

Note that this study used watchful waiting, as opposed to active surveillance. Today, with the availability of the DCE-MRI, active surveillance will demonstrate even greater protection than watchful waiting did in men with low-risk disease.

I am not saying that active surveillance is always preferable to aggressive treatments such as prostatectomy or full gland radiation. These therapies play a crucial role for men with higher Gleason levels, abnormal DRE or worrisome findings. The key is to accurately differentiate which men need which treatment. And for men with low-risk cancer who are not comfortable knowing they harbor cancer in their prostates, the focal therapies can provide safer, less injurious ways to remove the cancer without causing lifelong impairments in bladder and sexual functioning. The key to all of this is obtaining an accurate diagnosis that defines the type and grade of cancer you have and pinpoints where it is located. PSA, DCE-MRIs, and if available, color Doppler ultrasound, are all the key players in accomplishing a level of diagnostic accuracy that has not been possible previously.

ANDROGEN DEPRIVATION THERAPY

A boy's prostate gland is tiny. With puberty and the first surges of testosterone from the testes, the prostate gland begins to enlarge until it is the size of a walnut. About seventy years ago, Dr. Charles Huggins discovered that removal of the testes markedly slowed prostate cancer progression. And so it became widely accepted that reducing testosterone in the body hindered prostate cancer growth.

Medications that reduce testosterone's impact on prostate cancer are known as "androgen deprivation therapy," or ADT. Occasionally, they are called TIP for "testosterone-inhibiting pharmaceuticals," or simply referred to as "hormone therapy." ADT drugs block the stimulating effect of testosterone on prostate cancer cells. Generally, an ADT approach is preferred before chemotherapy because it is less toxic and generally more effective initially.

Today, ADT is used most often at the later stages of treatment for aggressive cancers, after prostatectomy or radiation therapy, sometimes after metastases have already spread outside the prostate gland. It is often overlooked for men with low or intermediate-risk prostate cancer. Back when my doctors told me I had intermediate-risk prostate cancer, not one of them mentioned this frequently effective approach. Yet this approach has many advantages when used for intermediate-risk disease. The main benefit of ADT is that it can allow men to avoid surgery or radiation for years or decades, and sometimes altogether.

How ADT Works

Treatment with ADT most often involves drugs that provide three types of synergistic, anti-testosterone effects. A drug frequently used for turning off testosterone production in the testes is Lupron (leuprorelin, Eligard). The drug is administered as a monthly or long-acting quarterly injection.

Another group does not lower testosterone per se, but instead blocks the androgen receptor at which testosterone impacts prostate cells and prostate cancer cells, thereby reducing testosterone's effect on the cells. The best-known androgen receptor blockers are Casodex (bicalutamide) and Nilandron (nilutamide).

The third group, the 5-alpha-reductase inhibitors such as Avodart (dutasteride) and Proscar (finasteride), block the chemical conversion of testosterone to dihydrotestosterone, which is five times more potent. By doing so, these drugs greatly reduce the potency of the testosterone reaching the prostate cancer cells.

When ADT is used for advanced prostate cancer, its effectiveness usually lasts three to six years, at which point the cancer may develop resistance to the drugs' effects. For men with early, intermediate-risk prostate cancer, the effect can extend ten years or more.

ADT's impact can be rapid and dramatic. Within eight months, many men with newly diagnosed prostate cancer see drops in their PSA levels to far below one ng/ml, often as low as 0.05 ng/ml, meaning that the activity level of the prostate cancer has been reduced to near zero.

Case Reports on ADT

Mark Scholz, M.D., co-author of the excellent *Invasion of the Prostate Snatchers* and a pioneer in ADT for intermediate-risk prostate cancer and sometimes in concert with active surveillance for low-risk disease, writes "over the years we have seen hundreds of men with excellent responses to ADT." Here are three of the many cases he has described:

- A man with a PSA of thirty-four was found to have Gleason 6 prostate cancer. After starting ADT, in two months his PSA was 0.3. He discontinued ADT two years later after a biopsy showed no residual cancer. His testosterone levels returned to normal a year after that. He has remained off ADT for fifteen years while continuing with active surveillance.

- A seventy-eight-year-old man had a PSA level of 33. Digital rectal exam revealed multiple palpable areas suggestive of prostate cancer. Biopsy determined he was intermediate-risk. He began ADT therapy, which reduced his PSA rapidly. The man continued ADT therapy for eighteen months, then discontinued. His testosterone level recovered quickly. Multiple color Doppler ultrasound tests have revealed stable areas of prostate cancer. He has never required additional ADT. At age ninety, his PSA level remained at a very low 0.06 ng/ml.

- A sixty-four-year-old man with PSA 12 was found to have an intermediate grade prostate cancer in one area of his prostate gland and low-grade cancer in two other areas. He began ADT treatment, and five months later his PSA was too low to be measurable. He discontinued ADT therapy. Six years later, a biopsy showed a recurrence of his intermediate-grade cancer. ADT was restarted, his PSA dropped again, and one year later his biopsy was clear. ADT was discontinued, and his condition remained stable.

Although the typical ADT triad is comprised of drugs such as Proscar, Casodex, and Lupron, Ralph Blum, the second author of *Invasion of the Prostate Snatchers,* did it differently. He agreed to take Lupron only. However, Blum also took Casodex for a few days before starting Lupron. The Casodex blocked the brief flare of testosterone that can cause unpleasant side effects when initiating treatment with Lupron. Today, doctors often prescribe ADT by starting one or two drugs at a time rather than all three simultaneously. They then add a third when the first drug loses effectiveness.

Four weeks after Blum began Lupron, his PSA had dropped from 18.3 to 10.3 ng/ml. Seven months later, his PSA was 0.125. He discontinued Lupron for four months. When his PSA level crept back to 1.05, he restarted Lupron. He went off and on Lupron for many more years, ultimately deciding to have radiation therapy. The delay his ADT afforded was worthwhile, because during his years on ADT, the accuracy and effectiveness of radiation treatment improved greatly.

Many doctors start ADT with Avodart, which they favor over Proscar. If it becomes necessary, Casodex may be added when Avodart's effect wanes. Third comes Lupron, if needed. Drugs, dosages, and regimens can vary considerably between different doctors.

How Does ADT Rate Overall?

A study of ADT treatment in men with newly diagnosed prostate cancer revealed the following results. The study included seventy-three men, average age sixty-seven, with an average PSA of 9, and a majority of men with DRE findings suggestive of prostate cancer. Most of the men were intermediate-risk and some were high-risk. All of the men took ADT for nine months or longer. After twelve years follow-up, twenty-one (29 percent) of the men never required any further treatment. Twenty-four men (33 percent) required periodic ADT to keep PSA levels below 5. Other men ultimately elected to have invasive treatment (surgery or radiation). And three men had died three, eight, and eleven years after starting ADT treatment.

The main finding of the study was that 29 percent of the men with intermediate or high-risk prostate cancer never needed any further treatment after their initial course of ADT, and another 33 percent were maintained with intermittent ADT treatment. In other words, forty-five men (62 percent) never needed surgery or radiation or other invasive treatment.

In all cases, testosterone levels gradually returned to normal after discontinuation of ADT. With today's superior monitoring abilities using DCE-MRI and/or color Doppler ultrasound for following the progression of prostate cancer, the results with men on ADT will likely be even better. Over time, it has become clear that for men with intermediate-risk prostate cancer, ADT is another option to consider.

The Downside of ADT

The results of ADT for prostate cancer are impressive, and all it takes is a few pills a day or a monthly or quarterly shot. But the fact is that if you have intermediate-risk prostate cancer, there are no easy treatment choices. Most men who have intermediate-risk prostate cancer require treatment. The choices are prostatectomy, one of the many forms of radiation therapy, one of the focal therapies (if the cancer is localized)—or ADT.

Taking pills is certainly easier than invasive treatment. However, as you might imagine, taking pills that inhibit testosterone has many undesirable effects on the male body and mind. First and foremost, ADT markedly reduces libido. Your sex drive may drop to nearly zero. Erectile dysfunction drugs like Viagra can help produce an erection, but many men don't bother because they have no desire for sex. Blum writes that he couldn't imagine not having any desire for sex, but when he was on ADT, even though Viagra worked for him, "I couldn't dredge up enough desire even to want sex." Not every man experiences this side effect to this degree, but many do.

Other ADT side effects include loss of muscle mass, fatigue, weight gain, night sweats and daytime hot flashes, breast growth (often not reversible), osteoporosis (bone loss), joint pains, and increased emotionality.

New ADT Drugs
for Advanced Prostate Cancer

Two new drugs, Zytiga (abiraterone) and Xtandi (enzalutamide), were approved by the FDA for the treatment of "castration-resistant prostate cancer," meaning that standard ADT treatments no longer worked. The term originated from a time when the only form of ADT was castration, which greatly lowered testosterone levels. When castration no longer worked, or in modern times, standard ADT no longer works, the prostate cancer is called "castration-resistant." Because Xtandi and Zytiga are extremely potent blockers of testosterone, they can have many side effects. Be sure to ask about this if your doctor recommends either of them for your prostate cancer. For example, Xtandi can increase the risk of seizures.

Xtandi was purposefully designed to overcome the androgen receptor resistance that occurs with many men on long-term ADT. Xtandi works by blocking the androgen receptor of prostate cancer cells approximately five times more tightly than Casodex (bicalutamide). In addition, resistance to Xtandi may develop more slowly than with standard ADT drugs. In studies, Xtandi was shown to markedly reduce PSA levels and to extend life significantly more than placebo in men with castration-resistant, metastatic prostate cancer.

Zytiga is also used as a treatment for castration-resistant prostate cancer that is metastatic. The drug blocks the production of androgen in both the testes, adrenal glands, and the tumor itself. Studies have shown that Zytiga significantly slows the progression of metastatic prostate cancer, delays the time when men had to start chemotherapy, and modestly improves survival times. Because of its many adverse effects, Zytiga is taken with prednisone, a form of cortisone.

Some men say they can minimize the muscle loss, fatigue, and weight gain by regular exercise with weights and a healthy diet. If hot flashes and sweats are bothersome, other medicines can block this adverse effect. Yet other side effects can be more difficult to reduce.

These problems seem monumental to most men, but before rejecting this approach, consider the adverse effects with the other options. Surgery: 50 percent impotence and 8 percent incontinence, which are often permanent; all of the other adverse effects and risks of the surgery; and return of cancer in 25 percent. Radiation IMRT: 35 percent impotence, 2 percent rectal burn, 2 percent urethral inflammation, and return of cancer in 25 to 30 percent.

The fact is, the adverse effects of ADT can vary greatly from man to man. For this reason, ADT should be started on a trial basis. For example, Lupron can be effective for many men, while others are greatly affected by fatigue or severe hot flashes. If you and your doctor decide to try Lupron first, start with the monthly injection, rather than the extended-release three-month injection. If severe side effects hit, you know they will subside within a month, rather than having to wait three months.

Many doctors today prefer to start ADT with Avodart because adverse effects are somewhat less. Avodart blocks dihydrotestosterone, the primary and most potent stimulus of prostate cancer among a man's hormones. When this drug benefit wanes, doctors often add or replace Avodart with Casodex. Today, Lupron is often held for last.

On the positive test for ADT, some men with intermediate-risk disease only need it once and others intermittently. Some men can go off ADT for months or years at a time. Testosterone levels typically rise again. Sex drive, and normal sexual functioning return in most men, but not all. Long-term loss of normal sexual functioning has been reported with Proscar (finasteride) and Avodart (dutasteride) lasting months or years after the drug has been stopped.

CHEMOTHERAPY

If you need to speak to a doctor about chemotherapy, your prostate cancer is high-risk and possibly metastatic, or spreading. You want to be sure the doctor is knowledgeable and highly experienced. Some urologists specialize in the chemotherapy of high-risk prostate cancer, but the majority of urologists do not. The same can be said about oncologists, who are doctors specializing in the treatment of cancer. Most oncologists treat many types of cancer.

My recommendation is to find an oncologist who specializes in treating prostate cancer, or at least an oncologist whose practice includes a lot of cases of prostate cancer. Don't hesitate to ask the doctor about his experience with your type and degree of prostate cancer, as well as his experience in prescribing the drugs I have discussed in this chapter and chemotherapeutic agents.

Also be sure to read Chapter 7 on the new genetic tests that are available today for improving the accuracy of biopsy interpretation and for enhancing cancer aggressiveness grading. Most of all, if you may need chemotherapy, read about the new genetic tests to identify the most effective chemotherapy drugs based on the genetic profile of each man's prostate cancer.

XOFIGO FOR BONE METASTASES

The recent FDA approval of the drug Alpharadin was a major breakthrough for prostate cancer treatment. The name has since been changed to Xofigo. Developed by Bayer Pharmaceuticals in partnership with Norweigan company Algeta ASA, Xofigo is an intravenous injection that contains radium-223 chloride, among other chemicals, to destroy cancer that has metastasized, or spread, to the bones.

Xofigo is the first drug of its kind, a drug that fixes specifically to calcium and other minerals in bone that allows it to deliver radiation directly to cancer metastases. Because radium-223 is chemically similar to calcium, it readily attaches itself like a magnet to bone. The alpha particles are highly lethal to cancer cells harbored there. Xofigo is intended for men who have been treated with surgery or radiation, or medication therapy to lower testosterone levels, or chemotherapy. It is not designed for men whose prostate cancer has spread to other organs of the body.

Greater Effectiveness, Fewer Side Effects

Cancer experts agree that Xofigo represents a therapeutic step forward. Commenting on recent scientific reports, medical oncologist Jean-Charles Soria, M.D., Ph.D., stated, "I think that [radium-223 chloride] will become a major player in prostate cancer management." Michael Baumann, M.D., professor of radiation oncology at the University of Technology in Dresden, Germany, added, "This is a very important finding. It is certainly practice-changing."

Xofigo's properties allow for a marked reduction in adverse effects compared to earlier isotope therapies that target cancer metastases in bone. Strontium 89, which emits beta particles that cause greater peripheral damage, has been used infrequently because of its many adverse effects, especially suppression of bone marrow cells. Samarium 153, also a beta emitter, causes fewer problems but has still been withheld except for a very advanced metastatic bone disease.

Unlike the above therapies, alpha particles have a very limited range, only two to ten cells deep, thereby causing much less injury to surrounding health tissues. The half-life (how long it takes for half of the substance to leave the body) of Xofigo is just eleven days, which makes it ideal as a targeted, limited, radioactive cancer therapy. Residual Xofigo is rapidly dispatched to the intestinal tract and eliminated.

Most importantly, Xofigo is the only direct radioactive agent demonstrating improvement overall in studies of men with prostate cancer bone metastases. In the Alpharadin in Symptomatic Prostate Cancer Patients (ALSYMPCA) trial, men receiving Xofigo demonstrated a median survival time of 14.9 months versus 11.3 months for men receiving placebo. This large trial involved 921 subjects at over 100 treatment facilities in nineteen countries. Treatment consisted of monthly intravenous infusions of Xofigo or placebo over six months. The results were so encouraging that the FDA sought a priority review and granted early approval.

Although an increase of 3.6 months in longevity may seem small, it is statistically significant. Moreover, many men experienced greater benefit, and it should be remembered that all of the subjects had very advanced prostate cancer. Now that Xofigo has been approved, doctors will likely use it earlier in men exhibiting bone metastases. Such metastases occur frequently in men with advanced prostate cancer, especially those with prostate cancer resistant to testosterone blocking therapies ("castration-resistant prostate cancer"). The most common side effects in the study were nausea, vomiting, diarrhea, and swelling of the legs, ankles, or feet. Other adverse effects included reduced red and white blood cell and platelet counts.

11

Focal Therapies

For decades, the medical approach to treating prostate cancer has been based on the premise that if prostate cancer is found in biopsy, it likely exists in many parts of the prostate gland. This explains why doctors have so often recommended radical treatments that entail removing the entire prostate gland or irradiating it, even to men with low-grade, Gleason 6 cancer. This is why overtreatment has been and continues to be so rampant.

Yet as Dr. Dan Sperling, M.D., writes, "Radical treatments themselves pose inherent risks: post-treatment urinary, sexual, and bowel morbidities (side effects). The recent debate over routine PSA screening of healthy men stems from a well-placed concern that men with a rising PSA are rushed into invasive, blind needle biopsies that entail risks of infection, false negative, and under-staging. A positive biopsy triggers an intense period of decision-making with whole-gland treatment often behind the physician's first recommendation."

In the past, we did not have the technological capability to differentiate the men who actually needed whole prostate treatment (prostatectomy or radiation) from the men who didn't. Before DCE-MRI and color Doppler ultrasound, a man who declined radical treatment was making a risky wager. Today, the availability of the DCE-MRI has reversed the risk. In my case, when the MRI and color Doppler ultrasound both showed a modest-sized, solitary tumor in a safe area of my prostate gland, a tumor that was not near any vital structures, it became much easier for me to consider a less aggressive approach.

Quietly, more men have been opting for focal treatment of their prostate cancer, which aims to effectively treat the cancer while causing the least amount of damage to the prostate gland and the surrounding areas.

The treatment modalities most often used are cryotherapy or high intensity focused ultrasound (HIFU). As the prostate DCE-MRI has become available, men have chosen these techniques with greater confidence. A newer method, MRI-guided focal laser ablation (destruction by intense heat), is available now. It too is applied in a targeted manner with DCE-MRI guidance during the procedure.

Today, many experts and patients alike are asking: Why treat the whole prostate if only one part of it has evidence of cancer? Proponents of focal therapy compare it to a lumpectomy that many women choose for localized, low-grade breast cancer. The main advantage of focal therapy is that while destroying the cancerous lesion in the prostate, healthy tissue including the nerve bundles that control sexual and bladder functioning can be spared. For example, the most vexing adverse effect with HIFU of the whole prostate gland is urinary stricture (severe narrowing of the urethra), but this problem can be avoided when HIFU is used for focal treatment.

CRYOTHERAPY

Cryotherapy (cryoablation) is a non-surgical method of destroying prostate cancer cells by freezing them. The use of cryotherapy began fifty years ago and methods have improved greatly in recent years. Today, cryotherapy is performed using 3D and Doppler ultrasound in fusion with DCE-MRI imaging, allowing accurate identification and measurement of areas of prostate cancer.

Cryotherapy involves no cutting and little blood loss. The treatment is done through the wall of the rectum and takes a couple of hours. Cryotherapy does not involve any radiation, and it may be repeated if the cancer returns locally. It may also be used for salvage treatment of recurrent prostate cancer following prostatectomy or radiation. Radiation therapy can also be done if cryotherapy fails.

The most vexing adverse effect from full prostate cryotherapy is erectile dysfunction. This side effect occurred very often with early forms of full prostate cryotherapy. The shift from total to focal cryotherapy has reduced this problem greatly. Urinary incontinence and injury to the rectal wall are infrequent adverse effects.

There is a wealth of information about cryotherapy and its practitioners on the Internet. See the *Resources* section for more information.

Results From Studies

Studies of cryotherapy have demonstrated improving results as the emphasis has shifted from full-prostate treatment to focal treatment and as techniques and imaging methods have advanced. The emphasis for this approach has also shifted away from high-risk prostate cancer to low and intermediate risk cases.

For example, in a study by Bahn et.al., focal cryotherapy assisted by color Doppler ultrasound was conducted with thirty-one men with unilateral prostate cancer. Six years later, 93 percent of men showed no elevation in their low PSA levels, and 96 percent had negative biopsies. Sexual potency was maintained by 48 percent of the men, and another 41 percent regained potency with medication. In other words, adequate potency was obtained in 89 percent of the men, a far better number than with prostatectomy or radiation therapy.

FOCAL LASER ABLATION (ALA)

Initially developed to treat brain tumors, MRI-guided focal laser ablation is now approved for treating cancers in soft tissues, including spinal cord, muscle, kidney, liver, and prostate. Laser treatment uses light energy delivered by a probe positioned into the core of the tumor. As the intensity of light increases, the temperature of the probe rises and destroys the cancer cells. The doctor will also burn a margin of normal prostate tissue surrounding the tumor to make sure all of the cancer cells are destroyed.

The DCE-MRI imaging plays a key role in ensuring that the laser treatment is delivered to the proper area. The laser probe is inserted into the man's body via the perineum (between the testicles and anus) and directed by the doctor between other pelvic structures and toward the prostate. Once in the prostate gland, the laser probe is threaded using MRI guidance into the proper area of the gland and then into the tumor. The entire focal laser ablation (FLA) procedure takes two to four hours, and most of it is used for accurately positioning the probe. Once there, the intense heat of the laser destroys the tumor in about ten to fifteen minutes. As this occurs, the changes of the cancerous tissue from the laser's intense heat can be seen on the MRI images. This helps the doctor to administer the correct amount and duration of laser-generated heat.

Today, there are a handful of practitioners in the United States who perform focal laser ablation for prostate cancer. One of them is Dr. Dan

Sperling, who states that with MRI guidance, he is able to identify prostate cancer tumors as small as four millimeters and then destroy them with FLA.

Compared to HIFU and cryotherapy, laser therapy seems a much simpler and direct approach. Dr. Sperling told me, "Focused laser ablation of prostate cancer isn't much different than performing a biopsy." Except that a biopsy only requires taking twelve or so pieces of prostate tissue, which is accomplished in about ten to fifteen minutes.

Dr. Scott Eggener, a urologic oncologist at the University of Chicago Medical Center, calls focused laser ablation "the equivalent to women with breast cancer having a lumpectomy."

Dr. Sperling states that focal therapy is rapidly presenting itself as a middle ground, energetically sought by patients and cautiously championed by a minority of clinicians. Advances in imaging technology now make it possible to clearly detect smaller and smaller tumors, and advances in targeted ablation enable effective ablation of even a small focus of disease.

FLA with MRI guidance is also available under the direction of Sharif Nour, M.D., at Emory Healthcare, Atlanta, GA, and so does the group at Desert Medical Imaging, Indian Wells, CA. The University of Texas Medical Branch also offers FLA. Its chairman of radiology, Eric Walser, M.D., has been performing this procedure for three years. "The problem is, most men who test positive, even if the risk is one in 1,000 of dying of prostate cancer, still just want to get it out of there," says Dr. Walser. "Our approach pairs the most advanced MRI imaging to identify cancer-suspicious areas in the prostate and the most advanced laser technology to remove them, with virtually no risk of impotence or incontinence."

HIGH INTENSITY FOCUSED ULTRASOUND (HIFU)

Robotic high intensity focused ultrasound, or HIFU, is a recently developed medical technology that aims to kill cancer cells with high frequency sound waves. It is also used to treat other prostate-related diagnoses, including benign prostate hyperplasia.

HIFU destroys cancerous prostate cells by heating them to nearly 212 degrees Fahrenheit while leaving nearby structures unharmed. HIFU is not a form of radiation therapy, so it doesn't have any of the adverse effects of radiation on surrounding tissues. HIFU is performed with a probe through the rectum and into the prostate, so no cutting is involved, little blood loss occurs, collateral damage is minimal, and recovery is relatively quick. Indeed, HIFU is performed as an outpatient procedure. Treatment typically takes two to three hours.

HIFU can be tailored to the needs of each patient. It can be used to destroy the entire prostate gland, one of its lobes, or one specific area of the prostate. HIFU can be performed on all stages of prostate cancer and on all Gleason scores. It can also be used as a salvage treatment when cancer returns after prostatectomy, radiation, prior HIFU or other types of treatment.

Adverse Effects with HIFU

As with robotic prostatectomy, the HIFU doctor can see the area being treated, thereby avoiding vital structures such as the seminal vesicles and neurovascular bundles. This capability allows for lower rates of adverse effects. After HIFU, men will require a urinary catheter for two to four weeks. Incontinence or urinary retention (inability to urinate) occurs in a small percentage of men.

The most common significant adverse effect with HIFU is urinary stricture, a scarring of the urethra through which urine flows. Stricture occurs in approximately 25 percent of men after HIFU prostatectomy. This happens much less frequently in men receiving single lobe or focal HIFU, as do most other adverse effects. Sexual dysfunctions and bladder control difficulties can occur with whole gland HIFU as often as with surgery or radiation treatment. When used for focal treatment, HIFU causes fewer of these problems.

Total prostate HIFU cannot be performed on men whose prostate size is over 40 cc. In men with larger prostates, medication is often prescribed to shrink the prostate gland before proceeding with HIFU treatment.

A Lack of Long-Term Studies

A major downside of HIFU is the lack of results from long-term studies. One of the most recent publications describes a study of 157 men with various degrees of prostate cancer treated with HIFU. After five-year follow up, 66 percent of low-risk men lacked any sign of cancer recurrence, as did 40 percent of intermediate-risk and 21 percent of high-risk men. Men without any sign of cancer spread were 74 percent, 46 percent, and 29 percent, respectively. These results do not compare with those following prostatectomy or radiation therapy. The authors commented:

"HIFU treatment does not provide effective oncologic outcomes even in low-risk patients with prostate cancer, as well as in intermediate or high-risk groups."

Another study showed a cancer-free rate of 69 percent seven years after HIFU treatment. This rate does not equal the results following prostatectomy or radiation therapy. At the same time, these results should be considered preliminary because they reflect men treated with HIFU in the early and mid-2000s, when clinicians had limited experience with a still developing technology. Today, many doctors have implemented the use of DCE-MRI guidance in performing HIFU, which should improve results with this therapy.

My first urologist, Dr. Summers, disdained HIFU, calling it something like "doing surgery with a hot curling iron." However, I was interested in this new technology and spent considerable time reading about it. In addition to the three doctors I mentioned above, I also talked to two HIFU patients who spoke highly of their experiences.

The use of HIFU will likely increase as the emerging diagnostic technology such as the DCE-MRI makes focal treatment a popular choice for localized prostate cancer. A recent, small study using HIFU for focal therapy in twenty men with low or intermediate-risk prostate cancer showed that persistent adverse effects were fewer than seen with prostatectomy or radiation therapy. One year after HIFU treatment, 95 percent of men continued to have erections sufficient for vaginal penetration; 90 percent of men were continent without urinary leakage or the need for pads.

You have the opportunity to ask about these results and other questions with doctors who perform HIFU. Many doctors and medical centers are seeking subjects for FDA-approved clinical studies of HIFU. Consult the *Resources* section for more information.

PART 3

Weighing the Evidence and Making a Decision

12

What Does Your Data Say?

Making a decision about treating your prostate cancer is not always simple. Even if you and other men have the very same results, you may get a different recommendation from your doctor than a man with similar results gets from his doctor. Even with similar input from their doctors, different men may choose different treatments. This is why it is important to organize your test results and then consider the appropriate treatment choices.

When you have finished your tests, lists all of the results together and see how they add up.

TABLE 13.1. YOUR TEST RESULTS		
Test	**Results**	**Risk Level**
PSA levels		
Positive biopsy cores		
T Grade		
Gleason score		
Color Doppler ultrasound		
DCE-MRI findings		
Carbon-11 PET/CT Scan (if done)		
Extenuating factors (if any)		

The next table shows how my data looked.

TABLE 13.2. MY TEST RESULTS		
Test	**Results**	**Risk Level**
PSA levels	15.3, 13.4	Intermediate
Positive biopsy cores	4 positive for cancer	Intermediate
T Grade	T1c	Low
Gleason score	6	Low
Color Doppler ultrasound	Small solitary lesion, no spread	Low
DCE-MRI findings	Small solitary lesion, no spread	Low
Carbon-11 PET/CT Scan (if done)		

Extenuating factors (if any)
#1: 7cc prostate inflated PSA results, making PSA more accurately 11 to 12 ng/ml, slightly above the low-risk ceiling of 10.
#2: Four biopsy cores showing cancer was above the two required for active surveillance; yet Scholz and also Katz allow three of twelve cores to be positive, and because one of my cores was only one percent cancer, Scholz felt they fit the low-risk category. Other experts disagree, stating that two positive cores or fewer are required for low-risk status

Consider one more factor when analyzing your findings: Which test results are most important?

Looking at my results, I considered the Gleason score of 6, indicating a less aggressive cancer, the most important finding. The DCE-MRI and the confirmatory findings with the color Doppler ultrasound were the next most important. These tests showed and confirmed that I have a small, solitary tumor in a relatively safe area of my prostate gland, not near any vital structures or showing any indication of spread outside of the prostate. Putting it all together over five months, my treatment choice became much easier: active surveillance.

It is important to remember that no single test is enough to decide where you stand or what to do. None of the tests for prostate cancer are 100 percent accurate, but rather are 75 to 90 percent reliable. How do you deal with this imprecision? As Dr. Scardino of the Sloan Kettering Cancer Center put it, "I don't rely just on the digital rectal exam, the PSA, the biopsy results, or the MRI. But if we put all that information together, we can get a pretty good idea of what's going on." In fact, this isn't some new method of evaluation and diagnosis. The basic medical approach to diagnosing any patient is: history, physical exam, laboratory tests, and other tests. Every medical student learns this. So why the problem in obtaining a DCE-MRI or color Doppler ultrasound? If the test doesn't jive with the other findings, you and your doctor can always ignore it.

Your case may be *typical,* in which all of the findings fit nicely into one risk category. Or it may be *atypical* like mine, with some results fitting into one category, and other risks fitting another. Atypical cases are common in medicine, sometimes so common that they outnumber the textbook cases. *This is why it is important to obtain all of the tests you can and as many opinions as you need.*

If your findings are similar to mine, doctors stuck in today's outdated model will almost invariably recommend surgery or radiation. They will look at your PSA levels and biopsy cores and make their recommendation to you, just as they recommended prostatectomy or radiation for me.

The problem with the current model is that it has not caught up with the new twenty-first century technologies. Medical guidelines are determined based on long-term studies that are replicated and confirmed. For example, a long-term study of the DCE-MRI can take many years, and to have the results confirmed by other studies takes additional time. Then the urology associations have to review the data and draw up new guidelines.

Meanwhile, conservative urologists, which include most urologists today, will remain slow to embrace the new tests, and insurance companies may not pay for them yet. Hadn't Dr. Summers, my urologist, who did a good job in determining that I had prostate cancer, discounted the utility of a DCE-MRI? Hadn't he refused to order this test, even though I offered to obtain it elsewhere and pay for it myself?

Your urologist may act the same way. Remember, urologists are most often surgeons, so they will have a particular point of view. Be prepared for this. If you don't agree with your doctor's analysis of your situation, stay calm, thank the doctor for his or her input, and seek a second opinion.

ASSESSING THE DOCTOR YOU CHOOSE

The surgeons and radiologists I consulted were highly recommended, intelligent, and experienced people. They were truly concerned about me and really wanted to help. Yet to my mind, they were strictly following the twentieth century model: high PSA and positive biopsy, go directly to prostatectomy or radiation.

At first, until I learned otherwise, that's how I looked at my case, too. As I mentioned earlier, I actually tried Rapid Arc IMRT radiation, but the beam was improperly designed for the severe nerve injuries in my legs. The photon beam hit the nerves descending from my spine, aggravating my condition. My setback was acute and serious, and I had to immediately discontinue treatment. This experience was a blessing in disguise, because it shocked me into thinking twice and twice again about the risks of treatment and whether, with my DCE-MRI findings, I needed treatment at all.

Unlike the surgeons and radiologists, Dr. Scholz paid attention to the DCE-MRI report and performed the color Doppler ultrasound that confirmed the MRI results. This willingness to use up-to-date technology is one reason I like him. Scholz said the cancer was small and located in a relatively safe area of the prostate gland. Because of this, he said, there was a 90 percent likelihood that it would never bother me. Scholz is one of the top prostate cancer oncologists in the country. He is one of the top experts on active surveillance and has evaluated hundreds of cases like mine. I could not have chosen a more appropriate doctor for my case than Scholz.

Yet I had to consider, he could still be wrong. I like Scholz and look forward to my next appointment with him. At the same time, all doctors have their biases and blind spots. By the very nature of his writings, Scholz clearly leans away from prostatectomy and toward active surveillance. I had to consider this fact, too.

If your doctor recommends surgery or radiation based solely on your PSA and biopsy findings, which many doctors still do, you should take pause and get a second opinion, if possible from a doctor who is not a surgeon and not in the same healthcare system. You should ask your doctor about the DCE-MRI for the prostate gland. Remember, this is different than the standard MRIs used today. Has your doctor heard of the DCE-MRI? Would he or she consider giving you an order for the test? If not, is the doctor agreeable to your obtaining another opinion from an expert who knows about the DCE-MRI, color Doppler ultrasound, genetically-based tests, and other recent breakthroughs?

Even though I am Gleason 6 and have a localized tumor, I still meet doctors today who recommend prostate surgery or radiation. My DCE-MRI and color Doppler ultrasound findings do not alter their views. They are not even aware of the genetic tests for when there is doubt. You may need to consult with several doctors. Some men create their own medical team consisting of their primary doctor, urologist, prostate surgeon, radiation specialist, and prostate cancer oncologist.

If you are Gleason 7, for example, you want to have a doctor who knows the difference between Gleason 3 plus 4 versus Gleason 4 plus 3. Remember, the numbers represent the levels of aggressiveness. Gleason 3 plus 4 indicates the most prevalent cancer in your prostate is Gleason 3, whereas with Gleason 4 plus 3, the most prevalent cancer is the more aggressive 4. Some doctors recommend very different treatments for these two types of Gleason 7 cancer. You want a doctor who understands these distinctions and can discuss them with you.

Perhaps your findings are severe, with a very high PSA level or a Gleason score of 8 or above. You are high-risk, so the tests I am recommending should be performed as part of your diagnostic work-up. A DCE-MRI is important to delineate the extent of your cancer. Is it on one side or both? Is it encroaching on the prostate capsule? Has it spread elsewhere? The new Carbon-11 PET/CT scan is key for determining whether there are metastases. All of these details are essential because the treatment of a Gleason 8 to 10 prostate cancer can be quite different depending on whether the cancer has grown beyond the capsule and into surrounding tissues or has metastasized to distant sites.

WHAT DOES THE SCIENCE SAY?

You may also find it helpful to read the reports of studies that are relevant to your type of prostate cancer. For example, a study in the *New England Journal of Medicine* was key to my choosing active surveillance as my current treatment. As discussed in the section on active surveillance (Chapter 9), this study unequivocally showed that for men with low-risk prostate cancer, watchful waiting was just about as effective in ten year survival as prostatectomy. This finding does not mean that all men with prostate cancer should choose active surveillance, but it is a reasonable consideration for men with low-risk disease. My view is that if watchful waiting was effective in this study, today's active surveillance will be more so. Watchful waiting was limited to PSAs and biopsies, whereas my active surveillance program also included follow-up color Doppler ultrasound and DCE-MRI testing. These tests are a big improvement over yesterday's watchful waiting, because they can improve the speed and accuracy of identifying any worsening of my prostate cancer.

The study mentioned above also found that, of the 365 men who underwent prostatectomy, a large majority of those with low-risk cancer had no other cancers in their prostate glands, or only small, insignificant ones. A conservative doctor would say yes, that's true, but the men with significant bilateral cancer were saved. I agree, but rather than doing prostatectomies on all of these men, why not use the DCE-MRI to sort them out first?

Dr. Scardino writes, "The level of treatment should match the risk posed by the cancer." This is why the diagnostic tests, especially the DCE-MRI are so important. Unless you get this and all other important testing, how can you and your doctor know the risk posed by your cancer?

The newer tests have an important impact on me in another way. By using them as part of my active surveillance, I no longer feel that I am flying blind. Psychologically, this is a big relief.

WHY LOW-RISK MEN CHOOSE HIGH-RISK TREATMENT

It is unfortunate that today, a large majority of men who are low-risk and who would be good candidates for active surveillance or focal therapy nevertheless choose to undergo prostatectomy or radiation treatment. Both of these therapies can cause serious, permanent adverse effects that greatly reduce men's quality of life. The unnecessary damage occurs so often—about 80,000 men each year who get aggressive treatment for low-risk disease—that the medical associations have recommended we stop PSA testing. Is it right for us to abandon them?

Why do these men with a low-risk prostate cancer choose more intensive and risky treatments than they need? One reason is that they feel acutely vulnerable. Being given the diagnosis of "cancer" has that effect on many men, and the instinct is to take immediate action. With the old model, with only PSA levels and biopsy results to guide them, these men feel very much in the dark about their prostate cancer. As I learned all too well, it is extremely stressful not to know how big your cancer is, where it is located, whether it is in one or both lobes, and whether it has spread. It is difficult to live with the knowledge you have a cancer inside of you that may kill you, yet know so little about it.

I expect that, as doctors begin implementing the DCE-MRI and genetic testing as diagnostic tools, a much larger percentage of men will select active surveillance. In an article in the *New York Times* on genetic testing, Dr. Eric A. Klein of the Cleveland Clinic said, "Even if we can only convince 15 to 20 percent of men that we have enough confidence and that they don't need to be treated, that will be a big step forward." The availability of the DCE-MRI (or multiparametric MRI) testing is also expanding.

Focal treatment is also gaining greater favor. Prostatectomy and radiation will remain important therapies for some men, and the new diagnostic tests will improve their results by sorting prostate cancer patients properly before radical treatment is chosen hastily. When these developments become routine, prostate cancer treatment will have truly entered the 21st century.

MY PROSTATE CANCER EXPERIENCE

My plan was to follow the active surveillance protocol to the letter. I monitored my PSA levels on a regular basis. A test in the months following my biopsy indicated a PSA level of 12.4 ng/ml. A few months after that, my PSA level was 13.0 ng/ml. These levels were slightly lower than the previous 15.3 and 13.4. The difference between them is negligible. Basically, my PSA levels were holding steady. As long as they did not escalate, I was content.

In the back of my mind, I sometimes thought about having the cancerous nodule in my prostate gland treated focally. Surgery and radiation are performed only on the full prostate. And while HIFU and cryotherapy can also be used to treat the whole prostate, they are more frequently used for focal treatment, as is focal laser ablation. Still, even these focal therapies had risks I would have rather avoided. Instead, I preferred to play for time, hoping I would be in the 70 percent of men in active surveillance who never need treatment.

Then, my PSA nearly doubled again, suddenly shooting up to 26 ng/ ml. I was shocked. I contacted my doctor. He told me that with prostate cancer, PSA levels rarely shoot up like that. PSAs rise more gradually. The most likely cause was an infection or inflammation. Did I have any sign of these? I had no signs of infection, but I do have an inflammatory disorder that had been causing more symptoms lately.

Dr. Scholz suggested I take Cipro or Levaquin, the best antibiotics for prostate infections, for three weeks. He didn't know that I had written one of the first medical journal papers on the severe and long-lasting side effects that these drugs cause, albeit rarely. I asked him if we could wait a little longer as I increased my anti-inflammatory therapy. The next PSA was 22, and a month later it was back to 14. I also got another color Doppler ultrasound test followed by a DCE-MRI, the 3.0 Tesla type at UCLA. The results were inconclusive. All was again quiet.

Still, I continued to watch as new studies were published and new advances in technology emerged. The odds that I would need intervention someday were 30 percent, so I needed to stay on my guard. Once you have had prostate cancer, or any cancer, no matter what treatment you choose, you are always on active surveillance for the rest of your life.

13

Thirty Questions to Ask Your Doctors

Prepare for your meetings with your doctors. Bring the following list of questions and circle the ones you want to ask. The questions should be relevant to the purpose of the meeting. If you try to ask all thirty questions at one meeting, you will wear your doctor out. Doctors are human after all, so be fair and respectful of the doctor's time. Too many questions may provoke frustration.

Bring a notepad. If you have a spouse, significant other, or close family member or friend, consider bringing one of them. Studies have shown that people remember only a fraction of what doctors tell them. A notepad and a companion can really help.

Bring an open mind. Different doctors have different expectations and points of view. It is certainly reasonable to ask follow-up questions or request the basis of a doctor's opinion or recommendation, but remain calm and respectful. If you disagree with the doctor's approach or recommendations, seek a second opinion, rather than arguing with the doctor. If possible, the second opinion should be with a doctor from a different group or institution. I say this because many groups and institutions have created their protocols that all of their doctors follow. In order to obtain a truly independent second opinion, you may need a doctor not associated with your first doctor's organization. If this is not possible, get a second opinion from a different type of doctor in your healthcare system, such as an oncologist.

Also bring information you have gathered from books or the internet. Doctors are sometimes resistant to Internet information, but a good doctor will be open to data from respected sources such as medical institutions, medical journal articles, the National Institutes of Health (NIH), the American Urologic Association, and books written by experts and supported with references.

Most of all, try to remain positive. The survival rate of men after ten years with prostate cancer is 95 percent.

QUESTIONS TO ASK YOUR DOCTORS

1. Is my PSA level normal or elevated?

2. If it is elevated, how elevated? What might it mean?

3. Other than cancer, are there other possible causes of my high PSA level?

4. Can we repeat the PSA test before initiating other tests?

5. Can you do the digital rectal exam and the ultrasound now to accurately measure my prostate size?

6. If my prostate gland is enlarged, how much might it affect the PSA results?

7. If my PSA levels are both significantly elevated, what does this mean? What is the next step? Antibiotics? Biopsy?

8. Can you refer me to a good prostate cancer support group? Remember, you can access all of the lectures from my support group, Informed Prostate Cancer Support Group (ipcsg.org).

9. If a biopsy is needed, can we arrange a targeted one instead of a random (blind) one?

10. Can we obtain a DCE-MRI test to determine whether a tumor may exist before doing the biopsy?

11. Do you perform a color Doppler ultrasound for prostate cancer? If not, do you know of any of doctors who do?

12. If a tumor is seen, can you use the DCE-MRI or color Doppler ultrasound to perform a targeted biopsy?

13. If the biopsy is negative, should we consider one of the new genetic tests to confirm the biopsy interpretation?

14. If my biopsy is positive for cancer, what Gleason score do I have and what does it mean?

15. Should I get a second opinion on my biopsy cores and Gleason score?

16. Should we consider genetic testing to confirm the grade and aggressiveness of my prostate cancer?

17. Is there any sign that the cancer has spread?

18. For men with high-risk cancer: Would a Carbon-11 PET/CT scan be helpful in determining whether I have metastases?

19. What treatment do you suggest for me? If prostatectomy or radiation therapy, can I speak to the surgeon or radiologist?

20. I have read about other types of radiation therapy: SBRT, brachytherapy, proton therapy. Can you tell me about them?

21. What are the risks of treatment failure and of adverse effects with these aggressive treatments?

22. Are there alternatives to surgery or radiation therapy I should consider? What about androgen deprivation therapy (ADT)?

23. Do you think that focal therapy might be appropriate for my prostate cancer?

24. Have you heard of cryotherapy, focal laser ablation, or high intensity focused ultrasound (HIFU)? Might one of these be worth considering for my career?

25. Am I a candidate for active surveillance?

26. Even though you have advised active surveillance, I am uncomfortable with the thought of cancer within my prostate gland. What other choices to I have?

27. I have intermediate-risk prostate cancer. Many treatments have been recommended: prostatectomy, radiation, ADT—which one do you recommend?

28. I have high-risk cancer with signs of metastases: what do you advise?

29. Am I a candidate for Xofigo?

30. What about genetic tests for selecting the most effective chemotherapy medications?

So now you've asked the doctor these questions. I have an important question to ask you: Are you with the right doctor? You have a serious disease. You have a right to ask questions and receive full answers. If your doctor is unable or unwilling to answer your questions, find another doctor who will.

Conclusion

f you ask Richard, a sixty-five-year-old with prostate cancer, what the most important part of evaluating the disease is, he answers without hesitation, "The accuracy of the diagnosis." He says this because several years ago, his PSA went over 6 ng/ml, and cores from a blind biopsy revealed a Gleason 6 cancer on one side of his prostate gland. Repeated PSA results remained steady, so Richard chose active surveillance, although his urologist recommended his prostatectomy.

A year later, he consulted with Dr. Duke Bahn, who performed a color Doppler ultrasound and targeted biopsy. The more accurate targeted biopsy showed bilateral prostate cancer with a Gleason 7 cancer in one lobe and Gleason 8 in the other.

His cancer had advanced to the point that Richard was no longer a candidate for prostatectomy, and instead radiation and androgen deprivation therapy were recommended. ADT is no picnic. Reducing a man's testosterone to almost zero can lead to osteoporosis, hot flashes, depression, breast enlargement, diabetes, obesity and high blood pressure, not to mention diminished libido and impaired sexual functioning.

Now Richard wonders if his original blind biopsy was accurate. Was active surveillance the correct initial treatment? Apparently not. Should he have chosen prostatectomy instead? If he had obtained the color Doppler ultrasound sooner or a DCE-MRI, would his treatment choices have been more appropriate? Could he have avoided ADT? Would his long-term prospects have been better?

"One thing that I feel certain about is the need for complex diagnostic testing, including the new modalities that are now available," Richard told me. "Too much testing is better than too little, because prostate cancer can be an insidious disease and difficult to diagnose accurately. Many cases like mine deviate from the established norms. The more you learn about your cancer, the better your chances of successful treatment."

My view is that a DCE-MRI and/or color Doppler ultrasound should be done as part of the diagnostic workup of *all* men who might have prostate cancer. It should be used just as we use standard MRIs today in so many other areas of medicine to help determine diagnoses before resorting to invasive methods. A biopsy is an invasive method, so it should be targeted, not blind.

And when a biopsy reveals prostate cancer, genetic testing should be considered to confirm that the Gleason is correct. Genetic testing should also be helpful to ensure that a negative biopsy is truly negative. The only questions about genetic testing are whether it is reliable and affordable.

THE PROSTATE CANCER TREATMENT RENAISSANCE

Imagine when the diagnostic technologies and new therapies like these become widely used, almost everything about prostate cancer will change. Soon, patients and their doctors will wonder why there ever was a debate about the DCE-MRI and MRI-guided biopsy, about genetic testing and Xofigo, and how did we ever get along without them. These next ten years are going to be the renaissance of prostate cancer care, a time of amazing departure from the past in the diagnosis and treatment of this very common and all-too-often lethal cancer in men.

It is already underway. My good friend Charles had his PSA level tested and found it had rose to nearly 4.5 ng/ml. This is only slightly above normal, but it was double the previous PSA level a year before, which was worrisome. His urologist recommended a biopsy, which did not detect cancer. However, the day after the biopsy, Charlie developed chills and fever. He was already taking an antibiotic for the biopsy, but it obviously had not prevented infection from the biopsy. His doctor switched antibiotics, yet Charles worsened. Two days later, he was in the hospital receiving intravenous antibiotics. The first one didn't work, the second caused a severe rash, and meanwhile Charles' condition deteriorated. He almost died.

Finally, a third antibiotic brought the infection under control. It was a close call for Charles, because the last antibiotic began causing kidney failure. If the drug hadn't controlled the infection quickly, it would have had to be discontinued, and at this point there were few other treatment choices.

I recently asked Charlie about his latest PSA level. "I am putting it off," he admitted. "I know I shouldn't, but I am worried it will come back elevated and I will have to undergo another biopsy. I dread that."

Charles knew I had prostate cancer but didn't know the details of my journey. I gave him the short version and then suggested he get a prostate DCE-MRI. He took a minute to think this over, then he said, "You know, that's not a bad idea. If the PSA remains elevated, I will need a biopsy again, and a prostate DCE-MRI might show us where to look. Even if the PSA is normal, I will still worry that we might be missing something." He smiled. "I've had MRIs for my shoulder and lower back. Why not get one for the prostate and see what's really going on?"

I added, "And if the DCE-MRI shows no cancer, then you can wait on the biopsy without worry. If the MRI shows no suspicious areas, you can get a guided biopsy. With a guided biopsy, they will only need a few cancers from the lesion. With a blind biopsy, they will take twelve or fourteen cores. So your risk of injury and infection would be much less with a guided biopsy. The fewer biopsy cores, the better, especially with you, but really with all men."

"That makes a lot of sense," Charles said. "It's nice to know I have options."

Charles did get a DCE-MRI, which showed a small abnormality, possibly cancer, in a safe area. Charles' PSA had dropped, so Charles and his urologist agreed to monitor his PSA levels and repeated the DCE-MRI before doing another biopsy. In essence, even though prostate cancer had never been formally diagnosed, Charles underwent active surveillance.

KNOWLEDGE IS POWER

The goal of this book has been to alert you to the breakthrough tests and treatments available today for men with prostate cancer. Each test you obtain can provide additional information that can make your treatment decision easier and more precise. In my case and in other men I have mentioned here, the DCE-MRI or color Doppler ultrasound changed everything. Knowing specifically the size, type, location, and absence of spread of my prostate cancer allowed me to consider an option that had been off the table: active surveillance. I have been following this method for twenty-two months and feel comfortable with it. At least, as comfortable as a man who has been diagnosed with prostate cancer can be.

More than half of the men diagnosed with prostate cancer today are candidates for active surveillance, yet most of them undergo prostatectomy or radiation despite the risk of long-term harm to their quality of life. In addition, prostatectomy and radiation treatment are not cures for 20 to 25 percent of men who undergo them. Yes, some men do require a prostatectomy or radiation, but others who undergo these treatments don't really need them. Current methods do not provide most men with enough information to make a truly informed decision. Many men are not even told about the focal therapies that would make sense for them. Making a diagnosis based solely on PSA levels and a blind biopsy, as most doctors do today, are simply not enough. The new tests, which can give you a picture of what you have and what you need to do, can change that.

Consider that 1,200,000 men in the United States undergo a prostate biopsy each year, yet only half of them need it. Prostate biopsies are usually safe, but as you saw in Richard's case, prostate biopsies do have serious risks, and nearly one in 1,000 are fatal. Why rush into a biopsy, which is a surgical procedure, before finding out via a prostate MRI or color Doppler ultrasound if you actually need one?

This is why I encourage you to obtain *all the tests you can, and all the second opinions you need* to be fully informed about what you have and what you need to do. *You have cancer.* After reading this book, you are well informed about the prostate cancer innovations that have come about and fully prepared to ask questions about tests and treatments. If ever there was time for you to be assertive and take control of your situation, it is now. I wish you the best of luck.

Glossary

Occasionally, this book uses terms that are common in discussions about prostate cancer treatment, prevention, and research, but may not be completely familiar to you. You may also hear these terms when working with doctors, especially urologists and oncologists, as well as other healthcare professionals. To help you better understand prostate cancer literature and participate in discussions with your physician, definitions are provided below for words that are often used by those who diagnose and treat prostate cancer.

Anecdotal. Evidence collected in a casual or informal matter and relying heavily or entirely on personal testimony, rather than scientific analysis. In medical terms, anecdotal evidence is based on an individual's reports or observations of their personal experience with a disease, including symptoms and treatment, but is not necessarily backed by scientific evidence.

Benign prostate hypertrophy (BPH). Enlargement of the prostate. BPH is a common condition that occurs in aging men, particularly between the ages of fifty-one and sixty. An enlarged prostate is not usually an indicator of cancer, and some men with the condition suffer from few, if any, issues.

Biopsy. The removal of tissue from a living body for the purpose of medical examination. A doctor may order a biopsy if he or she discovers an area of concern in the body. Biopsies are typically done to look for cancer, but can help identify many other conditions as well.

Bilateral cancer. Cancer that occurs in each of a pair of organs, such as both kidneys, lungs, breasts, ovaries, etc., at the same time.

Colonoscopy. A procedure in which a flexible fiber-optic instrument called a *colonoscope* is inserted through the anus in order to examine the colon for signs of intestinal issues, as well as screen for colon cancer.

Contraindication. A condition or factor that indicates against the advisability of an otherwise typical remedy or treatment due to the harm it would cause the patient. For example, certain medications are fine to take on their own but *contraindicated* for simultaneous use due to adverse drug reactions, such as warfarin, a blood thinner used to treat blood clots, and aspirin.

Cyclotron. An accelerator in which charged particles, such as protons and ions, are propelled by an alternating electric field in a constant magnetic field. Cyclotrons are used for cancer treatment to help stop or slow tumor growth through radiation, while minimizing damage to surrounding healthy tissue.

Gleason scoring system. A grading system devised to evaluate the aggressiveness of prostate cancer. Cores, or cancerous tissue obtained via biopsy, are assigned a number on a scale from 1 through 5 to indicate abnormality. Cells closer to 1 on the scale closely resemble normal prostate tissue and are considered "low-grade," while cells closer to 5 are more mutated and considered "high-grade." The final Gleason score is the sum of the two areas of the prostate that make up most of the tumor. For example, a Gleason score of 2+3=5 means most of the tumor is grade 2 and the rest is grade 3 to make a total score of 5.

Localized tumor. Cancer that is limited to the place where it initially started, with no sign that it has spread to other parts of the body.

Metastasis. The spread of cancer cells from the original tumor to a different part of the body. During metastasis, cancer travels through the blood or lymph system and forms a new tumor in other organs or tissues in the body.

Magnetic Resonance Imaging (MRI). A test that uses a powerful magnetic field and radio waves to create detailed images of the organs and tissues in the body. Doctors use MRI imaging to diagnose and monitor a range of conditions in the body.

Multifocal cancer. The presence of more than one tumor within the same quadrant (area) of the body.

Nanogram (ng). A unit of measurement equivalent to one billionth of a gram.

Neurovascular bundles. A group of nerves, veins, and blood vessels that travel together within the body. In the male reproductive system, the neurovascular bundles are located adjacent to the prostate and are responsible for erection.

Oncologist. A medical practitioner specializing in the diagnosis and treatment of cancer. There are multiple types of oncologists, including *medical,* who treats the cancer using chemotherapy or other treatments, *surgical,* who removes tumors and cancerous tissue during operation, and *radiation,* who treats cancer patients using radiation therapy. There are also oncologists who specialize in different types of cancer, such as gynecologic (uterine and cervical cancer), pediatric (children's cancer), and hematologic (blood cancer).

Oncology. The branch of medical science dealing with cancer.

Pathology. The study of the causes and effects of disease and illness.

Pathologist. A specialist who interprets and diagnoses the changes caused by disease in tissues and body fluids. Pathologists study the origin, nature, and course of all kinds of diseases.

Photon. A bundle of electromagnetic energy. Light is made up of photons. In radiation therapy, the energy produced by photons is used to kill cancer cells.

Placebo. A harmless pill, medicine, or procedure with little or no physiological effect that is used for a patient's psychological benefit. Placebos are also used as a control in an experiment or test in order to determine the effectiveness of a drug.

Proctology. The branch of medicine dealing with the structure and diseases of the anus, rectum, and colon.

Proctologist. A doctor specializing in the diagnosis and treatment of conditions affecting the anus and rectum.

Prostatectomy. A surgical procedure that involves removing all or part of the prostate gland. *Radical* prostatectomy is the removal of the entire prostate gland and surrounding lymph nodes in cases of localized prostate cancer. *Simple* prostatectomy is typically performed on men with urinary problems or extreme cases of BPH to remove the part of the prostate that is blocking the flow of urine.

Proton. A tiny, positively-charged electric particle that exists in the nucleus of every atom. Similarly to photons, protons are used in radiation therapy in order to kill cancer cells.

Radiation therapy. The treatment of disease, especially cancer, using X-rays or other forms of radiation. There are many different kinds of radiation therapy, the most common being *external beam* radiation therapy, in which high-energy beams are emitted from a machine to a precise point in your body. Radiation damages the genetic material of cells—both cancerous and normal—controlling how they grow and divide.

Renal failure. Sudden loss of kidney function.

Testosterone. A sex hormone that stimulates the development of male sexual characteristics, sex organs, and sperm. Testosterone is produced mainly in the testes.

Ultrasound. An external imaging method that uses high-frequency sound waves to produce images of structure within your body. Also known as a sonogram, ultrasounds are typically used on pregnant women to observe a fetus in the uterus, but are also useful for examining muscles, tendons, and internal organs.

Unilateral cancer. Cancer affecting only one of a pair of organs.

Urologist. A doctor specializing in the study and treatment of the function and disorders of the urinary system, including conditions relating to the bladder, urethra, and uterus.

Urology. The branch of medicine that focuses on the treatment and conditions involving the male and female urinary tract, as well as the male reproductive organs.

Resources

There are a number of medical centers and organizations that are devoted to diagnosing, treating, and preventing prostate cancer. Below, you'll find the names and contact information of the various cancer treatment centers, hospitals, and medical professionals that I've mentioned throughout this book. All of the organizations listed below are dedicated to fighting prostate cancer using innovative approaches to diagnosis and treatment. Be sure to give them a call or check out their websites to see all of the treatments they have to offer.

The internet contains a wealth of information regarding the new prostate cancer treatments I've introduced to you, which are evolving and improving every day. If you don't see a treatment center near you listed in this Resources section, check the availability of these services and more at the major hospital and cancer centers in your area by Googling the name of the treatment you're seeking followed by the name of your city. If you're not looking for anything in particular right now, try less specific search terms such as "prostate cancer treatments" or "prostate cancer oncologists" plus the name of your city.

PROSTATE CANCER TREATMENT BY STATE

ARIZONA

Phoenix Molecular Imaging
4540 E Cotton Gin Loop #150
Phoenix, AZ 05040
Dr. Fabio Almeida, director
(602) 331-1771 | phxmi.com/
   home.html

Phranq Tamburri, M.D.
Longevity Medical Health Center
1382 N 32nd St., Suite 126
Phoenix, AZ 85032
(602) 493-2273 | longevitymedical.
   com

CALIFORNIA

Desert Medical Imaging
74785 Highway 111
Suite 101 Wall Street West
  Building
Indian Wells, CA 92210
(760) 776-8989 |
  desertmedicalimaging.com

Chinn Urology
Douglas Chinn, M.D.
65 North First Ave., Suite 102
Arcadia, CA 91006
(626) 574-7111 | chinnurology.com

Prostate Institute of America
Duke Bahn, M.D.
168 North Brent St., Suite 402
Ventura, CA 93003
(888) 234-0004 | pioa.org
Loma Linda University

*Proton Treatment and Research
  Center*
11234 Anderson Street
Loma Linda, CA 92354
(800) 766-8667 | protons.com

**Mark Scholz, M.D. & Richard
Lam, M.D.**
Prostate Oncology Specialists, Inc.
4676 Admiralty Way, Suite 101
Marina Del Rey, CA 90292
(310) 927-7707 | prostateoncology.
  com

Rolling Oaks Radiology
4516 Market St.,
Ventura, CA 93003
(805) 644-7300 |
  rollingoaksradiology.com

Scripps Proton Therapy Center
9730 Summers Ridge Rd.
San Diego, CA 92121
(858) 549-7400 |
  scripps.org/services/cancer-
  care_proton-therapy

**Sharp Hospital and Medical
Center**
Multiple locations in the San
  Diego area
(800) 827-4277 | sharp.com

Sperling Prostate Center
2001 Santa Monica Blvd.,
  Suite 590W
Santa Monica, CA 90404
(561) 325-6396 |
  sperlingprostatecenter.com

**University of California,
Los Angeles (UCLA)**
UCLA Department of Urology
David Geffen School of Medicine
10833 Le Conte Ave.
Los Angeles, CA 90095
urology.ucla.edu/spore

**University of California,
San Diego (UCSD)**
Moores Cancer Center
3855 Health Sciences Drive
La Jolla, CA 92037
health.ucsd.edu/cancer

**University of California, San
Francisco (UCSF)**
Prostate Cancer Center
Ron Conway Family Gateway
  Medical Building
1825 Fourth St., Fourth Floor
San Francisco, CA 94158

ucsfhealth.org/clinics/prostate_
cancer_center

**University of Southern
California, Los Angeles**
Multiple locations in Southern
California
(310) 794-7700 | urology.ucla.edu

Veteran's Hospital
VA San Diego Healthcare System
3350 La Jolla Village Dr.
San Diego, CA 92161
(858) 552-8585 | (800) 331-8387 |
sandiego.va.gov

CONNECTICUT

Yale Medical Group, New Haven
Multiple locations in Connecticut
(203) 785-2815 | medicine.yale
.edu/urology/programs/
genitourinary/prostate

FLORIDA

Michael Dattoli, M.D.
Dattoli Cancer Center
2803 Fruitville Rd.
Sarasota, FL 34237
(877) 328-8654 | dattoli.com

Stephen Scionti, M.D.
Scionti Boston Prostate Center at
Sarasota Medical Center
5741 Bee Ridge Rd. 500
Sarasota, FL 34233
(866) 866-8967 |
sciontiprostatecenter.com

Sperling Prostate Center
Multiple locations in Florida

(561) 325-6396 |
sperlingprostatecenter.com

**University of Florida Health
Jacksonville**
655 West 8th St.
Jacksonville, FL 32209
(904) 244-0411 |ufhealthjax.org/
cancer/prostate

ILLINOIS

**Northwestern Medicine Chicago
Proton Center**
4455 Weaver Parkway
Warrenville, IL 60555
(877) 887-5807 |
chicagoprotoncenter.com

**University of Chicago Medical
Center**
5841 S. Maryland Ave.
Chicago, IL 60637
(855) 702-8222 | uchospitals.edu/
specialties/cancer/urologic/
prostate/index.html

INDIANA

Indiana University Health
Multiple locations in Indiana
(800) 248-1199 | iuhealth.org/
cancer/prostate-cancer

MASSACHUSETTS

Massachusetts General Hospital
Mass General Department of Urology
165 Cambridge St., 7th Floor
Boston, MA 02114
(857) 238-3838 | massgeneral.org/
urology/patient_care/prostate
cancer.aspx

MARYLAND

Johns Hopkins University
The James Buchanan Brady Urological Institute
600 North Wolfe St.
Baltimore, MD 21287
(410) 955-6100 | urology.jhu.edu/prostate/cancer.php

MINNESOTA

Mayo Clinic
200 First St. SW
Rochester, MN 55905
(507) 284-511 | mayoclinic.org/patient-visitor-guide/minnesota

NEW JERSEY

Procure Proton Therapy Center
103 Cedar Grove Ln.
Somerset, NJ 08873
(877) 967-7628 | procure.com/New-Jersey-Explore

NEW YORK

Robert Bard, M.D.
Bard Cancer Center
New York, NY 10022
(212) 355-7017 | bardcancercenter.com

Memorial Sloan-Kettering Cancer Center
Multiple locations in New York
(800) 525-2225 | mskcc.org/cancer-care/types/prostate

NYU Langone Medical Center
Smilow Comprehensive Prostate Cancer Center
135 East 31st St., 2nd Floor
New York, NY10016
(646) 754-2400 | nyulangone.org/locations/smilow-comprehensive-prostate-cancer-center

Sperling Prostate Center
Multiple locations in New York
(561) 325-6396 | sperlingprostatecenter.com

OHIO

University of Cincinnati Medical Center
Multiple locations in Ohio
(513) 475-8787 | uchealth.com/services/urology/urologic-cancer/

Cleveland Clinic
Multiple locations in Ohio
(800) 223-2273 | myclevelandclinic.org/health/articles/prostate-cancer-basics

OKLAHOMA

ProCure Proton Therapy Center
5901 W Memorial Rd.
Oklahoma City, OK 73142
(888) 847-2640 | procure.com/Oklahoma-Explore

PENNSYLVANIA

Fox Chase Cancer Center at Temple Health
333 Cottman Ave.
Philadelphia, PA 19111
(888) 369-2427 | foxchase.org/
prostate-cancer

Sidney Kimmel Medical College at Jefferson University
Jefferson Diagnostic Prostate Center
1025 Walnut St.
Suite 1112, College Building
Philadelphia, PA
(215) 933-6916 | jefferson.edu/
university/jmc/departments/
urology/prostate_diagnostic.
html

Penn Medicine
Abramson Cancer Center
Multiple locations in Pennsylvania
(800) 789-7366 | pennmedicine.
org/cancer/types-of-cancer/
prostate-cancer

TEXAS

MD Anderson Cancer Center
Multiple locations in Texas
(855) 848-3596 | mdanderson.org/
cancer-types/prostate-cancer.
html

UT Southwestern Medical Center
Harold C. Simmons Comprehensive Cancer Center
5323 Harry Hines Boulevard
Dallas, TX 75390
(214) 648-3111 | utswmedicine
.org/cancer/programs/prostate

CANADA

Maple Leaf HIFU
Cleveland Clinic Canada
181 Bay Street, 30th Floor
Toronto, Ontario, Canada, 542 2T3
(877) 370-4438 | hifu.ca/index.htm

Sunnybrook Health Sciences Center
Multiple locations in Toronto
(416) 480-5000 | sunnybrook.ca/
content/?page=occ-prostate

FOR MORE INFORMATION ON GENETIC DIAGNOSTIC TESTS

ConfirmMDx
(866) 259-5644 | info@mdxhealth.com | mdxhealth.com

Mitomic Technology
(844) 321-6362 | info@mdnalifesciences.org | mdnalifesciences.org

ProstaVysion and QuadVysion
(877) 865-3262 | bostwicklaboratories.com

Prolaris
(855) 469-7765 | prolariscs@myriad.com | prolaris.com

OncotypeDX
(855) 677-6782 | myprostatecancertreatment.org

Decipher
(888) 792-1601 | genomedx.com

Caris Molecular Intelligence Profile and ProfilePlus Tests
(866) 771-8946 | carislifesciences.com

FOR MORE INFORMATION ON HIGH-INTENSITY FOCUSED ULTRASOUND

Focused Ultrasound Foundation
1230 Cedars Court, Suite 206
Charlottesville, VA 22903
(434) 220.4993 | info@fusfoundation.org | fusfoundation.org

The Focused Ultrasound Foundation is dedicated to conducting research on focused ultrasound technology and extending this valuable treatment option to the millions of patients who need it. The website is an excellent resource where you can learn more about the Foundation's mission, read up on focused ultrasound technology advancements and news, and more. You can also find treatment centers offering focused ultrasound technology, as well as clinical trials seeking participants in research for this ground-breaking treatment.

FOR MORE INFORMATION ON POST-FINASTERIDE SYNDROME

Post-Finasteride Syndrome Foundation
27 World's Fair Drive
Somerset, New Jersey 08873
contact@pfsfoundation.org | pfsfoundation.org

The Post-Finasteride Syndrome Foundation in Somerset, New Jersey is a non-profit organization dedicated to raising awareness and funds for scientific and clinical research into post-finasteride syndrome. If you'd like to learn more about Proscar and post-finasteride syndrome, the Foundation's website is a great place to start.

FOR MORE INFORMATION ON THE IPCSG

Informed Prostate Cancer Support Group, Inc.
P.O. Box 420142
San Diego, CA 92142
(619) 890-8447 | info@ipcsg.org | ipcsg.org

The Informed Prostate Cancer Support Group meets every third Saturday of the month from 10 A.M. to noon at the Sanford Children's Health Auditorium in San Diego, California. The group regularly hosts nationally respected experts to give lectures on a variety of topics, including prostate cancer research, treatment, and prevention. IPCSG offers more than thirty DVDs showing its informative lectures and Q&A sessions at its website under the "Purchase DVDs" tab. A good DVD for you to start with is Richard Lam, M.D., speaking in May 2013. I gave a lecture of my own in June 2013. The IPCSG website is an educational, informative resource for anyone who wants to learn more about prostate cancer.

References

Introduction

1. Fang F, Fall K, Mittleman MA, et al. Suicide and cardiovascular death after a cancer diagnosis. New England Journal of Medicine Apr 5, 2012;366:1310–18

2. Blum, RH, Scholz, M. *Invasion of the Prostate Snatchers: An Essential Guide to Managing Prostate Cancer for Patients and Their Families.* New York: Other Press, 2011.

Chapter 1: An Annual PSA Test

1. Carter, HB, Albertsen, PC, Barry, MJ, et al. "Early detection of prostate cancer: AUA Guideline." *American Urological Association* 2013: www.auanet.org

2. Jacobs, BL, Zhang, Y, Schroeck, FR, et al. "Use of advanced treatment technologies among men at low risk of dying from prostate cancer." *JAMA* 26 June 2013;309(24):2587 95.

3. Schröder, FH, Hugosson, J, Roobol, MJ, et al. "Prostate cancer mortality at 11 years of follow up." *New England Journal of Medicine.* 15 Mar 2012, 366(11): 981 90.

4. Loeb, S, Vonesh, EF, Metter, EJ, et al. "What is the true number needed to screen and treat to save a life with prostate specific antigen testing?" *Journal of Clinical Oncology.* 1 Feb 2011;29(4):464 7.

5. Blum, RH, Scholz, M. *Invasion of the Prostate Snatchers: An Essential Guide to Managing Prostate Cancer for Patients and Their Families.* New York: Other Press, 2011.

Chapter 2: Blind Biopsy, Targeted Biopsy, No Biopsy

1. Nam, RK, Saskin, R, Lee, Y, et al. "Increasing hospital admission rates for urological complications after transrectal ultrasound guided prostate biopsy." *The Journal of Urology.* 2013 Janl;189(1 Suppl):S12–7;discussion S17–8.

2. "The impact of repeat biopsies of infectious complications in men with prostate cancer on active surveillance: a prospective study. Abstract 1244." New Prostate –Cancer Infolink, 1 May 2013. http://prostatecancerinfolink.net/2013/05/01/risks-associated-with-serial-biopsies-for-men-on-active-surveillance-protocols/#comment-42083

3. Blum, RH, Scholz, M. *Invasion of the Prostate Snatchers: An Essential Guide to Managing Prostate Cancer for Patients and Their Families.* New York: Other Press, 2011.

4. Marks, L, Young, S, Natarajan, S. "MRI-ultrasound fusion for guidance of targeted prostate biopsy." *Current Opinion in Urology* 2013, Jan;23(1)43–50.

Chapter 5: The Dynamic, Contrast-Enhanced MRI

1. Chodak, G. *Winning the Battle Against Prostate Cancer.* New York: Demos Medical Publishing, 2011.

2. Cohen, JS. *Over Dose: The Case Against The Drug Companies. Prescription Drugs, Side Effects, and Your Health.* New York: Tarcher-Putnam, 2001.

3. Lazarou, J, Pomeranz, BH, Corey, PN. "Incidence of Adverse Drug Reactions in Hospitalized Patients: a Meta-Analysis of Prospective Studies." *JAMA* 1998;279(15): 1200 5.

4. Sackett, DL, Rosenberg, WM, Gray, JA, et al. "Evidence-Based Medicine: What It Is and What It Isn't. Center for Evidence-Based Medicine." 14 May 2004. www.ncbi.nlm.nih.gov/pmc/articles/PMC2349778.

5. Sackett, DL, Straus, SE, Richardson, WS, et al. "Evidence-Based Medicine: How to Practice and Teach EBM." Churchill Livingstone: Edinburgh, 2000.

6. Than, M, Bidwell, S, Davidson, C, et al. "Evidence-based Emergency Medicine at the 'Coal Face.'" *Emergency Medicine Australasia* 2005;17(4):300 40.

7. Miller, FG, Rosenstein, DL. "The Therapeutic Orientation to Clinical Trials." *New England Journal of Medicine* 2003;384:1383–1386.

8. Guyatt, G, Rennie, D. "Users' Guide to the Medical Literature: A Manual for Evidence-Based Clinical Practice." American Medical Association: Chicago, 2002.

9. Puech, P, Potiron, E, Lemaitre, L, et al. "Dynamic Contrast-Enhanced Cancer: Correlation with Radical Prostatectomy Specimens." *Urology* 2009;74:1094–1100.

10. Scardino, PT, Kellman, J. *Dr. Peter Scardino's Prostate Book.* New York: Avery Books, 2010.

11. Beck, M. "The Man, the Gland, the Dilemmas." *Wall Street Journal.* 31 March 2009.

Chapter 6: The Color-Doppler Ultrasound

1. "Dr. Duke Bahn on Color-Doppler Ultrasound." *Ask Dr. Myers.* 10 October 2013. https://askdrmyers.wordpress.com/2013/10/10/dr-duke-bahn-on-color-doppler-ultrasound.

1A. Sen, J. Choudhary, L, Marwah, S, et al. Role of Color-Doppler Imaging in Detecting Prostate Cancer. *Asian Journal of Surgery* 2008;31(1):16–19.

2. Narvatil, F. Letter, *Wall Street Journal.* 7 April 2012. prostablog.wordpress.com/older -stuff/articles/wall-st-journal-prostate-articles

Chapter 7: Genetic Diagnostic Tests

1. Pollack, A. "New Prostate Cancer Tests Could Reduce False Alarms." *New York Times.* 26 Mar 2013. nytimes.com/2013/03/27/business/new-prostate-cancer-tests-may-supplement-psa-testing.html?pagewanted=all&_r=0.

2. Foster, DJ. "New Biomarker Tests for Prostate Cancer." *PCRI (Prostate Cancer Research Institute)* Newsletter, Aug. 2013; 16(3): http://prostate-cancer.org/wp-content/uploads/insights/august2013/insights_august2013_%20new_biomarker_test.pdf

Chapter 8: The Carbon-11 PET/CT Scan

1. "C-11 Choline PET-CT Scan in Finding Metastases in Patients with Newly Diagnosed High-Risk Prostate Cancer." National Institutes of Health (NIH). http://clinicaltrials.gov/show/NCT00804245

Chapter 9: Aggressive Therapies

1. Sinnott, M, Falzarano, SM, Hernandez, AV, et al. "Discrepancy in Prostate Cancer Localization Between Biopsy and Prostatectomy Specimens in Patients with Unilateral Positive Biopsy: Implications for Focal Therapy." *Prostate* 2012, Aug. 1;72(11):1175–86.

2. Eifler, JB, Humphreys, EB, Agro, M, et al. "Causes of death after radical prostatectomy at a large tertiary center." *Journal of Urology,* Sept 2012;188(3):789–802.

3. Menon, M, Bhandari, M, Gupta N et al. "Biochemical recurrence following robot-persisted radical prostatectomy." *European Urology* 2010;58:838–846.

4. Eastham, J, Scardino, PT, Kattan, NW. "Predicting an Optimal Outcome After Radical Prostatectomy: the Trifecta Nonogram. *Journal of Urology,* June 2008;179:2207–10.

5. Katz, AJ, Santoro, M, Diblasio, F, Ashley, R. "Stereotatic Body Radiotherapy for Localized Prostate Cancer: Disease Control and Quality of Life at 6 Years." *Radiation Oncology,* 2013 May 3;8(1):118.

5A. Allen, AM, Pawlicki, T, Dong, L, et al. "An evidence based review of proton beam therapy: the report of ASTRO's emerging technology committee." *Radiotherapy and Oncology,* Apr 2012;103(1):8–11

5B. Terhune, C. "Blue Shield of California to Curb Coverage of Pricey Cancer Therapy." *Los Angeles Times,* 2013, Aug. 29: latimes.com/business/la-fi-hospital-proton-beam-20130829,0,1343046.story.

6. Zelefsky, MJ, Pei, X, Teslova, T, et al. Secondary Cancers After Intensity-Modulated Radiotherapy, Brachytherapy and Radical Prostatectomy for the Treatment of Prostate Cancer. *BJU International* 2012; Aug. 13:1464–1410.

7. Vora, SA, Wong, WW, Schild, SE, et al. "Analysis of Biochemical Control and Prognostic Factors in Patients Treated with Either Low-Dose for Localized Prostate Cancer." *International Journal of Radiation Oncology, Biology, Physics,* 15 July 2007; 86(4):1053–58.

8. Alicikus, ZA, Yamada, Y, Zhang, Z, et al. "Ten-year Outcomes of High-dose, Intensity-Modulated Radiotherapy [IMRT] for Localized Prostate Cancer." *Cancer* 2011, Apr. 1;117(7):1429–37.

9. Pradat, PF: Poisson, M, Delattre, JY, et al. "Radiation -Induced Neuropathies: Experimental and Clinical Data." *Revue Neurology* 1994 Oct;150(10):664 77.

6. Chen, AM, Hall, WH, Li, J, et al. "Brachial Plexus-Associated Neuropathy After High Dose Radiation Therapy for Head and Neck Cancer." International *Journal of Radiation and Oncology, Biology, and Physics* 2012, Mar 12: Epub.

7. Gikas, PD, Hanna, SA, Aston, W, et al. "Post-radiation Sciatic Neuropathy: a Case Report and Review of the Literature." *World Journal of Surgery and Oncology, Biology and Physics*, Dec 2008;11(6):130.

8. Johansson, S, Svensson, H, Denekamp, J. International *Journal of Radiation and Oncology, Biology, and Physics*. Apr 2002; 52(5):1207 19.

9. Rubin, DI, Schomberg, PJ, Shepherd, RF, Panneton, JM, "Arteritis and Brachial Plexus Neuropathy as Delayed Complications of Radiation Therapy." *Mayo Clinic Proceedings*, Aug 2001;76(8)849 52.

10. Lalu, T, Mercier, B, Birouk, N, et al. "Pure Motor Neuropathy After Radiation Therapy: 6 cases." *Revue Neurology*, Jan 1998:154(1):40 4.

11. Royal College Radiologists. "Management of Radiation-induced Brachial Plexus Neuropathy. *Oncology* May 1996;10(5):685, 689.

12. Stoll, BA, Andrews, JT. "Radiation-induced Peripheral Neuropathy." *British Medical Journal*, 2 Apr 1966;1(5491):834 7.

Chapter 10: Non-Invasive Therapies

1. Blum, RH, Scholz, M. *Invasion of the Prostate Snatchers: An Essential Guide to Managing Prostate Cancer for Patients and Their Families*. New York: Other Press, 2011.

2. Scholz, M, Lam, R, Strum, S, et al. "Primary Intermittent Androgen Deprivation as Initial Therapy for Men with Newly Diagnosed Prostate Cancer." *Clinical Genitourinary Cancer* 2011. Dec;9(2):89–94.

3. Parker-Pope T. "Choosing Watchful Waiting for Prostate Cancer." *New York Times*. 23 July 2012.

4. Marks L. "Ultrasound-MRI Fusion for Targeted Diagnosis of Prostate Cancer: Use of Artemis Device to Evaluate Organ-Confined Lesions." http://casit.ucla.edu/body .cfm?id=222.

5. Wilt, TJ, Brawer, MK, Jones, KM, et al. "Radical Prostatectomy vs. Observation for Localized Prostate Cancer." *New England Journal of Medicine*, 19 July 2012; 367(3):203–2012.

6. Parker-Pope T. "Questioning Surgery for Early Prostate Cancer." *Wall Street Journal.* 18 July 2012.

7. "Dr. Duke Bahn on Color-Doppler Ultrasound." *Ask Dr. Myers.* 10 October 2013.

https://askdrmyers.wordpress.com/2013/10/10/dr-duke-bahn-on-color-doppler-ultrasound.

8. National Institutes of Health. *The Role of Active Surveillance in the Management of Men with Localized Prostate Cancer.* NIH Consensus and State-of-the-Science Statements. 7 Dec 2011, 28:1:6

9. U.S. Food and Drug Administration. "FDA Approves New Drug for Advanced Prostate Cancer." 15 May 2013: www.fda.gov.

10. Bayer Pharmaceuticals. A Phase 3 Study of Radium-223 Dichloride in Patients with Symptomatic Hormone Refractory Prostate Cancer with Skeletal Metastases. *ALSYMPCA.* Identifier NCT00699751. Clinicaltrials.gov, a Service of the U.S. National Institutes of Health.

11. Parker, C, Nilsson, S, Heinrich, D, et al. "Alpha emitter radium-223 and survival in metastatic prostate cancer." *New England Journal of Medicine* 2013, Jul 18;369(3): 213–23.

12. Marchione, M. "Drug Cuts Prostate Cancer Risk, Study Finds." *Associated Press, San Diego Union-Tribune* 2013, Aug 15:A13.

12A. Thompson, IM, Goodman, PJ, Tangen, CM, et al. "Long-Term Survival of Participants in the Prostate Cancer Prevention Trial." *New England Journal of Medicine* 17 July 2003;349;215–224.

13. Scardino, PT. "The Prevention of Prostate Cancer—the Dilemma Continues. *New England Journal of Medicine.* 17 July 2003;349:297–299.

14. *Physician's Desk Reference,* 67th Edition. Montvale, NJ: PDR Network, 2013.

15. Reinberg, S. "Sexual Side Effects from Propecia, Avodart May Be Irreversible." *USA Today.* 13 Mar 2011. http://usatoday30.usatoday.com/news/health/medical/health/medical/menshealth/story/2011/03/SSexual-side-effects-from-Propecia-Avodart-may-be-irreversible/44787684/1

16. Traish, AM, Hassani, J, Guay, AT, Zitzmann, M, Hansen, ML. "Adverse Side Effects of 5[alpha]-Reductase Inhibitors Therapy: Persistent Diminished Libido and Erectile Dysfunction and Depression in a Subset of Patients." *Journal of Sexual Medicine* Mar 2011;8(3):872–84.

17. NPR News. "Evidence Supports Pill to Prevent Some Prostate Cancers." 14 Aug 2013. http://www.npr.org/blogs/health/2013/08/14/212046489/evidence-supports -pill-to-prevent-some-prostate-cancers

Chapter 11: Focal Therapies

1. Sperling, D. "Focal Laser Ablation of Prostate Tumors. *Choices, the PAACTUSA Newsletter.* Dec. 2012:14–17. paactusa.org.

2. Beck, M. "The Man, the Gland, the Dilemmas." *Wall Street Journal.* 31 Mar 2009.

3. "Dr. Duke Bahn on Color-Doppler Ultrasound." *Ask Dr. Myers.* 10 October 2013. https://askdrmyers.wordpress.com/2013/10/10/dr-duke-bahn-on-color-doppler-ultrasound.

3A. Bahn, DK, Silverman, P, Lee, F, et al. "Focal Process Cryoablation Initial Results Show Cancer Controls and Potency Preservation." *Journal of Endourology* 2006;20(9): 688–92.

4. Springen, K. "New Hope for Men with Prostate Cancer." ChicagoMag.com. July 2011: www.chicagomag.com/Chicago-Magazine/July-2011/New-Hope-For-Men-With-Prostate-Cancer.

6. Dannenmaier, M. "Nonsurgical Prostate Cancer Treatment: a First of Kind in Texas." *Galveston County Daily News*. 14 May 2013. http://www.utmb.edu/newsroom/article8543.aspx

7. Sung, HH, Jeong, BC, Seo, SI, et al. "Seven Years' Experience with High-intensity Focused Ultrasound for Prostate Cancer: Advantages and Limitations." *Prostate*. 15 September 2012;72(13):1399–1406

8. Zini, C, Hipp, E, Thomas, S, et al. "Ultrasound and MR-guided Focused Ultrasound Surgery for Prostate Cancer." *World Journal of Radiology* 2012, June 28;4(6) 247–252

9. Ahmed, HU, Freeman, A, Kirkham, A, et al. "Focal Therapy for Localized Prostate Cancer: a Phase I/II Trial." *Journal of Urology* 2011;185(4):1245–55.

Chapter 12: What Does Your Data Say?

1. Blum, RH, Scholz, M. *Invasion of the Prostate Snatchers: An Essential Guide to Managing Prostate Cancer for Patients and Their Families*. New York: Other Press, 2011.

2. Katz, AE. *The Definitive Guide to Prostate Cancer 2011*. Rodale Press: New York, NY.

3. Scardino, PT, Kellman, J. *Dr. Peter Scardino's Prostate Book*. New York: Avery Books, 2010.

4. Wilt, TJ, Brawer, MK, Jones, KM, et al. "Radical Prostatectomy vs. Observation for Localized Prostate Cancer." *New England Journal of Medicine*. 19 July 2012; 367(3) 203–2012.

5. Pollack, A. "New Prostate Cancer Tests Could Reduce False Alarms." *New York Times*. 26 Mar 2013: nytimes.com/2013/03/27/business/new-prostate-cancer-tests-may-supplement-psa-testing?pagewanted-all&_r=0

6. Cohen, JS. "Peripheral Neuropathy with Fluoroquinolone Antibiotics." *Annals of Pharmacotherapy*. Dec 2001;35(12):1540–47.

Index